CREATING
AND SUSTAINING
Small Learning Communities

SECOND EDITION

To my Dad, Bob Sammon, who never stopped teaching or learning.

GRACE SAMMON

CREATING
AND SUSTAINING
Small Learning
Communities

Strategies and Tools for Transforming High Schools

SECOND EDITION

CORWIN PRESS
A SAGE Publications Company
Thousand Oaks, CA 91320

For information:

Corwin Press
A Sage Publications Company
2455 Teller Road
Thousand Oaks, California 91320
www.corwinpress.com

Sage Publications Ltd.
1 Oliver's Yard
55 City Road
London EC1Y 1SP
United Kingdom

Sage Publications India Pvt. Ltd.
B 1/I 1 Mohan Cooperative Industrial Area
Mathura Road, New Delhi 110 044
India

Sage Publications Asia-Pacific Pte. Ltd.
33 Pekin Street #02-01
Far East Square
Singapore 048763

Printed in the United States of America

Library of Congress Cataloging-in-Publication Data

Sammon, Grace M.
Creating and sustaining small learning communities: strategies and tools for transforming high schools/Grace Sammon.—2nd ed.
    p. cm.
Includes bibliographical references and index.
ISBN-13: 978-1-4129-3789-4 (cloth: alk. paper)
ISBN-13: 978-1-4129-3790-0 (pbk.: alk. paper)
   1. School improvement programs. 2. Career academies. 3. Individualized instruction. I. Title.
LB2822.8.S26 2007
373.12—dc22   2006102762

This book is printed on acid-free paper.

07   08   09   10   11   10 9 8 7 6 5 4 3 2 1

Acquisitions Editor:	Lizzie Brenkus
Editorial Assistants:	Desirée Enayati and Ena Rosen
Production Editor:	Laureen A. Shea
Typesetter:	C&M Digitals (P) Ltd.
Cover Designer:	Rose Storey
Graphic Designer:	Karine Hovsepian

Contents

List of Artwork

List of Tool Kit Files

Number (Reflects Chapter and Sequence)	Name	Type of File
1.1	Creating SLC Presentation	MS PowerPoint
2.1	What Should a Graduate—Teacher—SLC Look Like?	MS PowerPoint
2.2	Data Tracking Tool	MS Excel
2.3	Data SLC Implementation Assessment	MS Excel
2.4	Data SLC Implementation Assessment With CTE	MS Excel
3.1	FAQ Frequently Asked Questions	MS Word
3.2	Teacher Readiness	MS Excel
4.1	Initiative and Partnership Identification and Alignment	MS Excel
4.2	SLC Punch List	MS Excel
4.3	SLC Punch List 5 Bin Sort	MS Excel
4.4	Strengths and Deficits Map	MS Word
4.5	Checklist for Ninth Grade	MS Word
5.1	Creating Teams—Roles and Responsibilities	MS Word
5.2	SLC Staffing	MS Excel
5.3	Sample SLC Teacher Selection Interview Questions	MS Word
5.4	It Was the Best of Times	MS Word
5.5	Imagine That	MS Word
6.1	SLC Pathways Course and Experience Planning	MS Word
6.2	Curriculum Planning Templates	MS Word
6.3	Brief-Cases Teacher Sheet	MS Word
6.4	DBL Experience Log	Adobe PDF
7.1	Department Instructional Facilitator Roles and Self-Assessment	MS Word
7.2	Instructional Leadership Team Roles and Self-Assessment	MS Word
7.3	Data Table 7.3 Whole-School Data	MS Word
7.4	Data Table 7.4 Content Area Data	MS Word
7.5	Data Table 7.5 Classroom Course Data	MS Word
7.6	Use of Time	MS Excel
7.7	Lessons Shared	MS Excel
9.1	Placement Checklist	MS Word
10.1	Listen, Learn, Lead	MS Word
10.2	Prides, Pitfalls, and Priorities	MS Word
10.3	Informational Interview Questions	MS Word
10.4	Measuring Up Evaluation	Adobe PDF

Preface

Let us put our heads together and see what life we will make for our children.
—Tatanka Iotanks (Sitting Bull, Lakota)

Welcome to an adventure in effective school redesign. Whether you are a district leader, school board member, school administrator, teacher, guidance counselor, school improvement facilitator, member of a school improvement team, business or community partner, or consultant, this book will lead you through the steps necessary to developing and sustaining small learning communities (SLC) within large high schools that lead to improvements in school climate, more effective professional practice, and academic achievement for all students. Creating your SLC and bringing them to scale successfully will be a long journey and a great adventure. It will require a comprehensive reform of the entire school, and a complete overhaul of the way we have done the business of educating our youth. It is a journey that will take years, and it begins with vision, commitment, understanding, and collaboration. The good news is that, even at the very start, you are not alone. There are many traveling with you. Educators across the nation are already committed to recreating, reforming, and revitalizing their large, comprehensive high schools by creating smaller, more personalized learning environments for their students. These are your fellow journeyers—those working in high schools who feel the necessary urgency to be restless for both the structures and the practices that lead to a high school culture committed to continuous improvement.

Several pivotal works highlight the growing focus on high school reform. Breaking Ranks I and II (National Association of Secondary School Principals, 1996, 2004); the American Youth Policy Forum's 2000 "High School of the Millennium"; and the best thinking of representatives from the U.S. Department of Education, the Council of Chief State School Officers, the National Association of Secondary School Principals (NASSP), Bill Daggett's International Center for Leadership in Education (ICLE), the U.S. Chamber of Commerce, and the American Federation of Teachers all outline the following as necessary key elements for schools to best prepare our students for the future:

- High academic standards that meet the community's definition of meaningful knowledge
- Learning opportunities that prepare youth for lifelong learning, civic involvement, and leadership
- Caring and competent adults who help students through the challenges of adolescence

- A laser-like focus on data
- Ongoing, varied assessments of student learning
- Opportunities for learning situations with adults, including work or volunteer activities
- Small, personalized learning settings
- Accountability to the community
- An environment where general and vocational tracks do not exist; instead, high academic achievement and a goal of postsecondary education are expected for every student
- Ninth and twelfth grade experiences that are focused on effective transition into and out of high school
- Shared and collaborative leadership.

For over thirty years, American educators have been weaving these elements into a process of reforming their high schools with the goal of establishing an atmosphere of challenge and support for students. A critical part of the reform—especially for urban schools—has centered on the reorganization of schools into small units to dispel the alienating effects of large schools, student apathy, falling test scores, disengaged school administrations, and unrelated curricular approaches. These smaller units within the large comprehensive high schools create structures for a more coordinated and concentrated approach to instruction, develop a personalized school climate for students, increase opportunities for communication between families and schools, and allow teachers a greater role in school leadership. The challenge for educators across the nation now is how to design and develop a teacher corps and a school culture that allow for a school to operate in a completely different manner than the classrooms we experienced during our own education.

Significant relevant research indicates that education is most effective when a true community of learners and leaders emerges in a high school. Increasingly, the research supports that this community is most effective when it exists in a small school environment with students engaged with teachers in a school-within-school setting of approximately 400 students. When educators, parents, students, and business/community and postsecondary partners join together in this manner, they make the high school experience one where excellence in teaching and nurturing each child to success are the focal points. In these settings, instructional practice is honed and the curriculum is integrated, is career related, and targets high standards. Here, the job of education is shared by supportive partners. Here, students find their own voice, build their skills, and develop a sense of community with their fellow students and their adult teachers. Teachers take on new roles as leaders in the school improvement process and commit to an introspective, data-driven process of reflecting on their shared practice. Community stakeholders demonstrate a vested interest in the success of students and the long-term success of the community. And families—however defined—find their own voice in a structure that welcomes and engages them as it also relies on their involvement to support student success.

Over the past three decades, we have seen a move from pockets of excellence for some students toward "whole-school reform," where all students have the opportunity to excel. We have seen that the move to implement SLC is as viable in our largest cities as it is in our smallest rural communities. There is a wide range of approaches to creating small learning environments for teaching and learning. For some, magnet schools, public charters, and learning "houses" have met the challenge successfully.

For others, the creation of school-within-a-school career academies has been the desired approach. Our nation is once again at a turning point, with a growing urgency to make whole-school reform statewide and to implement whole-district reform. Increasingly, the educational strategy used to raise the bar for all students is the creation of SLC, not because the creation of an SLC in and of itself leads to improvement, but rather because the effective implementation of an SLC creates the environment for a focus on data, students, and professional practice that leads to the improvements we seek to make.

I first wrote *Creating and Sustaining Small Learning Communities* in 2000. The near-decade of work that has intervened has necessitated an important shift in the emphasis of this completely revised book. The focus on school improvement has been altered dramatically as the educational and political landscape has continued to shift under foot. The changes brought about by research and legislation, as well as those reaped through the hard work of educators in the trenches, has brought a new perspective to the implementation of smaller learning communities and a need to update that work and the myriad of tools contained in the accompanying CD-ROM Tool Kit. We have moved into an era where structures and instruction must be addressed—not in separate or even parallel implementations, but in one seamless data-driven design. It can no longer be (if it ever could) about the simple creation of SLC. It must be about using SLC as a vehicle for creating high-performing high schools.

Over the years that have passed since the first edition of this book, a deep research base has developed, based on what works and what is essential for school improvement. Among the major changes is the unprecedented focus on data at the national, state, district, school, and classroom levels. While the first edition gave only a nod to the importance of data, this edition places the use of data front and center in a manner that borrows from a statement by Harvard's Tony Wagner: "no blame, no shame, no excuses." The emphasis on improving the instruction and educational outcomes for all of the nation's youth has grown as well with the advent of the standards movement, the "No Child Left Behind" legislation, and the simply astounding numbers of students who drop out, drift out, and leave our high schools unprepared to lead successful adult lives. While the debate about the need for reform rages in this country, and the national dialogue continues to focus on improving outcomes for youth through the structures of small schools, SLC, and redesigned, reconfigured, reformed, and converted schools, this text will lead you step by step through a process that will help you develop your own school improvement strategy. The book walks you through the five stages of effective implementation: formation, study and awareness, establishing structures, community engagement and commitment, and evaluation. It adds to the first edition's recommendation in the areas of the importance of mission, an effective planning process, professional development needs, defining roles and responsibilities, and the use of time. As in the original work, we will continue to look through the lenses of personalization, curriculum and instruction, partnership, and creating a climate for success; now we add a focus on data and reflective practice at each interval. We also provide assistance in navigating the sometimes complex political milieu that we know as American high schools. We distinguish between creating stand-alone small schools and establishing the varied types of SLC we see in the nation's high schools, including ninth grade and career academies. While the SLC you choose to create may not, for example, have a career or industry focus, you will undoubtedly want to enlist business partners and have your students involved with some type of career exploration or job shadowing. We will discuss the pros and cons of schoolwide, all-at-once implementation. This book is part education theory and part technical manual. It contains information, research, and best practices, as well as technical tools to power your efforts to lead other educators toward creating improved schools. We will spend most of our time empowering you to make good decisions and build the capacity of the educators you work with as you learn to create and sustain SLC.

Perhaps the biggest challenge in creating the type of educational setting we have outlined so far is determining who is responsible for implementing and effecting the changes necessary to transform the high school. In the rush for implementation, teachers will look to the school administration, the administration will look to the district, and the district will look for funding to support staff and services in order to provide the resources and training necessary. The business and community partners will look to the school to take the lead, and schools will turn to partners for support. Parents will want what all parents want: what is best for their children. Students will want to get on with the process of being teenagers, and they will trust us to provide them with a high-quality education that prepares them to succeed after high school. In today's educational arena, there is no time for waiting for someone else to single-handedly make a difference in the academic lives of young people.

If you are reading this book, you are part of the process. You are a key element of reforming your school into what we believe works best for all students: a small learning environment with high standards, an engaging curriculum, and a community partnership of support. While this book is specifically written for those who are mandated, by job or consulting contract description, with leading the SLC development process within a school or district, it is in fact for all those who will work with SLC.

Creating and Sustaining Small Learning Communities is based on the premise that no one person or group can do it alone. A team approach must be established, and the individual gifts of the team members and participating organizations must be identified and maximized. We must act now. As a nation, we have been worrying that many children are "falling through the cracks"—indeed, many are falling into a chasm. We have to act now to stop the flow of our children into a future that holds little promise for those ill-prepared to meet it.

Creating and Sustaining Small Learning Communities is designed to help you do just that. While the format of this book is meant to be user-friendly and "step-by-step," the nonlinear nature of school improvement suggests that there will be times you will want to move back and forth throughout the chapters as you reflect on what you need to know and what you must be able to do to make the biggest strides. Before you begin working your way through the chapters, review the entire process of implementation and sustainment that is laid out for you here. Depending on your school's or schools' situation, there may be some activities that should be undertaken before others, committees that should be established, Tool Kit applications tried, or advisory boards that should be enhanced or put to work before they are suggested in the sequence of this work. Take stock of and value what you now have, then get to work.

The Tool Kit will help you to assess your current school design. It will also help share the message of SLC. Its built-in PowerPoint presentation walks you through the main SLC design elements and shows what it takes to effectively implement them. It will serve as a useful tool in professional learning settings. The Tool Kit also holds over 30 electronic files or folders that will aid you in the critically necessary process of documenting your efforts. With the Tool Kit, you will be able to assess your faculty's readiness for embracing a move to SLC, chart their staff development needs, place them in teams, measure the developmental growth of the SLC, and evaluate the impact of the experience on students.

In addition to your own work, you will want to be aware of and keep abreast of national trends and current research. You will find references to useful articles, resources, and books, as well as essential Web page and Listserv listings, in the Resources section.

This book and Tool Kit are based on almost twenty years' experience in working with small and large school systems in over thirty states. The lessons shared are those developed through great collaboration and struggles with state-level administrators, superintendents, district leaders, principals, teachers, parents, students, postsecondary institutions, labor organizations, community-based organizations (CBO), government agencies, and businesses. Throughout this book, we share the lessons we have learned and the best practices we have developed in working with some of our nation's most challenged schools. From coast to coast, in urban centers, in suburban communities, and on tribal lands, the questions are the same. How do we develop a learning atmosphere for our students that encourages their individualized growth, has high standards, and prepares them to take their places on a global stage after they leave high school? How do we develop a teacher corps that is not only skilled in its own discipline, but can work across disciplines and with a variety of business and community partners? How do we share the challenge of education between business and schools? What school structures allow for this school climate to be created?

The journey of improving your school will be taxing. You will be amazed, perhaps, at the resistance you will meet from those who are holding on to a status quo that has placed only some of our students in a successful postsecondary position. You may also be amazed at the number of times you will want to give in to the ineffective spinning of the hamster wheel of reform—where we work as hard as we can but do not attain the progress we imagine—because it will seem easier to whirr than to push through to success. Be prepared. We must now commit to success for all students. From this moment forward, move away from the idea that you are "reforming" your school or district. Move away from the idea that you are "moving toward small learning communities." Instead, commit to a practice of continuous improvement. Create effective, data-driven, personalized SLC for teaching and learning. Be restless, along with your fellow travelers, to research, establish, assess, and continually seek to improve the structures and practices that will lead to effective environments for teaching and learning. I look forward to walking part of the journey with you through the pages of this book and with the help of the Tool Kit materials.

Acknowledgments

The original edition of this work, *Creating and Sustaining Small Learning Communities*, was dedicated, in part, to the many administrators and teachers who let me learn with them along the way. I still owe this group my thanks. They would be surprised at how their work continues to live in the number of times I tell their stories. Nearly a decade after the original work, I have been blessed with the good fortune of working in many more schools, and at increasingly deep levels of school reform. Over the years, I have worked at shifting the focus from one of high school reform—with a focus on deficits—to one of committing to a process of continuous improvement. That journey has brought an increased number of state and district superintendents, national reformers, principals, and classroom teachers into my work and me into theirs. In each of these venues, there are always students who keep me centered. At each juncture, we push each other to be better. I owe my thanks to all. This edition owes special thanks to the principals and school improvement facilitators in Houston, Texas; Wingate High School, Ft. Wingate, New Mexico; and Westgate High School in New Iberia, Louisiana.

Specifically, in the writing of this book, I would like to thank those who provided peer reviews—they taught me anew the importance of my own reflective practice and a commitment to continuous improvement. Lizzie Brenkus and Laureen Shea of Corwin Press make the process of creating books a positive journey. My thanks also to many good friends who cheer me on and tolerate the hermitage that is writing; to my daughter and son, Katie and Brian Loewe, who help me keep my language honest and inclusive; Cynthia Conwell, who has been an outstanding friend, resource finder, first reader, and moral compass for excellence; Curt Gilroy, who brought a detailed eye and a sharp No. 2 pencil to my work; Kim Stephanic, for her thinking on quality instruction; and Tonia Essig, without whom I truly could not have completed the comprehensive rewrite of this work. She was reminder, editor, and research aid. She consistently freed me from countless tasks that would have taken me away from its completion.

Always, thankfully, there has been my dad. He is the setter of high standards, the master editor, and the one who will have asked me the day this book goes to the publisher, "When are you writing your next one?"

Corwin Press gratefully acknowledges the contributions of the following reviewers:

Randel Beaver
Superintendent
Archer City ISD
Archer City, TX

Robert L. Blake
Principal
Mainland Regional High School
Linwood, NJ

Darin S. Drill
Principal
Cascade High School
Turner, OR

Daniel C. Elliott
Professor
Department of Distributed Learning
Azusa Pacific University
Azusa, CA

Douglas Gordon Hesbol
Superintendent
Laraway CCSD #70C
Joliet, IL

Mary Beth Lambert
Associate Director
Coalition of Essential Schools
    NW/Small Schools Project
Seattle, WA

Rodney Muth
Professor
Administrative Leadership and
    Policy Studies
University of Colorado
Denver, CO

Brinton S. Ramsey
Research Coordinator
Coalition of Essential Schools
    NW/Small Schools Project
Seattle, WA

Leslie Standerfer
Principal
Estrella Foothills High School
Goodyear, AZ

Cathy Wallach
Research Coordinator
Coalition of Essential Schools
    NW/Small Schools Project
Seattle, WA

Steve Zsiray
Principal/CEO
InTech Collegiate High School
North Logan, UT

About the Author

Grace Sammon, president and founder of GMS Partners, Inc., is an educator, school reformer, consultant, "coach," speaker, and internationally recognized author. She has spent nearly twenty years working in one of the United States' toughest institutions, the American high school. She has inspired change and fostered improvement in schools, districts, and government organizations nationally through her upbeat advice and sound, practical recommendations.

GMS Partners, Inc. is an educational consulting firm dedicated to enhancing school communities through a focused effort on vision, alignment of resources, planning, coaching, professional development, and a commitment to continuous improvement. Under Ms. Sammon's leadership, GMS Partners, Inc. has worked in thirty-two states across the nation, with a focus on whole-school improvement. She is the cofounding director of the National Career Academy Coalition (NCAC) and the Executive Director of the Business Institute for Educators. Her clients have included schools and school systems at the state and district level, nonprofits, and the U.S. Departments of Defense, Education, Health and Human Services, and Navy.

Ms. Sammon has authored *Battling the Hamster Wheel:*™ *Strategies for Making High School Reform Work*, eight manuals on school-to-career transition, and articles on organizational change, school partnerships, and staff development. She created *Metro MANIA: The Great Train Ride Through Washington*, a board and street experience game to facilitate student use of public transportation while they gain an appreciation for the employment and cultural offerings of the nation's capital. She has also authored five integrated curricular pieces for use in middle schools and a teen pregnancy prevention curriculum and training manual.

She earned her Master's Degree in Education at The Catholic University of America. She has ten years' experience in higher education administration and has served as an adjunct university professor and a long-term substitute teacher. Her professional notes include listings in *Who's Who in American Education* and being named Outstanding Business Person of the Year by Future Business Leaders of America. In the spring of 1996, she was appointed to the U.S. Secretary of Defense's Joint Civilian Orientation Council. She has two children, Brian and Kate Loewe, who continue to inspire her with their commitment to justice and equity, and to improving the communities they serve.

The reason most people never reach their goals is that they don't define them, learn about them, or even seriously consider them as believable or achievable. Winners can tell you where they are going, what they plan to do along the way, and who will be sharing the adventure with them.

—Denis Waitley
Productivity Consultant

1

The Journey Begins

There are risks and costs to a program of action. But they are far less than the long-range risks and costs of comfortable inaction.

—John F. Kennedy

Chapter 1 Road Map

Purpose	To focus on the use of SLC as a critical tool for improving high schools. To arm the practitioner with the history, research, and current practices surrounding the use of SLC as the vehicle for high school improvement. To outline a framework for successful SLC implementation. To identify benefits and types of SLC.
Stage of Implementation	Formation—focus on data, personalization, and creating a climate for success.
Process and Action Steps	Review chapter. Review entire book and Tool Kit. Review Tool 1.1, add your own school/district data.
Tool Kit	1.1 Creating SLC Presentation
Reflective Practice	What are the reasons and resources motivating a move to SLC? What design best suits our improvement needs?
Outcome	Practitioner will be able to articulate the necessity for addressing school improvement needs through creation of SLC, will have developed thinking around appropriate terminology, and will be able to make initial presentation to fellow educators.

Welcome to a journey focused on high school improvement and school redesign. Over the course of these pages, through use of the electronic Tool Kit that accompanies this book, and through your own hard work as a facilitator and practitioner, you will find a map for improving the culture, climate, and educational outcomes for your school and district through the creation of small learning communities (SLC) within the large high school. This book is part educational research and best practice, with the goal of equipping you with the theory and background you need to effectively communicate and make decisions, and part technical tool kit to speed you on your journey—providing shortcuts with electronic files that will help you motivate, plan, implement, assess, and document. As you move into the formative stage of your work, you will gain background knowledge on school reform, research-based strategies, national trends, and best practices. You will assess and value the strengths already in existence in your school, and identify the colleagues with whom you will work most closely. You will move through the stages of formation, study and awareness, establishing structures, community engagement and commitment, and evaluation. You will work through over one hundred items for decision and possible action in a long "Punch List" of implementation strategies. You will pay attention to both structure and instruction, and you will become increasingly data driven. This is essential in that it is not the simple creation of the school-within-a-school small learning communities that makes the difference in student achievement and school climate, but rather the attention to a clear mission and reflective practice. Along the way, you will have the opportunity to define and refine your work and tailor it to your specific educational mission, objectives, and needs. Your work, motivated by an urgency and commitment to improving your school, will not be as straightforward or linear as working through a book in ten chapters and thirty-plus tools. With that in mind, you will want to preview the Tool Kit early on and become familiar with each section of this book in order that you may turn to relevant sections as the need arises. At the end, you will have a school or schools redesigned into SLC. This, however, will be just the beginning because the creation of SLC simply sets the stage for establishing practices focused on *continuous improvement*.

If you have been in education for more than a few years, you are already familiar with the cycles of "school improvements" that ebb and flow through our schools. In an era that calls for us to radically rethink high schools, it is important to reflect on where we have been in the last forty years, learn the lessons from the work of researchers and educators, and position ourselves for creating *effective* schools. Rather than seeking the silver bullet, we must focus on mission and purpose: equity for all students, and clear and measurable outcomes. Without these at the core of our work in school redesign, we are likely to miss the mark, creating hollow structures that meet SLC design elements but do not result in higher performing schools. In short, without reflective practice we miss the warning issued by the White Rabbit to Alice in Wonderland—"if you do not know where you are going, anywhere will do"—and we wind up back at the beginning, having worked very hard and having not met with the anticipated goal of the journey.

Throughout this book, you will note that the words *continuous improvement* are always presented in italic. This is to continually reinforce that any school redesign, reform, or program implementation's sole goal should be to make an improvement in the climate and results focused on teaching and learning. Viewed in any other manner, you help create a "been there, done that, waiting for the next thing to happen" attitude amongst your faculty. Begin now to frame your thinking not around "reform," and not simply about the creation of SLC, but rather on building a commitment to *continuous improvement*.

BACKGROUND

The move to "small" has grown steadily since the late 1960s, with the start of the first career academies in Philadelphia, Pennsylvania. National momentum was brought on by the U.S. Department of Education's redesign of Perkins II, and the May 1994 passage by the United States Congress of the National School-to-Work Opportunities Act (NSTWOA), also known as the School-to-Work Act. The Act called for a sweeping change in American education. Building on the work already completed by Goals 2000 and the Secretary's Commission on Achieving Necessary Skills (SCANS), the School-to-Work Act invited all states and school systems to apply for funds to develop the required school-based and work-based learning systems that would:

- Address the school-to-career needs of *all* youth
- Create the opportunity to learn in a school-based educational setting that provides in-depth career awareness no later than the seventh grade
- Provide specific opportunities to interact with business and community leaders in a work-based career-focused program no later than the tenth grade, and
- Develop a sustained means of connecting these experiences through curricular innovations and supporting community structures.

The goal of the School-to-Work Act was to raise academic standards to provide *all* children with the opportunity to succeed in both the workplace and postsecondary educational opportunities. It was intended to increase young people's awareness of the variety of career opportunities open to them, to raise understanding and expectations about what students should *know and be able to do* in preparation for their future as lifelong learners and contributing members of society, and to develop a community of support that would change the way children learn and teachers teach through linkages with the educational, business, government, nonprofit, labor, and postsecondary communities.

Many schools and school districts chose to approach the move to school-to-work—known later as school-to-careers—by creating career academies within their high schools. Pragmatically, it was easier for large comprehensive high schools to deal with implementing such sweeping reforms if the changes could be addressed in smaller units rather than addressing the entire body of students, teachers, and programs of studies. Later in this text, we will draw a distinction between career academies, houses, and other types of SLC. For now, at their heart each comprises a small group of students, scheduled together, working with a small group of adults over a period of two to four years. Frequently, students are drawn to the program because of a career or academic theme or because of the special opportunities afforded them for internships or college experiences. Always, there is a commitment from the start that the smaller unit of teachers, students, families, and partners will create an atmosphere of support for each other's success. These school-within-a-school programs showed early signs of success in changing school climate, increasing student attendance rates, and raising high school completion rates. More often than not, these programs exist separately from the rest of the school, and they were originally implemented for just *some* students. They were known as stand-alone or "pocket" academies. The next generation of high school reform called for *all* students to be engaged in SLC throughout the school—"wall-to-wall."

As the NSTWOA legislation began to sunset, and the all-important supportive funding came to an end, we witnessed the emergence of two other federal initiatives: the Comprehensive School Reform Demonstration Act (CSRD) legislation of 1998, and the Smaller Learning Community (SLC) grants that began to be issued by the U.S. Department of Education in 2000. At the same time, major foundations such as Carnegie, Annenberg, and the Bill and Melinda Gates Foundation, as well as hundreds of other smaller regional funders, pumped significant money into large comprehensive high schools in an effort to make them small, more personalized environments for teaching and learning. Many of the mandates of NSTWOA were kept, but the emphasis began to shift subtly to a more solid "academic" base. And, while the intent of the NSTWOA was "*all* students," the terms of these newer initiatives' funding streams were and are far more prescriptive. Add to this mandate mix those created by No Child Left Behind (NCLB) for highly qualified teachers, students that pass state exit tests, and schools that must reach and maintain annual yearly progress (AYP), and we begin to feel rumblings to the foundation of education as we know it in this country.

Despite the trend to create smaller learning units—or sometimes even true, fully autonomous small schools—student enrollments are at an all-time high, and large, comprehensive high schools are still in vogue. This growth in student numbers is expected to continue for the next decade. Alaska, Idaho, Nevada, and New Mexico will see enrollments grow by more than 10 percent. By 2010, California will add 278,000 students to its rolls, while Texas will gain 219,000 students even before the mass transplantation of tens of thousands of students transported from flood-ravaged New Orleans. Across the country, it is now common to have high schools of 2,000 and 3,000 youths. In Los Angeles, Miami, and other cities, school populations can top 5,000. And in more rural communities, where it is unusual to have large groups of people together, even the large regional high school—small by city standards—can feel like a very big place. These schools exist at a time when the research points out that many of our schools are too large to effectively educate our youth; there is convergent research that supports a move to small, high-standards environments for teaching and learning.

Yet there are those who continue the argument for large schools. The rationale falls on the side of the plethora of courses and extracurricular offerings made possible when student numbers are high. While the numbers may breed increased services, they also have the potential to create an atmosphere that is the worst of what we are coming to know about American high schools. A U.S. Department of Education posting from the late 1990s noted that schools of 1,000 or more students experience 825 percent more violent crime, 270 percent more vandalism, and 1,000 percent more weapons incidents, compared with those which have fewer than 300 students. More recent studies point to the frightening statistic that, as a nation, we now graduate only 50 percent of African Americans, 51 percent of American Indians, and 53 percent of Latino and Hispanic students. For white and Asian students, the figures are 75 percent and 77 percent, respectively. Can we be satisfied that even our best results leave nearly 25 percent of the population behind?

The creation of *effective* smaller learning units *within the large, comprehensive high school* may, then, be the nation's best answer to combat these trends and the history of underachievement and alienation experienced by so many students in our high schools. These small learning units, by their very design, nurture a positive relationship between teachers, students, and the community. Those who seek to create them must begin with the understanding that providing a personalized, respectful, caring, high-expectations learning environment that leads to postsecondary success should be the birthright of all those attending public schools in the United States.

Mary Anne Raywid writes in her review of more than 100 studies on school size that the relationship between small schools and positive education outcomes has been "confirmed with a clarity and at a level of confidence rare in the annals of education research" (Raywid, 1999). Increases in standardized test scores are not necessarily a part of the research-based listing of student outcomes, although there are studies that reflect increases in grade point averages for academy students. It is unlikely that you will see academic gains through a structure that, in some cases, simply "rearranges the deck chairs." An SLC implementation that commits to working on structure and instruction at the same time will serve as a catalyst for school improvement. It is time to roll up our sleeves and begin in earnest to reform our schools around the key elements, principles, and practices that will successfully propel our students into the classrooms and workplaces of tomorrow.

THE MANDATE FOR SCHOOL REFORM

We have already noted the fact that, across the country, there are major reform initiatives being funded by state, local, and federal grants. Goals 2000, SCANS (discussed in Chapter 6), NSTWOA, CSRD, SLC, and Breaking Ranks I and II all fueled a revolution in funding for the revamping of schools. Yet, almost forty years into reform, the national data tell us that we are woefully unskilled as an educational community to meet the ever-demanding needs of a culturally diverse student population which must be prepared to take its place in a global economy. We are familiar with the staggering dropout rates—particularly of non-white students—but we sometimes fail to make the connection between those data and the impact on the broader community or nation. Indeed, in a recent Teachers College–Columbia University Week article we learned from researcher Alan Richard (2005) that "the United States could recoup nearly $200 billion a year in economic losses and secure its place as the world's future economic and educational leader by raising the quality of schooling, investing more money and other resources in education, and lowering dropout rates."

In the same article, economist Enrico Moretti states that a "one percent increase in graduation rates nationally would correlate with about 100,000 fewer crimes annually in the United States. Such a step would save the nation $1.4 billion a year in law-enforcement and incarceration costs." The article continues, "An increase in graduation rates by 10 percentage points would correlate with a 20 percent reduction in murder and assault arrest rates. It is hard to think of a better reason for investing in public schooling" (Richard, 2005).

And, while the data are clear that SLC positively impact dropout rates, this is not the only important data point. Students who remain in school must be taught to high standards in an increasingly information age–driven economy. We must, as educators, commit to creating a high-expectations learning environment for all students and to creating a "college-ready culture" in our schools. At the same time, we must not veer too far from the intent of the NSTWOA. We must be aware that not all of our students will seek or attain college entrance. At this midpoint in the first decade of the twenty-first century, record numbers of students are applying to colleges and universities, and the "pool" of college-aged students will continue to grow for the balance of the decade. The *CBS Evening News* recently reported that

> of the three million students graduating from high school this year, a record two thirds applied to college. That has forced universities nationwide to reject more students than ever. At the University of Virginia, the acceptance of applicants rate fell from 38 percent last year to 36 percent this year. At Northwestern, only 28 percent of students got in, while Yale accepted about just 8.5 percent of all applicants. The University of Pennsylvania had the largest admission drop, 21 percent accepted last year to less than 18 percent this time around. (Solorzano, 2006)

A majority of those who attend college will need some remediation; a significant proportion will not return for a second year of schooling. Add this to a labor market that is crying out for a skilled workforce and we must, as a nation, understand the need, and undertake a commitment, to prepare youth with a variety of valued postsecondary success plans.

The task is great. The research, and our own experience in school systems, tells us that the large school experience simply makes it too easy for students to fall though the cracks, and for teachers and administrators who are not *yet* up to the task of leading in a high-expectations culture to hide.

We will talk more about change and reform efforts in later chapters. For now, it is important to understand that, across the country, the mandate is clear—there is no turning back. There is a growing national commitment to reforming high schools, as evidenced in part by the commitment of the National Governors Association (NGA) to high school reform.

BENEFITS OF SLC

Research conducted by RAND, the Manpower Demonstration Research Corporation (MDRC), and Will Daggett's International Center for Leadership in Education (ICLE) all points to smaller learning environments bringing about improvements in student and school outcomes. Large school size adversely affects student involvement in school activities, attendance, and school climate. In addition, schools with large student numbers demonstrate evidence of increased school dropout rates, vandalism, and violence. The expectation for schools that transition from traditional large comprehensive schools to academies and SLC is that they will provide a nurturing environment, career-focused curriculum, access to adult role models, and work-based experiences for students. The anticipated result is higher expectations for student outcomes, increased achievement, increased numbers of students staying in school, and more positive postsecondary experiences. SLC, when done well and comprehensively, build in the rigor, relevance, and relationships that lead to the all-important *results* we seek in school improvement. Indeed, according to Dr. Michelle Fine of the City University of New York Graduate Center, "Small learning communities are the single most powerful intervention for young people" (Fine, 2000).

The 2006 MDRC report offers lessons from interventions in place in over 2,500 high schools across the country. They relate to:

- Creating personalized and orderly learning environments
- Assisting students who enter high school with poor academic skills
- Improving instructional content and practice
- Preparing students for the world beyond high school, and
- Stimulating change in overstressed high schools.

The report asserts that structural changes and instructional improvement are the twin pillars of high school reform. The MDRC research suggests that transforming schools into SLC and assigning students to faculty advisors can increase students' feelings of connectedness to their teachers. Extended class periods, special catch-up courses, high-quality curricula, and training on these curricula for teachers can improve student achievement. Furthermore, school/employer partnerships that involve career awareness activities and work internships can help students attain higher earnings after high school (MDRC, 2006).

Schools also report a myriad of positive results when they engage in SLC designs. Teachers report a sense of increased professionalism. In addition, schools report increased resources and commitment from business/community partners, increased student *and* staff attendance, fewer incidences of school disruptions, and increased graduation rates. Communities, too, register marked increases in appreciation for the benefits of SLC. Parents and guardians find it easier to be engaged in the high school life of their child and with their child's teachers. Business, labor, professional associations, and CBO all value the clear educational benefit of students staying in school and the opportunity to serve as good "corporate" citizens. They also see the benefit of establishing a more prepared and effective citizenry and workforce, and note the positive impacts on a community when youth are nontruant and engaged in fewer high-risk activities. Principals and teachers, in partnership with other designated practitioners, seek these improvements and are charged with enacting reforms and furthering a *continuous improvement* mandate.

WHO MAKES IT HAPPEN?
THE PRACTITIONER'S ROLE

In every district, in every school, there must be champions for *effective* reform. They must battle the tide and the constant spinning of a wheel that too often keeps them from meeting the mission they set. These are the change agents by job description, by consulting assignment, or by passion. Regardless of whether you are a state-level leader, superintendent, principal, member of a school improvement team, or one designated to marshal school improvement through SLC, the key practitioner role will be the primary force in partnering other administrators, faculty, and stakeholders to build school and community commitment to a data-driven process aimed *not at reform* but at *continuous improvement.* The practitioner—sometimes working in isolation, but more often with a team—will ensure that the effort to create SLC succeeds through a developed and coordinated effort of planning, staff development training, and program development. Practitioners help create school or district high-quality environments for teaching and learning. In addition, they are the individuals who help sustain improvements by seeking to make sense of the cycle of reforms and district mandates. They help seek appropriate grant funds and community resources, and they must be hold the rest of the stakeholders' feet collectively to the fire of accountability—helping all to stay the course in creating what we know is best for students. Let us be clear, however, that whole-school and whole-district reform is about a shared level of accountability. As we will see in subsequent chapters, it means everyone's roles and responsibilities are on the table of change. Individual principals have the primary responsibility for developing a school climate and the conditions that enable the school to meet the tenets and mandates that their state and district have set out to increase student performance as well as to prepare students to take an active role in the future of the community. The principals will share this authority with a cadre of professionals, and some version of a school restructuring team that will include parents, partners, and, where applicable, teacher union representatives. This work is not for the faint of heart. You will have to have many "messy" conversations. You will have to take risks and understand that some will meet with failure. The goal is *effective* SLC that embody a respectful, high-expectations climate for teaching and learning. To not take the risks is something this nation cannot afford. In Chapter 10, we review the practitioner's role as we look back and forward at how effective we were and need to be in improving school culture and outcomes through implementation of key elements for effective redesign.

KEY ELEMENTS OF EFFECTIVE REDESIGN EFFORTS

At the high school level, the transformation to SLC begins with the creation of a school climate that changes the way schools operate and the way communities address the continued educational needs of their youth. This change in climate demands:

- Developing a mission and commitment framework to which all can ascribe
- Establishing practices that change the school management structure to one of shared leadership and that keep students at the center
- Focusing on curriculum and instruction that is "high standard" for all students
- Creating school and community partnerships that are truly collaborative working arrangements with shared vision and responsibility, and
- (For career academies) engaging students in a career-focused curriculum and continuously complex series of work-based experiences that are as equally valued by the school as the "academic" education components.

LOOKING AT DESIGN OPTIONS

As the number of SLC and career academies grows, spurred on by government and foundation funds, and as the new research on adolescents continues to highlight their specific developmental needs, we have new tools and solid research to guide our work in redesigning high schools. Nationally, there is no one model for the creation of SLC. Their variety is as individual as the schools and school systems in which they are housed. While the terms "academy," "career academy," "house," and "schools of" are sometimes used interchangeably, researchers and national practitioners tend to differentiate them as distinct, one from another. There are some shared elements, of course, the most common of which is cohort student schedules that keep students and teachers together for a period of years, thus creating familiarity and a common set of experiences. The design you choose will be based on what you want to accomplish in your schools to create the ideal graduate and what you believe to be true in regard to your students' ability to handle transitions between middle school, ninth grade, and the upper levels of high school. Regardless of the design or term upon which you decide, a commitment to common language is important in order that all stakeholders understand the design elements and the goals that design seeks to achieve. There is no convergent research on which approach meets with the greatest success for students. It is not the design, primarily, that contributes to effectiveness but rather engaging in a thoughtful process that requires a strong focus and commitment to quality implementation of what we refer to as the "big five" or "bins of work" that transforms high schools. These "bins" include:

- Personalization
- Data-driven management
- A curriculum- and instruction-centric approach
- Community partnerships, and
- Creating a climate for success.

In our work with schools, we explain the bins as follows.

Personalization

Successful high schools create personalized, flexible, and challenging learning environments that meet the needs of all students, regardless of race, gender identification, ethnicity, socioeconomic status, or educational need. Personalization goes beyond simply creating small structures; it means providing true support for each child. Personalization goes beyond the needs of students; it includes the development of professional learning communities (PLC) for educators as well.

Data-Driven Management

Successful high schools ensure that decision making is tied to analysis, and the understanding of meaningful data, and they are aware that data are used effectively at the district, school, and classroom levels to guide reforms, instruction, and student outcomes.

Curriculum- and Instruction-Centric

Successful high schools ultimately know that what happens in the classroom is the most powerful determinant of student success. Interventions in planning and coaching are designed to help district- and school-level administrators, department chairs, literacy and data coaches, and teachers to improve curricula and instructional methods.

Partnership Focused

Successful high schools create effective partnerships between all members of a school community, including district personnel, students, families, business and community leaders, unions, postsecondary education, and other stakeholders.

Creating a Climate for Success

Successful high schools commit to building continuous improvement efforts, creating a climate that will sustain teacher and student success. This involves attention to the many interrelated elements that comprise the operation of schools and districts, including alignment of policies and resources and creating effective professional development plans. At its core, a climate for success means honing a definition of effective high schools and a set of practices and policies that support them.

As a way of beginning your thinking about "design," it is helpful to use the "bins" to form reflective questions about what you need to know and to be able to address each of these areas of work. It also helps to begin to line up in your mind what you already have in place and where you will need to expand. Along the way, we will arm you with many tools that are examined through these lenses. Many U.S. high schools are seeking to address these issues through a reconfiguration of the traditional high schools noted below. Each of these are distinct from true *small schools* such as The Met in Rhode Island, the Julia Richmond multiplex school in New York, and several of Baltimore City's small high schools. The independent, stand-alone schools have answered the question of how we deliver high-quality, personalized instruction for students by creating independent schools that are small in size and number. For the traditionally large high schools, the answer is more frequently one of the following design options.

Academy

This tends to be a very general term that usually follows the same definition as an SLC (see below). It is sometimes interchanged with the more specific term "career academy."

Career Academy

This is an SLC that enrolls students and teachers who self-select to be part of the academy. Each academy has a broad-based career theme, an integrated sequence of courses, work-based experiences, and strong alliances with business and community partners. While these designs include a career theme, and may lead toward industry certifications, it is essential to understand that they are not intended either to force students into an early career choice or to churn out students who will necessarily pursue careers in the themed academy area. Rather, the career theme is used as a catalyst to garner student interest, focus learning, and build a coherent and relevant curricular experience. The additional payoff is a more informed postsecondary choice. Unlike the other terms in this section, there is a nationally approved "standards of practice" for career academies that was agreed to in the spring of 2005 by leading organizations including the Career Academy Support Network (CASN), the National Academy Foundation (NAF), the National Career Academy Coalition (NCAC), the National Center for Education and the Economy (NCEE), America's Choice, the Southern Regional Education Board (SREB) High Schools That Work, and Johns Hopkins University's Talent Development High Schools. The link to those ten key elements of successful practice can be found in the Resources section.

House

The term usually follows the same definition as an SLC (see below).

Magnet Schools

Magnet schools were begun as specialty and theme-based schools or schools-within-schools for purposes of desegregation without forced busing. They were the natural progression from the specialty schools of early America, such as the Boston Latin School and small focused alternative schools. A common theme or instructional strategy and a small group of committed, talented, career-interested students became the means to motivate families and students to leave their neighborhood school and attend magnets. The federally funded Magnet Schools Assistance Program (MSAP), begun in 1984, is still a national program today. Funds are disbursed from the U.S. Department of Education directly to school districts through a competitive grant process. In many communities, it has become commonplace for the "magnet" programs to be elitist, serving only the best students. This was not the intent and should be discouraged: cultural diversity, common purpose, and building on student interest and abilities make magnets especially well suited for SLC and career academies.

Major, Pathway, or Cluster

These terms usually refer not to a true school-within-a-school, like SLC, but to a sequence of career-related and/or academic courses that lead toward graduation. Students in a major, pathway, or cluster may or may not be scheduled together in a manner that creates an SLC; however, most SLC have some sort of pathway sequence. Often thought of as similar to a major in college, these sequences build knowledge and skills. In larger SLC, they are frequently used to define subteams of students and teachers. For example, in an SLC of 400 students focused on health and human services, you might further define the student's experience for those students who are interested in deeper study around medical issues as opposed to education and training.

Ninth Grade or Freshman Academies

These develop students' academic and social skills by providing a strong orientation, freshman transition course, advisory support, and the opportunity to learn in teams that promote individualized supports for student success. They usually have a career-awareness component. Ninth grade is the time for students to focus on study skills, create a six-year educational plan, begin to engage in service learning, select an upper-level SLC, and start a high school portfolio. While not all schools are choosing to create "ninth grade only" units for their students, there is a growing body of research that suggests that the developmental needs of ninth graders need to include a specialized program of studies and services, regardless of the designation of a stand-alone ninth grade program within the regular school. The most widely recognized proponent of stand-alone ninth grades—and where we have learned a great deal about its students' needs—is the Johns Hopkins University's Talent Development High School Ninth Grade "Success Academy." With specific structural, interpersonal, and curricular supports, this CSRD-approved model is demonstrating student gains in reading and mathematics scores, and also showing lower instances of absenteeism and dropout rates.

Regardless of how students are placed in the overall SLC design, ninth grade must include significant interpersonal and academic support for surviving the high school years and for establishing successful habits of the mind and heart.

Ninth and Tenth Grade "Introductory Houses"

Introductory houses are designed to continue the supportive structure found in the ninth grade–only academy for a period of two years. Some schools choose to loop their teachers with students. While this design has little research basis, we are seeing an increased number of schools exploring this as a design option, perhaps because of the intense focus on students taking the high-stakes state tests in the tenth grade year. Similar to the ninth grade design, students in these "introductory houses" select an "upper house," career academy, or SLC at the midpoint of the tenth grade year. This is sometimes described as the model many of us are accustomed to from our college experience, where we studied fundamentals during the first two years of college and then selected a major that determined the course of our final school experience during the sophomore year.

PLC

PLC are sometimes confused with SLC. PLC are decidedly different. These are groups of educators working together to focus on professional practice. The best SLC incorporate PLC into their practices. The term *PLC* has become common through the work of Rick and Becky DuFour and Robert Eaker (see Eaker, DuFour, & DuFour, 2002). A similar approach, made popular by the National School Reform Faculty (NSRF) and the Coalition of Essential Schools (CES; see Resources section), utilizes "critical friend groups" (CFG) to improve professional practices. Regardless of the specific approach your faculty may espouse, creating a safe haven for looking at student work, teacher assignments, data, professional readings, school decisions, and classroom practices will help teachers learn to work effectively in common planning times. PLC add the "personalization" element into the school experience for the adults. Here teachers read and study texts and materials together. PLC provide a venue for getting in and out of each other's classrooms, modeling, and giving feedback on instructional strategies and classroom management. Teachers in PLC are creating common assessments and examining results. Often, these groups operate in several rings of membership—by SLC, by department, and by grade-level teams.

Schools of . . .

These should not be confused with true, independently operated small schools. Some high schools, seeking to name their SLC efforts, create "schools of . . ." similar to what you might have experienced in college—for example, a school of fine arts or a school of engineering and architecture. This term evolved in large measure as a reaction to the school-to-work movement, when there was a concern that the career themes–tracked programs and the SLC movement were somehow only for under-performing students.

SLC

Designate any separately defined, school-within-a-school, individualized learning unit within a larger school setting. Students and teachers are scheduled together and frequently have a common area of the school in which to hold most or all of their classes. SLC may or may not have a career theme or a set sequence of courses for students. The most comprehensive SLC include: an administrative structure with a principal, lead teacher, and guidance counselor; a heterogeneous team of students and teachers (ranging in size from 350–500, with subteams of 150); a home base or specific section of the school; an academic focus or career theme; extra help for students; data to drive decisions; time used effectively, including common planning time for teachers; coaching support and focused professional development for staff; inculcated traditions, practices, and beliefs; freshman orientation and support; service learning and work-based learning opportunities; opportunities for student voice; advisory supports; postsecondary planning; and a senior project. The design of SLC have two primary formats—ninth through twelfth grade and tenth through twelfth grade, thus continuing the focus on personalization begun in the ninth grade programs described above. Ninth through twelfth grade SLC configure the high school experience into small nine to twelve silos of learning to avoid the multiple transitions faced by students coming from middle school to the high school's ninth grade program, and then transitioning again into one of the upper-level designs. Tenth through twelfth grade, or eleventh through twelfth grade, programs continue the commitment to small school environments by placing students and teachers in learning teams. Increasingly, these teams are clustered around industry areas that specifically set high standards for student performance and develop students' talents and abilities to pursue postsecondary education and employment. The Northwest Regional Education Lab (NWREL), at this writing, has extensive materials, assessments, school comparisons, and resources available on each of these elements at the Web site listed in the Resources section.

Throughout this book, you will see the term "SLC" used as an abbreviated reference for a single small learning community within a comprehensive high school. You will also see the same abbreviation, rather than the sometimes used "SLCs," to reference small learning communities as a group. The word "communi*ties*" is in and of itself a plural. While it may be difficult at first for the eye and mind to make the adjustment, we note it here and encourage similar usage as you implement your own programs.

Reflecting on the five lenses of personalization, data, instruction and curriculum, partnerships, and climate for success provides a focal point for determining the design elements that will best help you achieve the envisioned goals. To borrow from the noted author and documentarian Hedrick Smith, these implementations "cultivate hope in a sea of despair." They transform school culture and are proven to be successful catalysts—particularly in urban areas—for addressing issues of school reform and community and workforce development. They specifically offer students the opportunity to think about themselves and their futures differently. As an example, data from the MDRC, the NAF, and RAND (listed in the Resources section) tell us that students in career academies do not simply *just* finish high school. They emerge as school leaders, earn more credits toward graduation, and attend classes more than their nonacademy counterparts. Teachers report that, while they never worked harder than in an academy setting, they also feel more satisfied, more collegial, more respected, and more effective. Students demonstrate an increased interest in school, resulting in increased graduation rates.

Much of the research on SLC has been done on the early stand-alone "pocket" programs. The restlessness of the educational community to change, and the restlessness of the funding sources—be they government or foundations—to fund, has not provided an in-depth focus around the specific elements that lead to whole-school improvement. Perhaps the most specific data we have come from Daggett's (2004) work on schools meeting with improvement. He identifies nine characteristics of schools meeting with success. In his work, Daggett puts evidence of SLC at the top of his list. The challenge for the nation is how to transform the positive practices that are sometimes created in isolated units to a scale that can benefit all students. Creating and sustaining the best of what educators have learned in pocket academies and in past reform efforts—especially in an era of high-stakes testing—is the current challenge for whole-school, whole-district "reform."

At a Glance: Summing It Up and Next Steps

Practitioners, those tasked directly with the focus on school improvement, have the unique role of partnering with others and pushing the educational agenda. This push–pull must include a direct alliance with the district office, school boards, principals, and individual groups of teachers. All must serve as key resources on current district and national trends in school improvement, including creating a college- and career-ready graduate. A variety of resources are available to practitioners that will give them an excellent background on local and national initiatives. The Tool Kit CD-ROM includes [1.1 Creating SLC Presentation], which is a MS PowerPoint file. All Tool Kit file names are presented in brackets to call your attention to the file as a resource. The table of contents contains both an alphabetical reference and a chart that lets you know where the file is discussed in this text. This presentation summarizes the case for using SLC as the vehicle for high school improvement. It is designed to allow you to insert your specific school data to assist in building the case for change as you present it to other stakeholders and faculties. In addition, it lays out many of the design elements discussed and provides you with visuals that demonstrate the various types of configuration possibilities. A listing of additional support materials is included in the Resources section at the end of this book.

The journey of creating and sustaining SLC and career academies is captured here in sequence, yet implementation is rarely a linear process. Regardless of where you begin with this book, you will want to make a commitment to engage in and model reflective practice and to continually assess your progress against the rubric for SLC. It is only through the process of looking back and looking forward that we will not only know where we have been but where we are going. This is a journey fraught with challenges. One thing we have learned over the last six years, since the first edition of this book was published, is that if we are going to really gain the commitment and engagement of others, we need to start with data and honor what we have already accomplished successfully. Next, you will assess your current level of redesign elements with the Data SLC Implementation Assessment introduced in Chapter 2 and contained as a Microsoft Excel spreadsheet in the Tool Kit. It will provide you a quick sense of the critical areas for consideration as well as a means to place those areas in the framework of your own educational setting.

2

Formation, Study, and Awareness

The Sum of the Parts

Expectations is the place you must always go to before you get to where you're going. Of course, some people never go beyond Expectations, but my job is to hurry them along whether they like it or not.

—Norton Juster, *The Phantom Tollbooth*

Chapter 2 Road Map	
Purpose	To empower practitioners to lead a process of change by benchmarking current efforts and data, and by putting specific student outcomes in place.
Stage of Implementation	Continuing Formation, Embracing Study and Awareness, preliminary work in Establishing Structures—focus on climate for success and data.
Process and Action Steps	Understand the process of change. Utilize Tool Kit files to gather data and assess current improvement efforts. Begin to engage others in the redesign work through establishing teams.
Tool Kit	2.1 What Should a Graduate—Teacher—SLC Look Like? 2.2 Data Tracking Tool 2.3 Data SLC Implementation Assessment 2.4 Data SLC Implementation Assessment With CTE
Reflective Practice	What do the data tell us? Do we really understand and apply the implications of data? With which students are we succeeding and with which are we missing the mark? What structure will provide us with the best vehicle for focusing on *continuous improvement*?
Outcome	Data-rich environment has begun or is enhanced. Preliminary assessments have been completed. Initial team has been created. Decisions, even if preliminary, on design have been accomplished.

"**B**egin with the end in mind" has become an important strategic catchphrase that came into the vernacular largely through Steven Covey's *Seven Habits of Highly Effective People* (1989). In this chapter, we apply that concept to *effective* small learning communities by beginning with our intended end point in mind: the development of an ideal graduate and ideal teacher. We will assess our current school structures and see how they match up to those employed by effective smaller learning communities. Using data, we will ask the hard question of how close we are to establishing a school that is committed to continually improving its practice and meeting the needs of all students. At the end of this chapter, you will have a base for working with your colleagues. You will have rolled up your sleeves and dug deeply into the Tool Kit. You will have begun the essential first stages of "formation" and "study and awareness."

As a key practitioner, you will want to begin to note your own developmental steps in order that they can be mirrored and modeled with your school improvement team, school decision making team, leadership team, redesign team, or others with whom you will share the primary work around redesign in a move toward *continuous improvement*. This, in turn, will have to be modeled with the faculty or the district as a whole. One of your first steps will be the most important. Ensure that you plan time to bring others along with you on the journey toward creating ideal outcomes for students. Whether you are revising or revitalizing existing SLC, this process will likely require sweeping changes in practice. Therefore, we start this chapter by building an understanding of the process of change that we engage in as individuals and as a group.

UNDERSTANDING THE PROCESS OF CHANGE

Let us be honest. Too many of our schools are not working. They may be functioning well for some students some of the time, but they often miss the opportunity to positively impact all students' lives. A peculiar data phenomenon is that, when surveyed, "the nation" agrees that our schools are in crisis, and that the knowledge, skills, abilities, and social fiber of today's youth need to be improved. However, individual families and teachers still believe that *their own* schools are working—sometimes in spite of mounting evidence to the contrary. Across the nation, and most likely within your own district, the change process is driven by the need to rigorously attack specific school and community deficits, such as low state test scores, underperforming schools, high truancy and dropout rates, low graduation rates, unemployment, underemployment, and low postsecondary enrollment rates for youth. This is where we will begin our data discussion later in this chapter. How can we really know what is working and what is not without a good look at the data presented in a disaggregated manner by subpopulations? Relying on a gut sense does not lead to systemic change: we must be able to demonstrate evidence in the form of rigorously collected data.

Even in high-performing schools, questions are being raised about truly engaging the minds and hearts of students to help them become the lifelong learners our mission statements purport them to be. We know that, far too often, students can drop out mentally even though they may still arrive in our classrooms each day and perform at or above grade level. Developing SLC structures helps ensure that we leave no child behind.

Now, let us be really honest. The plates of American teachers are full. There is probably not one more minute in a day that can be filled with another initiative, strategy, plan, or practice. So, if we are going to achieve our goals for truly improving schools, we have to change the way we approach this work. The essential element of organizational change to keep in mind is *process*. However, before you dive into one more article on whole-school reform, organizational change, restructuring, redesigning, and reinventing your school, take a deep breath. Congratulate yourself for being a school leader who has been entrusted with the mission of leading your school and community through a time of unprecedented change in the culture of American education. Ever since 1983, and the groundbreaking *A Nation at Risk* (National Commission on Excellence in Education, 1983) report that focused on the poor performance of American students based on international comparisons, and the continued gaps between poor and minority students and white students, our educational system has been in a state of critical transformation.

The result has been a national discussion around vouchers and schools of choice, coupled with federal and state initiatives focused on the birth of NCLB, the standards movement, AYP, and placing a highly qualified teacher in every classroom. Added to the discussion have been the increasing demands and opportunities presented by a rapidly changing, technologically driven society, the concerns around the psychosocial needs of today's youth, and the challenge of the employer community for schools to be accountable for developing individuals who will perform successfully in the workplace. The result is a call for our educational leadership to design schools to fulfill a purpose for which they were never intended—that is, to leave no child behind, hold *all* children to high academic standards, and prepare them for life in a competitive, knowledge-based, global marketplace. To be a school leader today is to be faced with the challenge of changing your *entire* school climate to reap and sustain these results. Your mission, should you choose to accept it, is to effectively lead your administrators, teachers, parents, community partners, and students through a sustainable change process.

Before you begin to turn your school upside down with a change effort, survey your landscape, assess your strengths, and, as Dr. Nettie Legters from Johns Hopkins University's Center for the Social Organization of Schools (see Resources section) would encourage, "celebrate your progress." Undoubtedly, you are already doing positive and effective things in your school, *as evidenced by* the data tools you have utilized so far. For further progress, you must engage all your community stakeholders in this process. Invite parents, students, union leaders, school board members, faith-based groups, and representatives from business, central administration, and postsecondary institutions to the table. Schools must move from basic school partnerships to establishing true *alliances* with families, business, postsecondary institutions, and faith- and community-based organizations (FBO and CBO) in order to reap the results required by this new demand in American education. Chapter 8 will focus on partnerships and the critical role they play in school improvement. You will see that by involving all stakeholders in the survey process you lay the framework for building not a committee, but a team. You also establish a baseline for what is working within your school and who is helping to make it work. In your celebration of the positives, you narrow the field of what truly needs to be changed and validate existing positive practices. In seeking the positives, you will also undoubtedly identify areas of concern such as student attendance, student engagement, lack of resources, staff morale, test scores, college acceptance rates, teacher retention, and family involvement.

Armed with data from your own site, you can define your challenge; set clear, realistic, and measurable goals; and determine what resources are available for you to make the internal changes necessary in your school to reach them. In truth, we are all limited by the resources of time, staffing, and funding, but to allow perceived limits of these recourses to derail the change process is to fail before you have begun. Rather, measure the availability and quality of these resources. Equipped with that data, school leaders can then move to the most difficult step in the change process: that of creating a passion—a sense of urgency—in all of their stakeholders for the need to improve that allows for risk, further exploration, and the adoption of a reform model.

The Dance of Change, by Peter Senge and colleagues (1999), puts the process in perspective. Senge and his fellow authors highlight that there are six key steps in any change process, and they make it clear that the leader of the organization is responsible for creating a climate for successful change. First, there must be an investment in the need for change. Second, professional development must be extensive, ongoing, and focused on personal results. Individual teachers must be able to see direct benefits to themselves and their students, and see increases in the areas defined by the change process as needing improvement. This practice leads to what Senge et al. identify as the third step in the process: personal investment and an upward spiral of results, which naturally leads to the subsequent steps of an enthusiasm for and a willingness to commit to the process, an institutionalization of change practices, and measured results. Making a difference in the lives of our students is the outcome we seek in any reform. Envisioning the ideal graduate is an initial step in making that difference.

WHAT DO WE WANT A GRADUATE TO LOOK LIKE?

A big development in my thinking around creating SLC occurred when I worked as a consultant in Junction City, Kansas. Then–school principal Greg Springston led his staff through a process of school redesign for the purpose of *continuous improvement.* He began with a few simple questions that can help frame redesign work:

- What should a graduate look like?
- Are we producing that now?
- If not, what do we need to do to get there?

As you begin to engage others in your process of study, use these questions to get ideas percolating around the "end in mind." Clearly, in order to create an ideal graduate, we need to know what one looks like. We have a myriad of places to look for the characteristics that are valued and measurable in a high school graduate these days—characteristics that go well beyond acceptable performance on the state tests. These need to go much deeper than most of our pledges to create lifelong learners who are ready to take their place in a global marketplace. Our ideal graduate has to be a complex human being with a myriad of skill sets and a plan to apply them. These skills have to be discernable, and the structures we create as educators have to support their development.

In this section, you will begin to craft—at least in your mind—that ideal graduate. What does the ideal graduate look like? What should an ideal teacher look like, and what would an ideal SLC look like if we were "building" that student or teacher? Using the three questions as prompts, begin with your own thinking about the knowledge, skills, abilities, and character you want to nurture to success in your graduates. (See the Tool Kit for PowerPoint slides to facilitate this process.) Review your list. How deep did you go? I have often been struck by the fact that, even in meetings with superintendents, we only scratch the surface in developing a comprehensive graduate profile that sets the high expectations we espouse as being at the core of student outcomes. Rather, groups often ascribe to the minimum expectations of reading and performing at grade level on the state tests. To answer these prompts fully, we need to know what postsecondary "success" looks like—which means we need the input of postsecondary instructions, employers, and the military to help guide our thinking. It also requires—since we should not be expected to produce this ideal student on our own—that we map backward to the middle school and the ninth through eleventh grade experiences as the stepping stones to nurture our ideal student to graduation success. To create more "ideal" graduates, we must focus on ideal teaching.

WHAT DOES THE IDEAL TEACHER LOOK LIKE?

NCLB culture seeks to guarantee each child a highly qualified teacher. The focus on *continuous improvement* now falls squarely at the classroom door. Highly qualified has two sides: that which is transparent to the student and that which goes on behind the scenes. Behind the scenes, today's teachers must be unafraid and confident in their use of data to guide their practice. They must be encouraged to be restless for improvement in student outcomes and nurtured to their own success as they are continually challenged to examine their own and their colleagues' practices. They must be skilled in addressing the diverse learning needs and cultural norms of their students. In a high school culture where we know that teachers believe themselves masters of their discipline, we need to continually nudge the paradigm to include being masters of teaching today's youth. This entails extensive mission-specific professional development and a schedule that allows for coaching and common planning time.

As for the more transparent side of teaching—what the students experience in each day in class with teachers—give this one to the students to handle. As we have mentioned, the Tool Kit [2.1 What Should a Graduate—Teacher—SLC Look Like?] contains a template for asking what an ideal teacher looks like. Whether you use that template or hold informal focus groups with a diverse group of the students you serve, talk to the kids. They will define for you a teacher who is disciplined, is hard on them, is consistent, enjoys teaching, is fair, sets high expectations, and, perhaps, most of all, respects students. This anecdotal gathering of information is an important data point for setting the course for teacher expectations and for moving into discussions on data.

ARE WE PRODUCING THAT NOW?
THE DATA DISCUSSION BEGINS

Moving through the three prompt questions discussed above—either initially on your own or with a group—it may seem even harder to envision a structure and measurement system that will enable you to know whether you have arrived at creating the structures, systems, and practices that will lead to the creation of this ideal student. To ensure your best thinking, start now by gathering a team. It may be your school improvement team; it may be your key administrators; it could be a group of students. Facilitate a meeting with the goal of developing responses to the three slides. Push yourselves to ask the hard questions and establish early on a focus on data that provides evidence to support your thinking. Catalogue your efforts and note where you have convergent and divergent thinking. Review the responses and begin with what will be a mantra for you: "*As evidenced how? What would it look like? What data do we have that what we are saying is real?*" Here is where the hard discussions begin and where you, as a practitioner, begin to build the case for a commitment not to reform but to *continuous improvement.*

National data on schools not meeting AYP tells the story. Many schools are not yet equipped to meet the educational needs of our students as evidenced by the large numbers of students who fail to graduate and the frightening statistics of those that need remediation if they do enter college and the workplace. To begin a detailed discussion on data, pull out your school report card. If you do not know where it is, it is available to you on your state Department of Education's Web site. You might also check out the Great Schools Web site (see the reference in the Resources section). You will see a range of data elements from state testing data to demographics and attendance. You should also cross check this data with your school and district data. It is not uncommon for data points not to match. For you to "own" your data, you will want to begin collecting this information in a user-friendly manner. "User-friendly" is important so that you can communicate to colleagues, families, school boards, and granting authorities the urgency you feel in addressing issues related to improving your school. It will also be important to assist you to begin the data discussions with what Harvard's Tony Wagner calls a "no blame, no shame, no excuses" attitude (Wagner, 2003b, p. 137). We use the term "data-safe" discussions. There is no benefit in pointing fingers of blame or creating a feeling of shame about what the data tell us. Most classroom educators are wholly unfamiliar with the details of their data because the data have not been made relevant to them. The job of district and school administrators is to encourage data use in an atmosphere of support. The job of the practitioner is in large measure communicating over and over again about data. We must create safe places to understand data, learn how to question and interpret data points, and, from this point forward, commit to addressing areas for growth.

Begin with schoolwide data. In the Tool Kit, you will find a baseline data and mission management tool [2.2 Data Tracking Tool]. In MS Excel format, it allows you to calculate both whole-school and ninth grade data over time. This will be a critical element of your commitment to data-driven improvements and to going the distance. Through the use of this tool (see Tool Kit Snapshot 2.1), you are be able to establish baseline data and watch your average yearly and net changes across eighty whole-school and thirty-six ninth grade demographic, academic, and school climate data points. Like all Excel files, there are pages or tabs at the bottom of your screen when you open the file. The first page contains the directions for how to use the tool. When you move to the next tab, you will see something very similar to the example we have created for you here.

In this example, on the tab that reveals "whole-school data" we have documented one school's progress. Here you can see the school's growth in school size by looking at rows 5, 6, and 7 and columns I, J, K, and L. Please note that the columns reveal gains over time and columns R and S capture average and net changes. You can also see that this sample school is monitoring its ninth graders and ninth grade repeater students, noted across the board in rows 20 and 21. You can even make an assumption that they are working at addressing the needs of ninth grade students

Tool Kit Snapshot 2.1   Data Tracking Tool

Data Tracking Tool

School/SLC Name: _____   change measured in % from immediately previous period & aggregated in final columns

	Base 200x	Year 200x	+/- in %	Year 200x	+/- in %	Year 20x	+/- in %	YEAR 200x	+/- in %	Average Change	Net Change
DEMOGRAPHICS											
Total Number of students	1000	1000	0%	1500	50%		0%		0%	25%	50%
Males	400	400	0%	750	88%		0%		0%	44%	88%
Females	600	600	0%	750	25%		0%		0%	13%	25%
Staffing: Total School Staff			0%		0%		0%		0%	0%	0%
# of Administration			0%		0%		0%		0%	0%	0%
# of Instructional			0%		0%		0%		0%	0%	0%
# with Advanced Certification			0%		0%		0%		0%	0%	0%
# with Standard Certification			0%		0%		0%		0%	0%	0%
# with Provisional Certification			0%		0%		0%		0%	0%	0%
# of Counselors			0%		0%		0%		0%	0%	0%
# of School Safety Personnel			0%		0%		0%		0%	0%	0%
Number of students on free and reduced lunch			0%		0%		0%		0%	0%	0%
Number of ESL students			0%		0%		0%		0%	0%	0%
Number of Special Needs students			0%		0%		0%		0%	0%	0%
Student mobility rate (enter whole number as is 35 for 35%)			0%		0%		0%		0%	0%	0%
Class size 9th	300	302	1%		0%		0%		0%	1%	1%
9th grade repeaters	99	40	-60%		0%		0%		0%	-60%	-60%
10th			0%		0%		0%		0%	0%	0%
11th			0%		0%		0%		0%	0%	0%
12th			0%		0%		0%		0%	0%	0%
alternative school			0%		0%		0%		0%	0%	0%
ACADEMIC GAINS/DECLINES			0%		0%		0%		0%	0%	0%
Students earning Ds & Fs: Algebra I	200	300	50%	172	-43%		0%		0%	4%	-14%
Eng I	150	150	0%	145	-3%		0%		0%	-2%	-3%
Eng II			0%		0%		0%		0%	0%	0%
Eng III			0%		0%		0%		0%	0%	0%
Eng IV			0%		0%		0%		0%	0%	0%
Sci 1			0%		0%		0%		0%	0%	0%
Sci 2			0%		0%		0%		0%	0%	0%
Sci 3			0%		0%		0%		0%	0%	0%
SS 1			0%		0%		0%		0%	0%	0%
SS 2			0%		0%		0%		0%	0%	0%
SS 3			0%		0%		0%		0%	0%	0%
SS 4			0%		0%		0%		0%	0%	0%
Students earning 1 or more Fs	490	570	16%	200	17%		0%		0%	16%	29%

PLEASE NOTE: Calculating numbers of Ds and Fs by year is far less helpful that monitoring this data every four weeks and developing strategies for immediate intervention, support and improvements in instructional practice. You may wish to use this section for a semester to semester check.

DIRECTIONS \ **WHOLE SCHOOL DATA** / 9th Grade Data

who are repeating, or in need of repeating, the ninth grade. Looking at that data point over time/across columns shows numbers dropped significantly in year two. However, further study shows the school has not kept up with collecting that data, and we do not know how it is doing now. A third data point we can look at is in terms of the approach to instruction. We can see that they are paying attention by monitoring the number of students who are receiving D's and F's in Algebra and English I. Here, the raw numbers continue to be most serious in Algebra I. Please note, however, that while the numbers are most severe in Algebra, the percentage of students receiving D and F scores is dropping dramatically—perhaps reflecting a serious attempt to address students at risk of failing and those who are failing. We cannot make the same assumption for the English Department, where the net change in D's and F's is far less significant.

Inputting the specific data for your school now provides a comprehensive baseline data picture and will help build the case for *continuous improvement*. Monitoring the data over time will provide a platform for assessing program impact. As you begin to deepen your familiarity with and understanding of the data, you will also be able to identify the areas that can best be addressed through the development of effective SLC focused on data, personalization, instruction and curriculum, partnerships, and the commitment to a climate for success. The answers to the questions of how close we are to meeting, in serious numbers, the production of the ideal graduate and how many of our teachers are "ideal" build the case for change, even in high-performing schools. Even in discussions I have held at the school and district levels, administrators believe the numbers are below 20 percent. The emerging question that should be asked is: is this good enough? Educators can learn from the work done by Jim Collins in *Good to Great* (2001) where he studies corporate institutions that push past the mark of adequate success to one of excellence. Such examination builds an understanding of mission and vision as it relates to success for all students in a climate built on *continuous improvement.*

WHAT "REAL" MIGHT LOOK LIKE

The literature review, creating the ideal graduate, and baseline data discussions all open the door to a vision of what schools committed to *continuous improvement* through SLC might look like. Below is an outline of the development of one graduate profile and the scaffolding that will support its creation.

Graduates will be:

- College and career ready
- Ready to assume active roles as citizens and community members
- Instilled with a readiness and ability to learn more.

Therefore students will participate in a strong transition experience beginning in seventh grade that will include:

- Working with teachers and guidance counselors to identify student strengths, needs, and goals
- Mapping of curriculum horizontally and vertically across grade levels
- Identification of students not yet ready to fully succeed in the ninth grade

- A transition "Summer Bridge" academic, study, and personal skill development program
- Orientation to high school programs
- A guidance and career counselor support program that will be student-centered with high standards linked to community resources, technical centers, postsecondary institutions, and the business community.

These programs of studies will:

- Deliver a high-standard curriculum, by highly qualified instructors, in a flexible block schedule format that supports the mission
- Include career exploration and career and technical education (CTE) connections that begin in elementary school; are a significant component of the middle school instructional focus and guidance, beginning no later than seventh grade; and provide well-articulated CTE completer opportunities at the high school level
- Ensure high-quality curriculum and instruction that focuses on rigor and relevance
- Provide the extra help strategies for English language learners, special education students, students performing below grade level, and students who are performing below a "C" in any academic course
- Include accelerated learning opportunities for Honors, Advanced Placement (AP), International Baccalaureate, and dual enrollment in postsecondary institutions.

Students will experience an environment for teaching and learning that is delivered in SLC which are safe, respectful of all, equitable, and culturally rich in programs and services that meet the diverse needs and interests of *all* students. These SLC will involve a cohort of an administrator, guidance counselor, teachers, and students who stay together in a small school environment over the course of four years. These communities will include heterogeneous groups of approximately three to four hundred students. Each SLC will:

- Be career-themed, reflecting global workforce, industry, and academic standards
- Provide ninth grade students with a freshman experience and twelfth grade students with a senior transition experience
- Develop a six-year (four plus two) educational and career plan for each student
- Allow students to participate fully in an array of academic and enrichment experiences, including athletics and the arts
- Provide students with the opportunity to succeed through multiple diploma options, dual/college enrollment, and CTE certifications and to participate in community service and work-based learning experiences
- Support students through an advisory/family advocacy program
- Involve the cohort of teachers in regular common planning time that is focused on instruction and students' needs.

In reviewing this profile, enact your mantra: "What evidence would we have that what we are saying is real?" Each of these bullet points can be developed into an assessment that will determine whether the graduate, and thus the SLC community, has met their mark. Still further work leads to developing the *commitment framework*—the conditions and requirements necessary for success.

BUILDING A "COMMITMENT FRAMEWORK": AGREEMENTS NEEDED FOR SUCCESS

The process of committing to whole-school restructuring will take, by some research estimates, five to ten years. It will also require the engagement of the complete array of school stakeholders. In our years of working with schools, we have seen evidence of myriad groups slowing or stopping the redesign process for good reasons, bad reasons, and uninformed reasons. Part of the job of the practitioner is to make sure that as many roadblocks as possible are avoided. This means one-on-one, detailed, data-reinforced discussions. Conversations need to be held in order to help each individual and group to see the urgency for improvement and a path to get there. People need to see themselves as essential to the solution. This takes time; it also takes clarity of purpose. There can be no hidden agendas. If there are already decisions that have been made about a model, timeline, or implementation practices, be clear in your communication about them. If the educators who are expected to implement the changes are well informed at every step, and feel engaged in a respectful process, you will meet with better results. This means identifying and communicating what I used to refer to as the "nonnegotiables"—district, or school, leaders' requirements and expectations. Perhaps it is just a matter of semantics, but nonnegotiables seem to leave folks with a sense that they are not part of the process and are being mandated to act. Switching the language so it is asking for teachers to work within a *commitment framework*—even with the same policies or expected practices in place—can make all the difference in the world at the start of an engagement process. Be clear about what you are expecting of others and consider the commitment elements below.

From all parties, there needs to be a commitment to:

- Establishment of, and adherence to, a mission statement that reflects the climate, culture, and expected outcomes for your institution
- Collaboration and equality of partners
- Understanding data and being able to apply lessons learned from national, state, district, school and classroom level data
- Increased positive outcomes for *all* students, ensuring equity of expectations and services for all
- Bringing the best of what we know about education, youth, and the world of work to the dialogue
- A climate for teaching and learning that reflects equity, respect, and high expectations
- Alignment of policies and practices that lead to coherent implementation practices, and
- A commitment to a culture of continuous educational improvement.

From the school system, the need is for a commitment to:

- A redesigned school that is aligned to the system's initiatives and goals
- The type of hiring practices and school staffing that support success
- Ongoing, open communication with stakeholders on district policies and practices, and
- The activation of system resources that facilitate development, implementation, evaluation, and recognition.

From the principal, we must have a commitment to:

- Shared, participatory leadership
- The development of teaching and counseling staff who are assigned to the SLC by choice with the benefit of staff development, training, and common planning time
- Building the capacity of staff to lead
- The assignment of students to the SLC based on their stated interests
- Creation of a school climate and master schedule that support the unique nature and needs of SLC. This includes flexible class time and the ability to have frequent educational experiences out of the school building, and
- Appreciation of the benefits of true partnership with community, business, postsecondary, parents/families, and government partners.

From the teaching team, there should be a commitment to:

- Participating in a process of *continuous improvement* that will fundamentally redefine their role as teachers
- Participating in effective common planning time that is focused on classroom instruction and best practices
- Ongoing professional development in educational and, where appropriate, career-linked curricula and professional practice areas
- Integration of speakers, work-based experiences, careers, and postsecondary planning into the curriculum and classroom process
- A willingness and ability to work with business partners.

From the business partners, a commitment is required to:

- Working in a school culture very different from their own
- Seeking true partnerships with schools that result in enhanced learning for students
- Activating resources for the benefit of students
- Nurturing the program, teachers, and students to success.

From students, we need a commitment to:

- A desire to attend the SLC based on the unique nature, career theme, and/or requirements of the program
- Striving to exceed expectations and to participate fully in all aspects of the SLC, including work experience, exhibitions, senior projects, special training opportunities, summer work, and enrichment activities.

From parents, families, and guardians, there must be a commitment to:

- Being a partner in the education of their child
- Understanding the unique structure of SLC that provides many experiences beyond the classroom and traditional school format
- Working with the school and business and community leaders in a way that will result in increased benefits to students.

Here is what a commitment framework might look like in your district. To ensure this works effectively for *each* child, the district needs to be committed to the following:

- Setting high expectations for all students
- Instilling staff with a focus on improving student engagement, curriculum alignment, increased instructional rigor, curriculum relevance to real-world application, and improved relationships at all levels
- Being data driven at the district, school, and classroom levels, therefore addressing the academic needs of all learners
- Providing engaging, aligned, and rigorous instruction to all students
- Making sure that every student is known by and connected to at least one adult within the school
- Integrating college readiness and career preparation into each student's plan for success
- Aligning policies and practices to support continuous improvement at each school
- Creating a secondary improvement system that is embedded in a process of continuous improvement, not a *reform* or *redesign* strategy that will not transcend time and is not limited to a few schools
- Providing systemic and appropriate professional development for all staff
- Involving families, community partners, businesses, and postsecondary partners in the life of the school(s) and in the desired outcomes for students.

It will take a great deal of work to make the thinking involved in this comprehensive approach come off the page and become a viable design. Details still need to be defined, but it is possible to see how a framework begins to develop when we start with student outcomes and experiences in mind. This process clearly defines expectations for an outcome that will develop an ideal student. It requires excellence in management and teaching. It is the *what* and the *where*. It recognizes a requirement for district-level support. It sets the stage for the *how*, the *when*, and the *who* involved in building your local definition for SLC development.

BUILDING YOUR LOCAL DEFINITION: ESTABLISHING STRUCTURES

Many school systems have a rich history of pioneering and succeeding at great educational innovation. However, they do not necessarily have the same history with sustaining or supporting the reforms. Schools sometimes grow overly eager for improvement without taking the time to follow the practices of highly effective organizations. They are working as hard as they can but not meeting the objectives they set. They continually seek to employ one reform strategy after another. This has resulted in what Arnold Fege so aptly calls "innovation fatigue" (Fege, 2004). It is time we worked smarter, not harder. I believe we are at a tipping point where our own school statistics, current educational practices, and funds and initiatives from SLC grants and an array of other sources can coalesce for a serious commitment to best practices and *continuous improvement*.

Every system has a variety of programs that meet some or all of the elements of career academies and SLC as outlined in Chapter 1. The challenge for schools is to define what their SLC will look like, identify the elements that are currently working in schools, coordinate these with a revised implementation strategy, and sustain the gains made through an aligned approach and design.

Earlier in this chapter, we saw how one district built its definition of an SLC as an outgrowth of its concept of the ideal graduate. We also suggested looking at the other two slides in the Tool Kit [2.1 What Should a Graduate—Teacher—SLC Look Like?] and holding some initial discussions on what you would want in your ideal SLC. You may want to refer back to those tools now as you prepare to assess your current high school climate for teaching and learning. In the Tool Kit, we have created two MS Excel files [2.3 Data SLC Implementation Assessment] and [2.4 Data SLC Implementation Assessment With CTE]. Based on the data you input, these tools will help you to determine how close you are to the elements held central to *effective* SLC development and sustainability. Depending on the emphasis you are placing on CTE in your design, you will opt for one or the other of the files to begin your assessment. These data tools auto-calculate and capture composite data on the summary page. Each file has four common tabs or pages, as well as a summary sheet that automatically calculates the subsequent tabs. The tabs are labeled according to four of our five elements or "bins" of work: personalization, curriculum and instruction, partnerships, and climate for success. Each tab displays programmatic elements specific to one of the bins of work and the one for CTE should you choose a design focused on CTE. The missing bin in these files is data-driven management. However, you have already been introduced to that tool and have begun to gather your baseline data. In the 2.4 "With CTE" file (see Tool Kit Snapshot 2.2 on pages 30–35), there is an additional tab that focuses on the key elements of CTE and is displayed for you here.

Each implementation and assessment file begins the process of addressing the bins. You will want to use these in a variety of ways and refer to them often. They provide you with baseline data now and will also prove an important document for start-up faculty discussions, as you will see later.

How It Works

Determine which file is most appropriate for your work. If you are creating career academies or CTE-focused programs, you will want the "With CTE" file; otherwise, [2.3 Data SLC Implementation Assessment] is the file with which you will need to work. In reviewing each tab and the multiple items listed, you have the opportunity to rank each element. Your rankings are subtotaled in sections, tallied for the entire bin and then carried over to the summary page. Breaking down the data in this way should help you to narrowly focus on your real strengths as well as target areas that need specific attention. The summary page provides you with an overall score that puts you on a continuum from *traditional high school* to *effective and sustainable SLC*. It is critical that you *not* use a number ranking other than those listed for you: No Evidence—No—Rarely—Sometimes—Always. In responding, you *must* follow the letter code in the appropriate column. While the program is not case sensitive, the only formulas it recognizes for calculation are those which follow a letter format. Failure to complete the forms in this manner will nullify any calculations. N/E, N,

R, S, and A, respectively, are the only acceptable responses. The rankings have been assigned a weighted formula, and the result is a four-point scale ranking on each bin. Review, discuss, and determine the response you want to make to each area.

The goal of the assessment is to provide a baseline of data for planning and to serve as a vehicle for documenting challenges and growth. It is designed as a tool that provides practitioners with a means to review specific elements of their program. Its usefulness will be as broad as the intensity of the scrutiny for each question raised.

Let us take a moment to say what the instrument is and what it is not. In addition to the data collection element, one of its strongest uses is as a tool for generating discussion among faculty members about the various bins of work. We have used this effectively in dividing faculty teams for the purpose of deep discussion around one bin of the work and then bringing them together to share their perspectives, to be questioned about their thinking, and to reach consensus as a group on elements they feel are central to their design. In Chapter 4, we will introduce the "SLC Punch List" to further these discussions. If you want to skip ahead, or view this tool in the Tool Kit, you will see the breadth of the work that lies before us.

- It provides the opportunity for self-assessment, peer reviews, or an independent set of eyes to look at your work through the lens of the five bins of SLC work.
- It can be used for a single SLC or academy, or for a whole school. It does not, however, "cross assess" between multiple programs within a school.
- It is easy to use; generates effective, quick results; captures the key elements of your reform; and serves as a catalyst for engagement of stakeholders.
- The data cells are protected so that you can enter data but cannot change fields, or inadvertently alter the weighted values or the formulas that lead to the summary results.
- It is not linked to any specific model or research design. It has worked well with schools that want to focus on and address a process for creating SLC or career academies. You may need to consider other elements if you are implementing a reform strategy linked to a prescriptive reform model or have designed an SLC with a specific programmatic element. You may also want to access the SLC assessment offered at the NWREL site referenced in the Resources section.
- It is set up on a simple 4.0 scale that is easily recognized and understood by those in schools. It is decidedly *not* intended to give a school an A- to F-like ranking, a negative judgment, or a sense of failure. It is intended to operate as a developmental scale, where all schools—just like all students—can succeed.

Without careful review and discussion, it runs the risk of being an arbitrary assessment by one individual or a group of individuals. With review and discussion, it serves as a powerful tool to help shape all areas of SLC or academy implementation.

Here is what to look for: we have created a fictitious school and conducted an assessment. It may or may not look like "Our High School" or "Your SLC"; however, here are the results we garnered (see Tool Kit Snapshot 2.3 on page 36).

(Text continues on page 37)

Tool Kit Snapshot 2.2 Data SLC Implementation Assessment

Data SLC Implementation Assessment

Name of School:		Name of Academy: (if "pocket")		Date:

SUMMARY DATA

"GPA": 0.00

GPA Key

- 0-1 Traditional High School
- 2 Embarking SLC/Academy
- 3 Emerging SLC/Academy
- 4 Effective and Sustainable SLC/Academy

Personalized Structures	Elements	Sub Total: 0.00
Facilities	0.0	
Identity	0.0	
Staffing	0.0	
Schedules	0.0	
Selection	0.0	
Activities	0.0	

Curriculum and Instruction	Elements	Sub Total: 0.00
College and Career Preparation	0.0	
Approach	0.0	
Integration	0.0	
Assessment	0.0	
Technology	0.0	
Features	0.0	

Career and Technical (CTE)	Elements	Sub Total: 0.00
Curriculum	0.0	
Implementation	0.0	
Program Evaluation	0.0	
Learning Environment	0.0	
Management	0.0	

Partnerships	Elements	Sub Total: 0.00
Evidence of Partnerships	0.0	
Approach to Partnerships	0.0	
Parent/Guardian Involvement	0.0	
Organizations Represented	0.0	
Features	0.0	

Climate for Success	Elements	Sub Total: 0.00
Vision and Understanding	0.0	
Shared Leadership	0.0	
Commitment of Resources	0.0	
Professional Development	0.0	
Assessment and Research	0.0	

Notes:

School Data

Please refer to the Data Tracking Sheet for current data on school demographics, data on academic gains or losses, and information on school climate.

Data SLC Implementation Assessment

Summary: 0.00

Please enter the LETTER(s), NOT the number, in cells J–N to get accurate totals.

Personalized Structures	NO EVIDENCE / NOT RELEVANT / N/E = 0	NO / FALSE / NEVER / N = 1	POSSIBLY / Questionable / RARELY / R = 2	PROBABLY / SOMEWHAT TRUE / SOMETIMES / S = 3	YES / TRUE / ALWAYS / A = 4
Please enter the LETTER(s), NOT the number, in cells J–N to get accurate totals.					
FACILITIES — SUB GPA: 0.0					
SLC/Academy has a specific location within the building					
SLC/Academy area reflects culture, theme, career orientation					
SLC/Academy has facilities of high quality, are respectful and safe learning environments					
SLC/Academy has sufficient access to technology					
IDENTITY — SUB GPA: 0.0	0	0	0	0	0
SLC/Academy is designed on research-based strategies					
SLC/Academy has individualized mission/vision statement					
SLC/Academy has brochures, stationery, business cards					
Student size is approximately 400 students					
Students Identify strongly with their specific SLC/Academy. May have SLC school ID.					
STAFFING — SUB GPA: 0.0	0	0	0	0	0
SLC/Academy has a core of Math, Eng., Social St., Science teachers (MESS)					
SLC/Academy has its own guidance support					
Teachers have common planning time at least once per week					
SCHEDULES — SUB GPA: 0.0	0	0	0	0	0
SLC/Academy includes common planning for teachers					
Students are rostered/scheduled together for all major courses					
Schedules are flexible and allow for academic supports and out-of-school experiences					
SELECTION — SUB GPA: 0.0	0	0	0	0	0
Students enter SLC/academy based on their interest					
Teachers are assigned to specific SLC/Academy based on their interest and skills					
ACTIVITIES — SUB GPA: 0.0	0	0	0	0	0
Teachers serve as teacher guides to a specified number of students					
Advocacy/homerooms are in place w/a focus on personalization and academic support					
Program supports addressing transition are in evidence					
SLC/Academy has a specialized set of activities (work-based, service, graduation, etc.)	0	0	0	0	0

(Continued)

Data SLC Implementation Assessment

Curriculum and Instruction Summary: 0.00 Please enter the LETTER(s), NOT the number, in cells J-N to get accurate totals.

	NO EVIDENCE / NOT RELEVANT / N/E = 0	NO / FALSE / NEVER / N = 1	POSSIBLY / Questionable / RARELY / R = 2	PROBABLY / SOMEWHAT TRUE / SOMETIMES / S = 3	YES / TRUE / ALWAYS / A = 4
Please enter the LETTER(s), NOT the number, in cells J-N to get accurate totals. SUB GPA: 0.0					
PREPARATION					
Courses meet or exceed state college entrance requirements					
Course work includes Advanced Placement and/or postsecondary offerings					
Courses (as appropriate) meet entry level work requirements for career-related industry					
Courses are taught to state/local *standards*					
APPROACH SUB GPA: 0.0	0	0	0	0	0
Student body reflects a full range of talents and abilities					
Students work in, or are assigned to, teams with a team of teachers					
Extra supports are available for academic development (tutoring, mentoring, "double dose")					
Work-based and academic learning are equally valued by staff and students					
Time is taken to orient/train new students/staff/partners to SLC/Academy					
INTEGRATION SUB GPA: 0.0	0	0	0	0	0
Teachers are aware of what their team members are teaching and reference it in class					
Teachers plan together and develop interdisciplinary/theme units					
When appropriate, career elements are in evidence in the curriculum					
ASSESSMENT SUB GPA: 0.0	0	0	0	0	0
Instructional delivery and support are guided by a regular data review, prior to failures					
Student work is assessed in a variety of venues					
Students participate in their own assessments; families and partners are involved					
TECHNOLOGY SUB GPA: 0.0	0	0	0	0	0
Teachers use, model, and promote student use of technology					
Students graduate with a documentable set of technology skills					
FEATURES SUB GPA: 0.0	0	0	0	0	0
Coursework has a strong emphasis on literacy and numeracy					
Students have significant work-based and community experiences					
Students create a six-year high school–postsecondary plan					
Students have access to a well-equipped college and career center	0	0	0	0	0

Data SLC Implementation Assessment

Please enter the LETTER(s), NOT the number, in cells J-N to get accurate totals.

Partnerships SUMMARY 0.00	NO EVIDENCE / NOT RELEVANT / N/E = 0	NO / FALSE / NEVER / N = 1	POSSIBLY / Questionable / RARELY / R = 2	PROBABLY / SOMEWHAT TRUE / SOMETIMES / S = 3	YES / TRUE / ALWAYS / A = 4
Please enter the LETTER(s), NOT the number, in cells J-N to get accurate totals. SUB GPA: 0.0					
EVIDENCE OF PARTNERSHIPS					
Staff know that partnerships exist and regularly turn to and team with partners					
There are signs, advertisements, donation/recognition plaques at school					
Students easily discuss partners' roles in the SLC/Academy and cite experiences					
Partners know the names of teachers and understand the SLC/Academy structure					
APPROACH TO PARTNERSHIP SUB GPA: 0.0	0	0	0	0	0
Partners are involved with developing the vision, goals, and strategies for SLC/Academy					
Both partners and school staff commit to shared, defined leadership					
A specific individual at the school has responsibility for managing partnerships					
Partnership experiences are valued equally to "academic" experiences					
Partners receive regular recognition and thanks					
PARENTS/GUARDIANS/FAMILIES SUB GPA: 0.0	0	0	0	0	0
Families are valued equally to other partners					
They are surveyed and tapped as a resource for their interests, talents, work experience, etc.					
Parents have active role in leadership and assessment					
ORGANIZATIONS REPRESENTED SUB GPA: 0.0	0	0	0	0	0
Business organizations are in evidence (nonprofits, associations, labor, etc.)					
State and/or local government organizations are represented					
Postsecondary institutions support the SLC/Academy (comm. college, univer., trades)					
FEATURES SUB GPA: 0.0	0	0	0	0	0
There is an active business/community advisory board					
Teachers are actively involved in personal work-based experiences and externships					
Students have career-focused field experiences, covering all aspects of the industry					
Labor market trends influence curriculum					
Partners assess/evaluate student performance/student work					
Partners assist with student service learning activities					
Students have internship experiences	0	0	0	0	0

(Continued)

Tool Kit Snapshot 2.2 (Continued)

Data SLC Implementation Assessment

CTE ELEMENTS	NO EVIDENCE / NOT RELEVANT / N/E = 0	NO / FALSE / NEVER / N = 1	POSSIBLY / Questionable / RARELY / R = 2	PROBABLY / SOMEWHAT TRUE / SOMETIMES / S = 3	YES / TRUE / ALWAYS / A = 4
SUMMARY 0.00	Please enter the LETTER(s), NOT the number, in cells J-N to get accurate totals.				
Please enter the LETTER(s), NOT the number, in cells J-N to get accurate totals.					
CURRICULUM SUB GPA: 0.0					
Curriculum is competency based using the State Standard/Frameworks for its appropriate courses and programs.					
Curriculum is nongender/race biased; emphasizes = access to occupations and nontraditional occupational pursuits.					
Courses are sequential and enable all available certifications and graduation endorsements.					
Courses offer a broad range of appropriate student assessment options.					
Instructional materials and texts are current, approved, and present in sufficient quality for all students.					
The pace, scope, depth, and sequence of lessons are matched to students' abilities.					
Student evaluation procedures adequately measure student knowledge and skills gained from course participation.					
Program supports student success on state assessments for all content areas.					
Courses are aligned to student's prior academic experiences and provide opportunities for postsecondary articulation.					
IMPLEMENTATION SUB GPA: 0.0	0	0	0	0	0
Teacher/student relationships are based on mutual respect, and teacher expectations are realistically high.					
Career and technical student organization activities are integrated into the curriculum to enhance program outcomes.					
Teachers regularly participate in content-specific professional development, ensuring relevant content and delivery.					
Teachers serve in leadership roles at the local, state, or national levels.					
Effective and efficient teaching/learning strategies demonstrate what teacher considers appropriate options.					
Student assessment results are used in the formation of instructional strategies.					
Student achievement data drives decisions for modifications to curriculum and program implementation.					
PROGRAM EVALUATION SUB GPA: 0.0	0	0	0	0	0
All aspects of program are regularly reviewed to identify improvement strategies.					
Industry representatives meet regularly with teachers and serve as technical advisors for program direction and improvement.					
Systematic and continuous program evaluation process is in place to ensure teacher and student success.					
Program is aligned to district priorities.					
Annual goals are developed and monitored to ensure continuous improvement.					
LEARNING ENVIRONMENT SUB GPA: 0.0	0	0	0	0	0
Environment is supportive of student interactions and student abilities to question, inquire, design, and apply content skills.					
Environment is up-to-date and adaptable.					
There is evidence of a safety plan, regulations, and support that promote KSAs relevant to content area.					
The number of students in the laboratory-classroom does not exceed its capacity.					
There are sufficient materials and equipment to accommodate active participation by all students.					
The environment is stimulating and motivating.					
Facility layout is conducive to student monitoring.					
Conditions are clean and attractive, and appropriate resources are available.					
MANAGEMENT SUB GPA: 0.0	0	0	0	0	0
The number of fully trained and appropriately qualified teachers is adequate to implement the curriculum.					
There is evidence of interdepartmental, cross-department, and administrative collaborations and shared decision making.					
The annual budget allocation is sufficient to support high-quality program implementation.					
Long-term plans for equipment repair, replacement, and upgrades are in place.					
Resources are used for the effective promotion and marketing of program offerings.					
Purposeful links and partnerships with business and industry and the local community are evident.					

Data SLC Implementation Assessment

Climate for Success	SUMMARY 0.00	Please enter the LETTER(s), NOT the number, in cells J-N to get accurate totals.				
		NO EVIDENCE	NO	POSSIBLY	PROBABLY	YES
		NOT RELEVANT	FALSE	Questionable	SOMEWHAT TRUE	TRUE
			NEVER	RARELY	SOMETIMES	ALWAYS
Please enter the LETTER(s), NOT the number, in cells J-N to get accurate totals.	SUB GPA: 0.0	N/E = 0	N = 1	R = 2	S = 3	A = 4
VISION AND UNDERSTANDING						
Administration has a clear vision and understanding of data and plan for *continuous improvement*						
Faculty have a clear vision and understanding of data and plan for *continuous improvement*						
Partners have a clear vision and understanding of data and plan for *continuous improvement*						
Students have a clear vision and understanding of data and plan for *continuous improvement*						
SHARED LEADERSHIP	SUB GPA: 0.0	0	0	0	0	0
The district is involved in the development of the SLC/Academy(ies)						
The principal has restructured, empowering teachers and others to lead						
There is a regular forum for setting goals and objectives and for measuring success						
There is a coordinated effort among consultants, T/A providers, reform efforts, etc.						
Students are active in leadership forums for themselves and the SLC/Academy						
COMMITMENT OF RESOURCES	SUB GPA: 0.0	0	0	0	0	0
A needs survey has been conducted. It is known what is needed to succeed						
Technology is appropriately utilized in instruction						
There is a commitment of training and planning time to aid staff to develop programs						
PROFESSIONAL DEVELOPMENT	SUB GPA: 0.0	0	0	0	0	0
Staff training addresses the *continuous improvement* practices necessary to succeed						
Staff training is coordinated among consultants, T/A providers, reform efforts, etc.						
Staff are provided opportunities to build their individual expertise						
ASSESSMENT AND RESEARCH	SUB GPA: 0.0	0	0	0	0	0
Staff are cognizant of current research and trends for SLC/Academies						
Attendance data for students AND staff are readily available and codified						
Student grades and test scores are readily available and codified						
Student truancy, office referral, and awards data are readily available and codified						
Graduation rates are monitored						
Jobs, scholarships, and college placements are codified and followed up on						
SLC/Academy(ies) participate in third-party evaluation						
		0	0	0	0	0

Data SLC Implementation Assessment

Name of School: YOUR SCHOOL	Name of Academy (if "pocket")	OUR SLC	Date:	12-May

SUMMARY DATA | GPA: 2.34

Personalized Structures — Sub Total: 2.56

	Elements
Facilities	1.75
Identity	3.20
Staffing	2.00
Schedules	3.70
Selection	2.50
Activities	2.30

GPA Key

0-1	Traditional High School
2	Embarking SLC/Academy
3	Emerging SLC/Academy
4	Effective and Sustainable SLC/Academy

Curriculum and Instruction — Sub Total: 2.52

	Elements
College and Career Preparation	3.00
Approach	2.80
Integration	2.70
Assessment	2.70
Technology	1.50
Features	2.50

School Data

Please refer to the Data Tracking Sheet for current data on school demographics, data on academic gains or losses, and information on school climate.

Partnerships — Sub Total: 1.65

	Elements
Evidence of Partnerships	2.50
Approach to Partnerships	1.60
Parent/Guardian Involvement	2.00
Organizations Represented	0.00
Features	2.10

NOTES:

Climate for Success — Sub Total: 2.62

	Elements
Vision and Understanding	4.00
Shared Leadership	3.80
Commitment of Resources	1.00
Professional Development	2.00
Assessment and Research	1.60

Summary Data / Personalized Structures / Curriculum and Instruction / Partnerships / Climate for Success

"Our High School" is clearly on the road to SLC implementation. It has an "embarking" SLC program, as you can see from the rankings on the summary page. We can see that there are positive elements in place and also areas for growth. The subtotal rankings are fairly evenly distributed, although we can see that more work needs to be done in the area of partnerships by looking at cell H18. Despite the fact that the curricular area is strong, more attention needs to be paid to technology as demonstrated in cell F16. The school climate for success looks good with a strong commitment to shared leadership, and everyone seems to understand the vision (cell F25), if the assessment of the reviewer(s) is on target. However, look at cell F27: the commitment of resources is extremely low, and this will need to be addressed if real progress is to be made.

How to Make It Work for You

Once you have determined which file to use, determine who will be responsible for completing the assessment. Who should provide feedback? Who gets the final word? You may wish to provide printouts to various stakeholders, inviting them to be part of a hold-harmless peer review process. Explain that the process will be about taking a hard look at what you currently have in place, not what is planned. It is about trying to derive an accurate picture of where your programs stand. As such, you will need feedback and you will also need to make hard decisions.

On the summary sheet, you need only add the name of your school and a specific SLC if you are focusing on individual SLC assessment. Each page provides you with a framework for discussion. The "Curriculum and Instruction" bin will give you an overview of how you are addressing these areas. It is not a substitute for a comprehensive look at teaching and learning in every classroom through the use of walkthroughs and a "data in a day" protocol as described in other chapters. The last tab reflects the "Climate for Success" bin. It may indeed be the most difficult element to address. In an educational climate that so often asks for more to be done with less, it will be important to truly assess what supports are in place and what barriers exist. If the proper staff development, school leadership, vision, and resources are not in place, you will have to begin at the beginning. If your school community does not already have a culture committed to ongoing research and assessment, you will have to begin with data-safe conversations. Be prepared for the fact that assessing and then ensuring a climate for success will take time and extensive discussion. It is the pivotal piece in getting the real barriers and supports on the table.

At a Glance: Summing It Up and Next Steps

This chapter has addressed the initial steps in creating and sustaining SLC—*formation*—and set the tone for ongoing study and assessment. We have begun by understanding the change process and the creation of an ideal graduate. We asked students to help with defining the ideal teacher, and started where we must: with a look at data. Your work from the Tool Kit [2.2 Data Tracking Tool] and [2.3 or 2.4 Data SLC Implementation Assessment] regarding *embarking, emerging* or *established* began to codify the direction in which you will continue to work. Consider how the steps of this work are intertwined and lead you both backward for reflection and forward for practice. Be aware that there is a potential pitfall if you skip this step and operate with a checklist mentality of "did that assessment, now I'll move on." As a practitioner, you will be responsible for ensuring that the mission, goals, and changes that are written into your school improvement plans and grant applications are aligned in a coherent approach for addressing the *continuous improvement* goals of your school. Hopefully, you have now laid a solid foundation for a framework that will lead to a school in the throes of change as policy, practices, and roles and responsibilities all begin to shift.

In working to establish a common language, we deepened the talk about "bins" of work: data, personalization, curriculum and instruction, and a climate for success, and commonly held definitions for learning communities. The Tool Kit files have armed us with a baseline from which to work. However, we have only begun the process. In the next chapters we will continue with the processes of *formation and study* and *assessment*, and move to *engagement and commitment* to provide the scaffolding for our effective SLC. As a key practitioner, your job is to ensure that the structures are sound and that you meaningfully engage others in your work. Next, we continue to keep the end in mind, creating a school with a personalized environment, focused on high expectations for teaching and learning—by extending the circle of those engaged in the process.

3

Leading an Improvement Process

Changes in Practice Are Inevitable

It may be hard for an egg to turn into a bird: it would be a jolly sight harder for it to learn to fly while remaining an egg. We are like eggs at present. And you cannot go on indefinitely being just an ordinary, decent egg. We must be hatched or go bad.

—C. S. Lewis

Chapter 3 Road Map	
Purpose	To build the skills of the practitioner to lead a facilitated process of change through identification of needs, presentation, planning, and engagement.
Stage of Implementation	Study and Awareness and Engagement and Commitment—focus on climate for success.
Process and Action Steps	Assessing teacher readiness. Presentation to faculty. Change activity. Developing a professional development plan to support SLC. Engaging stakeholders.
Tool Kit	3.1 FAQ Frequently Asked Questions 3.2 Teacher Readiness
Reflective Practice	How do we ensure that each teacher sees his or her place in the *continuous improvement* SLC process? What knowledge and skills do we need individually and collectively to move forward?
Outcome	Practitioner will have assessment of staff professional development needs in place, will identify areas for staff training, and will have met with key stakeholders in the improvement process.

The practitioner serves as a change agent, working within the system and in a particular school or schools to build relationships as they work to address issues of structure, instruction, climate, and culture. It is important to understand and communicate at the beginning of the process that, in order to improve results, there is a need to change practice. This may be an obvious statement and one that can be agreed to by a group. However, *individuals* in organizations sometimes miss the fact that the change in practice needed for the organization to improve must *be their own*. This chapter is designed to give you specific tools and guidance on how to build engagement—sometimes referred to as a "buy in" with staff. Here, your role is to "push the envelope" for the existing reform practices and to ensure that the efforts underway are fully in line with the specific SLC definition being embraced by your school and district. You will need to set up structures safeguarding the alignment of the new initiatives with your school's mission and purpose. We will continue throughout this chapter with a focus on the SLC formation and study process so critical in creating *effective* SLC. We will also introduce a variety of new tools.

If this sounds like we are providing you with a magic wand or silver bullet, we are not. Real change is difficult to achieve. As individuals, we call for change in all aspects of our society—as demonstrated by our determination to take our car to a mechanic who has the latest computer diagnostic equipment, or entrusting ourselves only to a medical practice with access to the latest information and techniques in health care, or even our propensity to toss aside "old" technology when a new innovation comes along. However, when it comes to changing the way we operate in our own professional lives, we do not often see the need for it. In fact, according to Price Pritchett in his *Executive Library on Organizational Change* (Pritchett, 1993), most of us react by engaging in the old "fight or flight" response. We disengage from the process or undermine it. We entirely miss a third option of choosing to embrace change, and thereby open opportunities for success where we have previously met with failure. This last option is the one you must tap into and encourage!

Try this simple activity. Choose a time to introduce the topic of change at an upcoming staff meeting. This can be done when you present the [1.1 Creating SLC Presentation] or at another time when you are setting the stage for change in practice. Ask staff to stand and to pair off facing each other. Ask them, in silence, to observe each other for ten seconds. Instruct them to then turn their backs to each other and to change five things about themselves. Give them just ten seconds to do this. Have the pairs turn and face each other and document any noticed changes. Give them just a few minutes for this. *Repeat* the process. Undoubtedly you will find a range of reactions, so let the process play out. Tell group members they can sit down and debrief after the activity. What did they observe about change? "It's fun, it's easy, it's creative, it's observable" are all likely comments on the upside of change. The challenges will come in the reactions of "it's hard, it didn't make sense, I was willing to do it once but not twice, I liked the way I was—why did I have to change?" You will also observe that there are some people who will not comment on the activity at all because they chose from the outset not to engage in it. All three observations are helpful to the work that lies ahead. After debriefing, ask participants how many people took the time to rearrange themselves back to exactly the way they were prior to the request for change. It never fails: 100 percent of the participants will have reverted. This too is a telling sign. As the practitioner, you will need to be attentive to how easy it is to slip back into "school as usual" as your faculty will want to slip back into tried—if not true—practices that are comfortable.

Your own observations about the process will likely reinforce what you intrinsically know about your faculty or team. Around a third will be eager to make the changes necessary for children to succeed. A third will make the change once they see and understand the how and why of change, and the final third will listen to those few teachers who simply will not engage in the activity and thus get disenfranchised before they begin. This phenomenon is reinforced in organization research and in Robert Slavin's *Sand, Bricks, and Seeds: School Change Strategies and Readiness for Reform* (1997). Here he highlights the importance of matching the readiness of a school faculty for embracing change to specific types of organizational school reform. He states that those involved in comprehensive school reform must be able to determine which faculties simply need to be nurtured to success, which are able to follow and implement a model, and which are in such a state of unreadiness that no effective change can take place.

Leadership will be the defining factor in successful change. As a leader, you must understand that, as individuals, we shy away from the idea of having to change, and that we react even more strongly to the idea of continued change. However, it may be helpful to understand that individuals do embrace the idea of personal growth. Perhaps the decades of work around school reform and organizational change would have been made easier had the entire discussion begun by framing it around the opportunity to grow and to increase outcomes rather than changing behaviors. Your mission is to be the leader who encourages a desire for growth.

Daggett, Pritchett, Senge, and others all identify strong leadership not only as the key to initiating change but as critical to sustaining the gains won by the process. This means developing a sustained leadership structure that can create and communicate a vision for growth and translate that vision into action steps that can be adopted and embraced by a community of stakeholders. It entails the ability to forge true linkages and partnerships between groups and individuals committed to the success of the organization. It requires that a climate be created that reduces barriers to innovation and risk, and institutionalizes policies geared at sustaining the effort.

In life, the old adage goes, we can be certain of only two things: death and taxes. In fact, we can also be assured of a third: change. As a nation, we will constantly be addressing the educational needs of children. We can anticipate new legislation that will drive new initiatives. As a society, we will continually turn to our school leaders to keep a focus on increased, measurable growth in our schools. And if we are truly committed to *continuous improvement*, we are committing to a process that states we can always improve, grow, and change. So celebrate your successes, identify your areas of greatest need, find supportive partners, and take a deep breath: your mission is clear, and there is a lot to be done.

CREATING A THEORY OF CHANGE

Increasingly, schools are asked to explain their theory of change in grant applications and in other venues. We have found it essential to codify a process that leads to effective improvement in practice. Engaging in a similar process will help you to ensure sustainability of the efforts you are now planning to implement. We suggest the following:

Build a Case for Change

This process includes engaging stakeholders in looking at and sharing data in a format that can easily be understood by educators and the local community.

Create a Shared Vision to Guide Continuous Improvement Efforts

The creation of a shared vision requires a careful balance between district and school leadership. High school improvement cannot be "one more thing" added to the already full plate of educators. Districts must identify the systemwide mission, vision, values, and goals, as well as a set of principles and practices that should guide reform. Districts will want to identify the resources and support that will be available to schools to foster reform. At the same time, schools must be empowered to develop their own missions, visions, values, and goals within the district context. In this way, administrators and teachers at the school level can take responsibility for the reform and will be willing to be held accountable for results. Principals and teachers should be encouraged to pursue approaches and ideas that best meet the needs of their students within the context of the district's vision, mission, values, and goals, and for which they are willing to be held accountable.

Studies suggest that successful districts set expectations for schools, help develop the capacity of principals and teachers, create a collaborative environment, build effective data systems to support improvement, and seek to balance central control and school-based decision making.

Garner Stakeholders' and the Public's Support for the Vision

There are multiple ways to garner support for changes in practice that lead to improved schools. The first is to have skill and be prepared with data. The second is to have a deep understanding of the reform process. The third is to gain the trust of stakeholders by establishing a climate of respect that demonstrates that sought-after improvements will succeed through *facilitated support*, not embedded mandates or external structures. This approach respects the talents of staff while building their capacity. This requires support through resources and coaching, along with a commitment to ongoing communication.

Develop the District and School Policies and Practices to Support Continuous Improvement

District and school policies, regulations, and financing need to be reviewed and updated, or abandoned in support of the new vision for high schools. The district's standards and graduation requirements, for instance, may need to take into consideration student mastery of skills and knowledge to accommodate reform initiatives. This is a specific place where the data come into play. Collect the requisite data on student outcomes and measure them against district and state standards.

Create the Capacity to Undertake Improvement Efforts

Three key elements of capacity building must be targeted:

1. Expanding district and school administrators' capacity by providing specific on-site and off-site support, and developing in them the skills they need to lead reforms

2. Developing effective structures for teaching and learning

3. Focusing on improving teaching and learning.

When using technical assistance or external consultant support, establish that the role of these individuals or organizations must be in line with the mission and goals, focused on building the internal capacity of the staff, and part of a strategic approach—not just a "random act of consulting."

District departments have traditionally administered programs and initiatives, and monitored compliance. High school principals have been trained and expected to focus on building management, discipline, budgeting, personnel, and scheduling. But the skills that are needed to support school transformation must include the ability to create a vision, set goals, lead and manage change, build a team to plan and implement change, use data to inform decision making, create effective structures, address issues of teaching and learning head on, and align policies and practices to support change. These skills must be developed and nurtured at the state, district, school, and classroom levels.

Improving teaching and learning must be a process that is addressed parallel to the structures and policies that will foster gains in student achievement. Instruction needs to be an equally important objective of technical assistance. In the short term, this means focusing on what happens in the classroom. But it also means thinking creatively about how to use the community outside the classroom to support learning and how to change teacher preparation and certification programs. Too many reform initiatives get hung up in haggling over governance, scheduling, and the like; they fail to pay attention to the kind of learning that is or is not taking place in the classroom. Structure and instruction should complement one another, but changing the structure while ignoring instruction is a recipe for failure.

Adopt New Practices and Align Policies and Practices in a Way That Promotes Continuous Improvement Supported by Expert Technical Assistance

It is essential that the development of strategic planning, policy development, the development of SLC, scheduling to support reform, student advisories, portfolios, project-based learning, improving instruction, aligning instruction to state content standards and grade level expectations, senior projects, and student motivation all fit into one effective system of redesigning and reculturing schools. Schools and districts can best support schools with technical assistance through training, coaching, and facilitated work sessions.

WHERE TO BEGIN WITH BUILDING CAPACITY

Depending on your school's or school district's place on the continuum of moving toward a culture commitment to *continuous improvement*, you will have a varying set of "first steps" to accomplish as a key practitioner. All systems operate on a basis of networks and connections, and that may be especially true in your district. If you are a seasoned practitioner, review these steps and adjust as necessary. If you are new in serving as a school leader and practitioner, take the time now to begin your work by engaging in reflective practice and by working effectively and efficiently.

The first stage of your process of building effective SLC will be to continue with formative steps as you begin building awareness and support for the concept and assessing the readiness of the faculty. Throughout the nation, we see an amazing turn of events in school reform and school leadership. As the interest in smaller schools continues to grow, we see that a variety of individuals and stakeholders can have an immense impact on how a school operates. School improvement—and certainly the creation of SLC—cannot happen in a top-down or fully bottom-up manner. Building support has to include more than lip-service and a few staff development sessions that focus on changing the school and creating smaller learning units. Indeed, some national models require a faculty vote of support for a specific redesign or reform before they will begin to assist a school in the SLC implementation model. Building on the suggestion of presenting to the faculty, consider utilizing conference/planning periods, late starts/early releases, and professional development days to create a tailored sequence of activities that involve staff in the SLC implementation process and enlist their support. Practitioners will benefit from the extra set of eyes and ears in looking at school data, best practices, reform models, and the variety of SLC models that exist. If you have not done so already, update the [1.1 Creating SLC Presentation] discussed in Chapter 1, and contained in the Tool Kit, with your own data on slides four and five. Use the presentation to help build awareness, create a sense of urgency, and set the course for all that will follow. You will want to include:

- Discussion about current school data such as test scores, promotion rates, graduation rates, college placement, truancy, and staff attendance. Do a reality check. Ask how many of the faculty, and even of the administration, have an intimate knowledge of school data and trends.
- Provision of the information on models/types of small schools and academies and on national trends
- An outline of the strategies and manner in which teachers "in SLC" or "in academy" operate
- Consideration of challenging issues such as staff jobs, union contracts, changes in school schedules, and extra workloads
- Material candidly addressing areas of concern for special needs, English language learners, and Advanced Placement (AP) students
- A review of your local labor market data
- Visits to industry sites to see the opportunities and trends within neighboring industries
- Visits to school sites that have already implemented SLC
- Attendance at conferences and meetings that support SLC development
- Meetings with school district staff to gain a districtwide perspective on related initiatives and mandates.

In addition, you will want to be responsive to the many questions that will arise as part of this process. You may find it useful to create a frequently asked questions (FAQ) opportunity for staff to post their queries. That's what Junction City High School in Kansas did. With their permission, we have included their questions and answers in the Tool Kit [3.1 FAQ Frequently Asked Questions]. Please feel free to adapt them and post them, using appropriate technology, for faculty and families.

In these early stages of building momentum and planning for engagement and a change in practice, you will want to assess the areas that are already most in line with an SLC approach to implementation and assess what areas of teacher strengths already exist in your school. The Tool Kit contains an MS Excel file to help [3.2 Teacher Readiness]. It is a tool that we have designed to get teachers, partners, families, administrators, and other stakeholders dialoguing about their improvement work and their readiness for SLC. It focuses on the five bins of work with which we are becoming increasingly familiar: data, personalization, curriculum and instruction, partnerships, and climate for success. Completing this tool helps to set a course for professional development needs.

Let us take a minute and see what the tool is and what it is not.

- It is protected in order that you can enter data but cannot inadvertently change fields or weighted values.
- It offers the possibility of use for group discussion, planning, and data collection.
- It is not linked to any specific research design. It has worked well with schools that want to focus on and address a process for creating SLC.
- It is set up, as were our SLC assessment files, on a simple 4.0 scale that is easily recognized and understood by those working in schools. It is decidedly *not* intended to give a school an A- to F-like ranking, a negative judgment, or a sense of failure. It is intended as a developmental scale where all schools— just like all students—can succeed.
- Without careful review and discussion, it runs the risk of being an arbitrary assessment by one individual or a group of individuals. With review and discussion, it serves as a powerful tool to help shape all areas of SLC implementation, specifically that of staff development.
- It is not complete. The sheer size of the file required some narrowing of categories and questions. You may find that there are questions you wish to codify more specifically, such as standardized test scores or grant funds received. Special school elements should be noted in your overall assessment but they are not catalogued here.
- It can be used for a single SLC or for a whole school. It does not, however, "cross assess" between multiple programs within a school.
- It is easy to use, generates great quick results, captures the key elements of your reform, and serves as a catalyst for engagement of stakeholders.

Here is how it can work for you. First determine who will provide feedback on staff readiness. This file has been used in a private meeting with a principal in a candid discussion about staff readiness, with school improvement teams, with departments, and with existing SLC—all with different results based on their varied perspectives. Open the file. Tool Kit Snapshot 3.1 shows what you will see.

Tool Kit Snapshot 3.1   Teacher Readiness

	A–D	Basic (1)	New (2)	Developing (3)	Expert (4)	SCORE
1	*Teacher Readiness*					
2	School Name: "Our High School"				**Faculty N**	**140**
3	**Data Driven**	Basic (1)	New (2)	Developing (3)	Expert (4)	SCORE
4	Baseline of knowled AVERA 2.65	Row	Row	Row	Row	
5	Graduation rate	15	30	80	15	2.68
6	Ninth grade repeater numbers	20	20	80	20	2.71
7	Student attendance rate	20	80	20	20	2.29
8	Teacher attendance rate	10	40	20	70	3.07
9	# of students proficient on state test	10	40	20	70	3.07
10	Average GPA	50	60	10	20	2.00
11	Are AP up or down	10	10	10	80	2.71
12	**CLIMATE** AVERA 2.27					
13	Goals	5	25	70	40	3.04
14	Urgency	25	10	95	10	2.64
15	Know models	80	20	20	20	1.86
16	Are engaged	40	20	30	50	2.64
17	Work collaboratively	80	20	20	20	1.86
18	Common planning	90	0	40	10	1.73
19	**Staff Development**					
20	Site visits	10	10	10	110	3.57
21	Team building	110	10	10	10	1.43
22	Leadership	20	60	50	10	2.36
23	Extended period day	10	0	0	130	3.79
24	Partnership					0.00
25	Shared leadership structure	20	60	50	10	2.36
26	Alignment of policy and practice	60	30	20	30	2.14
27	**PERSONALIZED ENVIRONMENT FOR TEACHING AND LEARNING**					
28	AVERA 0.00					
29	Individual SLC are identified					0.00
30	Facility					0.00
31	Schedules support instruction					0.00
32	Advisories are in place					0.00
33	Teachers work in PLC or CFG					0.00
34	Students have 6 year plan					0.00
35	Leadership					0.00
36	Team balance					0.00
37	Student balance					0.00
38	Field experiences					0.00
39	**CURRICULUM AND INSTRUCTION**					
40	AVERA 2.54					
41	Evidence of focus on improvement	15	30	80	15	2.68
42	Standards based	20	20	80	20	2.71
43	Plan and practice for coaching	20	80	20	20	2.29
44	Data driven	20	80	20	20	2.29
45	Plan to reduce "general ed" class	10	40	20	70	3.07
46	College 2+2, etc. real opportunity	50	60	10	20	2.00
47	CTE certifications widely available	10	10	10	80	2.71
48	**PARTNERSHIPS**					
49	AVERA 3.94					
50	Partners: Business				140	4.00
51	Community				140	4.00
52	Parents				140	4.00
53	Postsecondary				140	4.00
54	Program Externships	10	10	10	110	3.57
55	Work-based Experiences				140	4.00
56	Service Learning				140	4.00
57						
58						

SAMPLE READINESS / YOUR READINESS LEVEL

As with the other Excel files, there are multiple tabs or pages in this file. The first page reflects the sample we have created for "Our School" with a faculty of 140. The second page is a blank form for you to complete as follows:

- Enter the name of your school. Enter the specific number of faculty on your staff. *This number is essential, and is preset at 1.* All data figures are calculated off the new raw number you enter here.
- The only data entries that you can make, beyond the name and faculty number, are the breakout of the faculty along a continuum of "basic," "new," "developing," and "expert." It is essential that, in entering the raw numbers, the totals reflect the same number that you indicated for number of faculty on your staff.
- Review the bin areas listed. Let us look at "climate for success." Here there are elements that are essential for the change process and cover many of the awareness elements we have discussed. Here you need to review how many faculty members understand the goals and timelines for the school. How many are ready for change and understand the national models and the models you are considering? How many already "buy in" to the process and support the move to continuous improvement? How many already reflect curricular strategies that are based on collaboration, integration, and common planning? You will need to consider what staff development has taken place and how many faculty members reflect the benefits of that training. In the staff development category, you should gain a good base for making the important staff development decisions we will discuss later. Lastly, under "climate," you will input how many members of the faculty feel empowered to be part of the process and the extent to which assessment and research are a regular part of the school culture.

Working though the items helps build on the development of a common language and how it will be used. It sets the tone for the next steps of creating and implementing your SLC: bringing others to the *continuous improvement* table. Take note of your results and plan, in partnership with school and district staff, a professional development plan based on the needs of this specific faculty and this review.

ESTABLISH RELATIONSHIPS

In large measure, the success of your implementation effort will be based on your ability to establish trusting, professional relationships with the range of individuals who care about the success of your school. There is a great deal of discussion in the SLC and school improvement field about who must approve or support the model. Every part of the school system should be—indeed, needs to be—involved. We know that the reality of what works in schools happens sometimes because of an excellent principal, and sometimes despite an ineffective one. In some instances, there is central school administration support; in others, "downtown" is simply not closely involved. You will want to both understand, and rise above, negative politics, "command and control" management styles, and infighting between warring factions. Accept at the beginning that schools and school systems are highly political and sometimes highly polarized places. Remaining focused on outcomes for students, rather than the sometimes distracting issues of the adults, will be the best course of action. That said, you will still need to be cognizant of who the players are and how to interact with them to create the win you need in your school and district. Here is a quick guide to negotiating some of these issues and stakeholders.

U.S. Department of Education and State Departments of Education

At least once per month, you will want to visit the Web sites of both the U.S. Department of Education and your state Department of Education. These will likely be your best source for new initiatives, grant funding, and support materials. They will be excellent data sources for information on your school or district's "report card" on graduation rates and standardized test scores. They will also provide you with the key contact persons within the departments who are responsible for, and aligned to, your current effort. Explore these Web sites and make contacts. Do not stop at a first level of review. Finding, for example, the person in charge of Allied Health programs for your state can be an immense help if you are considering establishing a health-related SLC or academy.

District Office and School Boards

Even more critical than dealing with the state and federal level, it is essential that you become familiar with the current mission and key initiatives of your school system. With superintendents changing on average every two years, you can be assured that other district personnel are also turning over at a rapid rate. Some systems are no longer run by superintendents but rather by Chief Executive Officers (CEOs) and Chief Academic Officers. This move has been made in part to stress the fact that the school system is no longer conducting "business as usual." Fiscal and academic accountability are the new driving forces.

If you are a school-level practitioner, keep abreast of who holds key positions that affect high school policy and practice, and the implementation of SLC. Invite those people into your school or region to meet you and your team, observe your implementation, serve on advisory boards, and generate community support. In making a list of those you want to involve or contact, please make sure you include those related to special needs students, guidance, English language learners, service learning, curriculum and instruction, staff development, and special projects or initiatives. You will also want to involve school board representatives in a similar manner.

Principals

If you are not the principal, as a practitioner you will need to establish a "right hand" relationship with the principal, who has primary responsibility for all aspects of the school. Principals' assessments are tied in large measure to the success of test scores and the establishment of a positive school climate. With the regrettable rotation of principals through so many of our high schools, it will be important to have a good working knowledge of all aspects of the school improvement process so that, in the event that there is a change of principals at your site(s), there is always someone with the institutional knowledge to continue building on best practices. If a school is changing principals, make sure you rally the other related stakeholders to help ensure that the next principal assigned can support the reforms and successes that have been put in place. In almost every school, the principal, in tandem with advisory or governance support, must submit a school plan that details the major initiatives, budget, staffing, and goals for the upcoming year. As a practitioner, you will want to ensure that your role, as well as the SLC formation initiative, is specifically included in the school plan. The plan will address capturing goals, statements of need, developmental action plans, objectives, and specified benchmarks for achieving the goal(s).

If you are not the principal, you also need to seek a regular schedule of meetings with the principal to outline and review goals, exchange information related to SLC and related initiatives, and plan strategies for whole-school involvement. As a practitioner, you should be involved in all aspects of the whole-school redesign and improvement process outlined in this book. Perhaps more than anyone else in the process, it is your unique mandate to stay abreast of current research and best practices, and to continually push the envelope for an improvement process that is coherent and aligned to mission, values, and goals. You should serve as the principal's primary resource on how to implement SLC and work-based experiences in the school.

If you are working with a number of schools, consider establishing a principals' and practitioners' network for the sharing of ideas, best practices, and frustrations. Regular meetings will develop an approach that quickly reflects lessons learned and best practices. Also consider peer review committees for assessing areas of strengths and the need for growth. You will learn more about this later.

The School Improvement Committee

Each school has its own version of a committee which shares responsibility with the district and school administrators for shaping school climate and service delivery. The team is usually composed of administrative leadership, union representatives, parents/guardians, teachers, community advisors, and students. In many cases, the team has approval authority for many key school issues and the creation of the school improvement plan that drives the areas of:

- Academic achievement—standardized tests
- Academic achievement—comprehensive program of study
- School climate—a safe, engaging learning environment; clean, well-maintained structures
- Programs of instruction
- Family and community involvement.

The individual school plans will have certain benchmarks for increasing these and will indicate the strategies that are intended to address each area. To create a plan for the creation of an SLC without working with the school improvement team and the school improvement plan only leads to confusion for staff and a disconnected improvement effort. It is essential then that you identify this group within your system, become involved in its process, attend meetings, and work with *the individual representatives*. Of key importance will be the stakeholders listed below.

Teachers and Support Staff

It is, perhaps, obvious that relationships have to be established with the faculty and support staff in order to get anything done at the school. It is, however, sometimes less obvious how these relationships play out in school improvement and in the establishment of SLC. You will need to pay special attention to the concerns of special education teachers and teachers of Advanced Placement (AP), International Baccalaureate, or magnet programs. Frequently, these groups can derail the implementation process with the belief that SLC are neither appropriate nor needed for these students. You will also want to spend time with department heads and assistant principals to talk about new leadership. All teachers will need time to understand changes in schedules and practices. As we will see in Chapter 7, everyone's role shifts in a school committed to a redesign focused on improvement.

Regardless of your current role as a practitioner, you will need to build credibility with the teachers in the school. Teachers respect those who have spent time working in the classroom. If you have not been there, or if you have not been there in a while, be prepared to take the time to learn about "life in the classroom." Only those who can reflect the knowledge of dealing with the multitude of demands of education and adolescent issues will be able to quickly gain the respect of the teacher corps. In a like manner, support staff will need to be both newly engaged to align their talents to a specific SLC and empowered to see their role in the educational life of the entire school.

Parents/Guardians/Families

Involve families in the up-front and follow-up implementation. Attend meetings, send home correspondence, make phone calls, and create or utilize a database or roster of parents. Be prepared to tap into this group as a resource.

You should be aware that there have been occasions across the country where families have challenged the implementation of SLC, and specifically career academies, insisting that they are a means of tracking or "dumbing down" the school experience. You must be prepared with the information that SLC formation is about high standards for *all* students. Reviewing research will arm you with important data that support this and sets the initiative squarely where it needs to be: on increased expectations for all students.

Effective family involvement also means family empowerment. Involved families can help foster school improvement and reinforce the need for hiring practices that keep, for example, an SLC-minded principal at the helm of the school. They, like school boards, can make sure that improvement practices are institutionalized so they do not vanish after the principal moves on. Typically, high school is a time where family involvement drops off sharply just at a time when students are facing life-altering decisions and benefit from having strong adults in their lives. By nature, schools designed for SLC are inviting environments. Families see them as an easier place in which to find ways of supporting their children. From going on field trips to making phone calls, to serving as speakers, job shadow hosts, and teacher mentors, the list of positive ways of involving families in school is limitless.

The Teachers' Union and State Associations

Depending on your state requirements, you may not have a teachers' union per se with which to interact or partner. You will undoubtedly have a professional association of some type that addresses the needs, working conditions, and concerns of teachers. Find out early on who in your building and district has the best information and/or designation as a union/association representative. Learn about the strengths and challenges of the school from this perspective. Ask about specific strategies or practices in place for staff development. Ask about such issues as the demographics of the faculty in terms of numbers, curricular areas, certifications, unfilled positions, and average age of retirement. These types of data will give you an important insight into the school culture and the challenges and issues that the teachers regard as important. Explore practices and schedules relating to the bargaining agreement, schedule of votes, important topics, and the history of the relationship between the district administration and the union.

It is critically important in meeting with the union or the association on change issues that you become sensitive to specific union/association issues that are of concern as they relate to SLC. There is no question that SLC implementation, or any change effort, requires that it is no longer "school as usual." Teaching strategies, schedules, and expectations all must change. Needs for increased planning, changed schedules, and position titles all may challenge union/association regulations and practices. The challenge is to engage the faculty in the process of change, provide the appropriate supports and training, and to assist them in their true desire to make a difference in children's lives.

Not paying attention to union issues and the negotiated agreement led us to seriously falter in one district. In Massachusetts, we were prepared by the administration with an hour-long discussion focused on the willingness of the teachers to move into SLC. To provide for planning time, we knew we needed to ease the union contract stipulation of their staying at school for ten minutes each day after the students left. The goal was for the teachers to leave with the students for two weeks, thereby "banking" a total of 100 minutes of time that could be used for a planning session. During the whole-faculty meeting, a great deal of the discussion was focused on the eleventh day. On that day, teachers wanted to know whether they were expected to meet for 100 minutes or 110 minutes due to the fact that on the eleventh day there was still a ten-minute block of time to be considered. The faculty voted down the proposal, and no common planning time was established! Across the country, we have ample evidence of school system strikes when labor and administrators are unable to settle even a fifteen-minute-per-day instructional time dispute. These instances are not cited to put the unions in a bad light, but to advise you of the depth and detail that will have to be addressed in the reform process.

Share the vision and task of SLC implementation with the union/association leaders and determine, along with the principal, the best way to address the inclusion of implementation practices and mandates in the overall school reform effort. Getting a "yes" early on with this critically important group will make the entire implementation process move far more effectively.

Business and Community Partners

Some research studies point to 90 percent of school/business partnerships failing within the first year, so getting them to work effectively will take time, effort, and ongoing commitment. In Chapter 8, we will outline the varied types of support that can be obtained when partners—informal and formal—are fully engaged in the implementation process. We also provide specific tips on managing these partnerships. We will highlight the importance of getting to know the individuals and intermediary organizations in your community which can help with creating a partnership support network for your site. At this point, however, it is simply important that you begin to address the essential need to have a relationship with the community partners that will assist the SLC effort. These relationships can be the essence of these learning communities, and specifically of career academies. Without the strong support of the community in a strategic, clear, measurable plan, critical relevance and skill-building opportunities will be lost.

Students

While it was obvious that teachers and staff needed to be included in the building relationships section of where to begin in building capacity, it *should* be even more obvious that anyone interested in making a difference in the lives of children should actually be *engaged* with them. Establish a forum where students' issues and interests are heard. *Genuinely* involve them in every aspect of the planning and later in assessing what is working and what should be sustained. Just as we saw with building the ideal teacher in an earlier chapter, student input will be invaluable for what can and cannot work. In addition, involving them in the process reinforces for everyone what the best of education should be: keeping children at the center, and providing an atmosphere and opportunity where they can learn and apply that learning to their own lives.

At a Glance: Summing It Up and Next Steps

The SLC implementation process will be iterative and time consuming, and will involve constant attention to honoring the concerns and needs of others while at the same time pushing a reform initiative. To *effectively* engage in a process of improvement means that change is inevitable—that understanding, couched in a deep respect for what is *in evidence* as currently working well and reaping positive results for students, will go a long way toward building the relationships required to bring systemic improvement to your school or schools. Work through a theory of change that is viable and includes:

- Building a case for change
- Creating a shared vision to guide improvement efforts
- Garnering stakeholder and the public's support for the vision
- Developing the district and school policies and practices to support a commitment to *continuous improvement*
- Creating the capacity to undertake improvement efforts
- Aligning policies and practices
- Adopting and sustaining new practices in a way that promotes *continuous improvement.*

This chapter aimed at placing everyone on the path to an awareness of a change in practice that leads to a culture of *continuous improvement.* In the next chapter, you will create teams that will embrace a detailed planning and implementation process. It is time for the move to SLC to take flight!

4

The Plan's the Thing

Establishing Structures

Let your mind take you to places you would like to go, and then think about it, and plan it, and celebrate the possibilities.

—Liza Minnelli

Chapter 4 Road Map	
Purpose	To enumerate and make decisions about the multiple details associated with each of the bins of work as they relate to establishing SLC structures.
Stage of Implementation	Engagement and Commitment, establishing structures—focus on data, partnerships, and a climate for success.
Process and Action Steps	Document initiative and partnerships that support SLC implementation. Create or refine existing committees to focus on *continuous improvement* and peer reviews. Work through comprehensive task listings and decide on a plan of action.
Tool Kit	4.1 Initiative and Partnership Identification and Alignment 4.2 SLC Punch List 4.3 SLC Punch List 5 Bin Sort 4.4 Strengths and Deficits Map 4.5 Checklist for Ninth Grade
Reflective Practice	What resources are in place to support our move to SLC? How do we codify the efforts that are in place? How do we create and manage an effective plan?
Outcome	Decisions have been made and there is a plan in place that is specific, measurable, attainable, relevant, and time bound.

Never underestimate the importance of a sound step-by-step strategic plan in accomplishing your goals and never be surprised that in most districts there are probably multiple such plans and initiatives already in place. While you would like to believe they are all coordinated and aligned, inevitably you will find that they are too often disconnected at best and competing at worst. Undoubtedly, you have already observed that there are multiple initiatives in play at your school site(s). Too often the literacy initiative runs separately from the afterschool effort, which runs apart from the dropout prevention effort, and so on. In the area of staff development alone, it is not uncommon for a school to participate in disconnected national and state conferences, district staff development, local staff development, and individual SLC-targeted training. Add to this mix the occasional "drive by consultant" that does not have a firm place in the school's redesign or *continuous improvement* structure, and the result is an array of goals, objectives, training opportunities, and curricular materials that overlap and become lost in the overall mission of improving teaching and learning.

Given the multiple federal, state, and local initiatives that abound, schools focused on improvement are beginning to see the need to align their efforts. Increasingly, there is an interest in coordinating the resources and demands of multitiered levels of programs, all geared to bringing about improvement. As a practitioner, you will want to see a coordinated process that will lead to effective implementation. As a practitioner, it is essential that you are committed to effective training that is aligned to the mission coordinated, is needs specific, and diminishes the chances for staff to simply attend workshops and then return to their classrooms for school as usual. This chapter focuses on providing you with the tools to get the right plan in place.

Be selfish here, as coordination now will obviate rounds of frustration and miscommunications. You should lead or support an effort to coordinate the multitude of strategies, practices, funding streams, and materials in play at your site(s). Finding out "Who is on first," who is responsible for what, and what the goals and deadlines are will provide a framework for success.

INITIATIVE ALIGNMENT AND PARTNERSHIP AUDIT

In the Tool Kit, we have provided you with a tool to do just that. The [4.1 Initiative and Partnership Identification and Alignment] MS Excel file is designed with two purposes in mind and is set up around several guiding questions. The "Initiative, Grant, Funding, Goals, Consultant, and Other Support Alignment" tab or page (see Tool Kit Snapshot 4.1) is to be used to capture the multiple initiatives that you have in play to support the redesign and improvement efforts already in play at your school(s). It is set up around seven guiding questions that—perhaps not so subtly— keep you focused on your main mission: improving teaching and learning.

Guiding Questions

- What do we have? Why?
- What do we need? Why?

Initiative, Grant, Funding, Goals, Consultant, and Other Support Alignment

Guiding Questions

1 What do we have? Why?
2 What do we need? Why?
3 Where will "it" fit in the school plan and schedule?
4 What is required of us to be in compliance?
5 How do these grants blend and complement each other?
6 How does "it" relate to meeting and exceeding school mission?
7 What evidence will you see that "it" is making a positive difference?

Grant Name	Grant ID Number	Period of Performance	Amount	District/ School Contact	Phone - E-mail	Goal 1	Goal 2	Goal 3	Goal 4	Goal 5	School Staff Involved	Consulting Staff	Responsibilities of Consultants	Allowable Activities	Line Items

- Where will it fit in the school plan and schedule?
- What is required of us for compliance?
- How do these grants blend and complement each other?
- How does it relate to meeting and exceeding school mission?
- What evidence will you see that it is making a positive difference?

The intent is that, once you have catalogued *each* initiative, grant, consultant support, and so on, you will enter into deep discussions with school leadership around funding streams, their goals, the consultants you use, and the way the puzzle of supports fits together. The other not-so-subtle message is that you get to free yourself from chasing after grants and initiatives that are not central to either the school mission or what you are trying to accomplish. By completing the matrix presented on this first tab, you will help to identify goals, timelines, responsible parties, and allowable activities. This will be useful for ongoing communication among planners as well as those tasked with implementing objectives. It can also serve as a coordination tool for staff development, reporting deadlines, and tracking funds. Committing to a coordinated process avoids duplicated efforts, focuses practices, and helps you develop an approach to systemic versus "drive-by" efforts. Of critical importance is some cross-knowledge among related practitioners, service providers, and consultants regarding how their programs relate, can support one another, and are going to be evaluated.

We recommend you set up a meeting for all those named in the matrix. Through the use of the Excel "sort" function, you are able to present the data in a variety of ways—for example, by goal or consultant. In creating sorts, you will want to make sure you use the sort commands under the word "Tools" in the uppermost task bar, not any sort capabilities represented as icons. Excel operates off a series of rows and columns, and treats each separately. Unless you identify a sort function from the task bar, your data will not stay together. You will want to perform multiple sorts in order that you can see what goals overlap and which are isolated. Share this discussion with teachers, families, students, and partners as a way of building awareness of the concentrated efforts in place for school improvement. This matrix should be updated regularly and revisited annually. As new projects, consultants, and administrators come to the school, they should be made aware of these initiatives in order to continue a commitment to aligning practices. Naturally, it should be reflected in future school plans. However, before you finalize your plans there is at least one more support system that should be codified: your partnerships.

The second tab of the Excel file, "Partnership Audit" (see Tool Kit Snapshot 4.2) follows the same premise as the previous tab and is centered on similar guiding questions. We will deepen our discussion around partnerships in Chapter 8. For now, be satisfied with capturing information on those who support your school, both in informal and formal ways.

Informal Partnerships

We are defining these partners as any individual, group, nonprofit business, for-profit business, postsecondary institution, faith-based organization (FBO), community-based organization (CBO), local or federal government entity, labor organization, or professional association that commits to, and works with, schools to

Tool Kit Snapshot 4.2 Partnership Audit

Partnership Audit

Guiding Questions

1 What do we have? Why?
2 What do we need? Why?
3 Where will "it" fit in the school plan and schedule?

4 What needs to be added/deleted? Why?
5 How does "it" relate to meeting and exceeding school mission?
6 What evidence will you see that "it" is making a positive difference?
7 Is it a real partnership? What is/can the school contribute?

Entity	Contact Name	Mailing Address	Phone	E-mail	Advisory Board	Speakers	Field Experiences	Teacher Externships	Student Work Placements	Student Needs Beyond Classroom	Long- and Short-Term Planning	Recognition and Scholarships	Training	Evaluation	Donations

enhance the educational experience of youth on a long-term or short-term project, or as-needed basis.

Formal Partnerships

In addition to the many informal supports that a school receives from interested and committed stakeholders, there are more formal relationships which are established to accomplish a specific task or objective over an extended period of time. There are also relationships formed through specific agreement to meet those tasks or objectives. These formal partnerships most often take the shape of established advisory boards, and comprise individuals who represent *all aspects of the industry*. Frequently, there is a signing ceremony or letter of agreement that establishes a formal partnership.

Consider both types of partnerships in completing the audit, and then run them through the following set of guiding questions.

Guiding Questions

- What do we have? Why?
- What do we need? Why?
- Where will it fit in the school plan and schedule?
- What needs to be added/deleted? Why?
- How does it relate to meeting and exceeding the school mission?
- What evidence will you see that it is making a positive difference?
- Is it a real partnership? What is the school contributing?

Once you have worked your way to this point of the process, you will have expanded your content knowledge in the area of school improvement and redesign, and established a firm foundation for your success. This is the time to take decisive action. Up until this point, as you have addressed your own skill set, you may have worked in isolation or with a small group. You have the research, you have begun to build awareness, you have established relationships, and you know the definitions of various models. It is time to begin to roll up your sleeves and get to the important work of laying out a *continuous improvement* plan that will reflect the specific elements that will become uniquely your school's path to effective SLC. It is now time to expand your efforts and begin sharing what you have learned with structured groups and the faculty as a whole. Remember too that you must spend time modeling a process of study, engagement, and building a plan.

CREATING WORKING TEAMS

If you have not done so already, this is the time to establish teams to help you get the work done. Unless you are opening a new school, it is unlikely that the teaming process—or indeed many of what might appear to be our step-by-step recommendations—can be undertaken in a linear manner. Undoubtedly, by this point you have already made some initial presentations to the faculty as suggested in Chapters 1 and 3 and held detailed discussions about data and initiatives. You may have already made general presentations to the school improvement committee, and perhaps the school board, as a way of both sharing and gathering information. Before you go further, you will want to carefully assess what committees currently exist, their missions, and whether they are meeting their goals. However, you do *not* want to create layers of teams or committees that overtax the same individuals or which step over each other as they are trying to do good work. In this section we are suggesting a tailoring of the committee structure to focus on teams which will work hard for *continuous improvement in teaching and learning through the creation of SLC*. We have specifically chosen the word "team" rather than "committee" to emphasize how important it will be to have a diverse skill group working together to achieve a common mission. Initial mission-critical teams might include those focusing on continuous improvement, instructional improvement, and peer reviews.

Once teams are established, set a standard for operation that includes posted agendas with a specified purpose and expected outcomes, strict adherence to timetables, and well-scribed minutes of meetings. Meetings should conclude with a summary, expected next steps, and the setting of the next meeting time and agenda. In working with teams, do not skip the step of focusing on the "how" of meetings. School communities are often woefully incapable of conducting effective meetings. Developing this skill, and seeking specific staff development and coaching on effective meetings, will pay off in your teamwork and, as we will see later, in the use of common planning time for faculty members.

We suggest the teams mentioned below as a baseline of support. In creating your teams, seek volunteers and expand your thinking beyond the usual suspects. Explain your use of the term "team." Make sure you involve all stakeholders from the "Building Relationships" section of the previous chapter. If you are going to give more than lip service to stakeholders' importance, this is the time—at the beginning—to seek their involvement. It is also important—though, we recognize, less appealing—to involve those individuals who are sometimes difficult to deal with—the naysayers and those opposed to SLC in general. These individuals can bring a powerful new element to the discussion. They provide a good barometer for how things are going in the school or district as a whole, and, when they are won over, they can be the most effective spokespeople to the community about the benefits of the redesign. This was made poignantly evident in Reading, Pennsylvania, when a teacher who was initially quite vocal in his opposition to the reorganization of the school and to the creation of a ninth grade academy gave testimony a year later to the entire faculty about his year in a ninth grade program. Unprompted, the teacher spoke of his improved connection with students and colleagues. He also said the magic words, "Student attitudes, behaviors, and academic skills all improved." No research study could have spoken as loudly to those who were questioning the broader implementation of SLC than the converted teacher's statement.

The Instructional Improvement Team

A hallmark of your work should be to identify and build capacity within school(s) and district(s). Capitalize on the momentum built by the work or funding initiative that has fostered your *continuous improvement* work to date. It may be a district mandate or the receipt of a grant. Whatever the impetus, use the energy to begin to focus on classroom practices for teaching and learning. We will learn more about the potential of this team in later chapters and the sections on Curriculum and Instruction and Sustainability. For now, consider that these teams will emphasize the importance of data as a tool to influence decision making, and to point out the need for individual and small-group coaching designed to improve student achievement.

The Peer Review Team

Once again, commit to building capacity. Create a team of school-based educators and district or consulting support. This team will carefully review data, past assessments, and reports, and will develop the skills needed to assist in monitoring implementation. Depending on where you are in planning and implementation, you may want to use this team to carry out the initial, or annual, Data SLC Implementation Assessment mentioned in Chapters 2 and 10. The Peer Review Team may need to be trained in how to conduct informational interviews, review data, and conduct effective site visits. The spirit of this work is to identify and share best practices and to provide recommendations on improvements. In districts that are engaging in this work across schools, you will want to consider a cross-district peer review team as well. In continuing with a focus on reflective practice that then influences action, peer teams should visit one another's campuses, review documentation, conduct interviews, and report out annually. We will read more about this in Chapter 7 on professional practice.

The Continuous Improvement Team

Perhaps separately from the School Improvement Committee, noted in the last chapter and usually mandated by district policy, create or recast a team focused on *continuous improvement* that consists, at a minimum, of administrators, school improvement facilitators, data coaches, literacy coaches, and career counselors. Build their understanding and skills as partners with the principal(s) and the district. Create a sense of urgency, and focus on the strategies necessary to create your *effective* SLC. As you will see shortly, the sheer volume of the team's work will demand initially weekly, then monthly, work sessions that focus on planning, implementation, skill building, benchmark adherence, and a sharing of training and resources with their school-based constituents—thus building capacity across the school. In districts that are engaging in this work across schools, you will want to consider a cross-district continuous improvement team as well.

Where should the teamwork begin? A good place to start is by reviewing all the tools used to date. Then it is on to the Punch List!

THE PUNCH LIST: 100+ THINGS FOR TEAMS TO THINK ABOUT AND WORK THROUGH

You are about to embark on very detailed work that requires building consensus, locking down dates, and setting objectives and timelines. If you do not already have some form of "operational calendar" for the school, or you are not tied into the school's master calendar, this is the time to set in place all the school details that will assist or prevent you from succeeding. Please go to the Tool Kit and open [4.2 SLC Punch List] (see Tool Kit Snapshot 4.3). Like some of the other Excel files we have previewed, the first tab introduces the tool and provides you with detailed instructions for its use. Here, you will see reference to the five bins of work already identified. You will also see reference to the language we have been using so far for your work in the area of *formation* and *study and assessment,* as well as the next stages of work—*establishing structures, engagement and commitment,* and *evaluation.* Here too, the details on performing effective sorts in Excel are described. The next tab is the Punch List itself, 113 items to think about, discuss, decide on, plan for, and act upon. Chances are you will not opt to include every element on the list in your SLC design—or at least not initially—but you will want to know at the outset the breadth of the work that leads to comprehensive redesign of schools and to effective SLC.

Let us take a minute and see what the instrument is and what it is not.

- It is largely "unprotected," allowing you to add items or delete them depending on your redesign.
- It is not linked to a specific SLC model, but can be adapted to any model.
- It is comprehensive and has been vetted in and by school systems across the country.
- It contains items categorized and identified by each of the five bins of work.
- It is presented to you here in a *possible* implementation scenario that begins with the formation stage. However, as we have already seen, this work is not linear in nature and you will find yourself criss-crossing stages of work. Also, due to some of the alphabetic preference sorting features of Excel, one item may appear to hold a higher importance within a suggested linear sequence. This is not the intent.
- Where there is a specific resource or tool available in the Tool Kit, it is referenced.
- Its purpose is to gain and document agreement on the elements listed in the left column, to determine who is responsible for each element, and to put specific due dates and timelines around each element.
- It suggests a long list of actions that is sometimes daunting to teams and to faculty members. With that in mind, the Tool Kit contains a variant on the file. The file [4.3 SLC Punch List 5 Bin Sort] is identical to the other one, with the notable exception of having been sorted by the bin of work—curriculum (and instruction), (community) partnerships, climate for success, data, and personalization.

How It Can Work for You

Consider the appropriate time to lay out this comprehensive scope of redesign work with your teams and with the full faculty. We recommend that it be presented early, in order to allow teams and faculty members to understand the breadth of the work. Become familiar with the codes that correlate to the bins of work.

Fill in the areas you have been working on or have accomplished. Doing this produces a sense of accomplishment and validates that SLC redesign values previous efforts.

Have the group you are working with review the entire document. Encourage discussion and questioning. Be prepared for comments suggesting it is overwhelming

(Text continues on page 72)

Tool Kit Snapshot 4.3 (Continued)

The Punch List: Developing, Opening, and Evaluating a Smaller Learning Community (SLC) School

This copy used with permission by: _____ Permission code:

To perform effective sorts, please position your cursor in Cell A7 and then select the sort criteria through Data, then AZ Sort options.

Big 5 BIN	Task/Issue Category	Category	Priority Stage	Date Due	Person Committee	Date Done	Notes
CS	Study union/negotiated agreement to ensure that issues are identified and addressed	1F					
CS	Create an SLC "Top Priorities/Objectives" Strategic Plan	1F					
CS	Create detailed "Three Year" SLC implementation timeline	1F					
D	Review school data to learn where there are deficits and strengths and what areas can be best impacted by getting to small and creating SLC	1F					
D	Study school data and determine implications for types of restructured school design	1F					
D	Establish baseline data and designate a Data Coordinator for ongoing data collection [Data Tracking Tool]	1F					
D	Discuss and determine details of SLC around core elements [Data SLC Implementation Assessment]	1F					
P	Design your "Ideal Graduate" [What Should a Graduate—Teacher—SLC Look Like?]	1F					
C	Determine plan for special education in all areas	2SA					
C	Identify "general ed" courses, develop a plan for decreasing the number	2SA					
C	Identify number of Advanced Placement courses, establish plan for increasing numbers	2SA					
C	Identify number of Honors courses, establish plan for increasing numbers	2SA					

The Punch List: Developing, Opening, and Evaluating a Smaller Learning Community (SLC) School

This copy used with permission by: Permission code:

To perform effective sorts, please position your cursor in cell A7 and then select the sort criteria through Data, then AZ Sort options.

Big 5 BIN	Task/Issue Category	Category	Priority Stage	Date Due	Person Committee	Date Done	Notes
C	Review graduation requirements, is it enough, what are the implications of changing?	2SA					
C	Study and make determinations about types of schedules—realize "it is just time!"	2SA					
CS	Design a process for deciding on students supports, including advisory, seminar, extra help	2SA					
CS	Set up protocols for running effective meetings	2SA					
D	Look at data regarding need for "double dose"/extra support in literacy and math	2SA					
D	Review teacher certification areas for strengths and deficits	2SA					
P	Establish goals for student orientation	2SA					
C	Align coursework, certifications, work-based learning, and extracurricular support [Curriculum Pathways]	3ES					
C	Create daily schedules	3ES					
C	Create professional community, critical friends, study groups, or other means for faculty to continually address academic performance and excellence	3ES					
C	Create strategies/courses to address literacy and numeracy	3ES					
C	Develop course descriptions	3ES					
C	Develop curriculum pathways	3ES					
C	Develop Freshman Transition course	3ES					

(Continued)

65

The Punch List: Developing, Opening, and Evaluating a Smaller Learning Community (SLC) School

This copy used with permission by: _____ Permission code: _____

To perform effective sorts, please position your cursor in cell A7 and then select the sort criteria through Data, then AZ Sort options.

Big 5 BIN	Task/Issue Category	Category	Priority Stage	Date Due	Person Committee	Date Done	Notes
C	Develop Senior Transition course/strategies	3ES					
C	Establish "Six-Year Academic and Postsecondary" plan	3ES					
C	Include appropriate technology training	3ES					
C	Plan repeater student support	3ES					
C	Provide professional development around career awareness, use of partners, curriculum integration [GMS: Quick Wins Curriculum]	3ES					
CP	Create a database of families, partners, faith-based organizations (FBO), community-based organizations (CBO), postsecondary, alumni	3ES					
CP	Create effective work-based learning program, consider credit bearing issues [Insights, Shadows, Mentors]	3ES					
CP	Determine WHY partnerships are needed; then seek appropriate supports	3ES					
CS	Appoint SLC Administrators/Teacher Leaders	3ES					
CS	Create detailed supply list	3ES					
CS	Create empowered subcommittees (e.g., facilities, curriculum, student support, ninth grade)	3ES					
CS	Define "core" for each smaller learning community	3ES					
CS	Design process for SLC "Themes/Design Structure" selection	3ES					

The Punch List: Developing, Opening, and Evaluating a Smaller Learning Community (SLC) School

This copy used with permission by: Permission code:

To perform effective sorts, please position your cursor in cell A7 and then select the sort criteria through Data, then AZ Sort options.

Big 5 BIN	Task/Issue Category	Category	Priority Stage	Date Due	Person Committee	Date Done	Notes
CS	Detail all renovation needs: new doors, movable labs, signs, card swipe, offices. . .	3ES					
CS	Determine administrative structure to guide and "operate" the academies	3ES					
CS	Determine appropriate strategy for integration and alignment of whole-school, SLC, and vocational centers	3ES					
CS	Determine classroom space and usage	3ES					
CS	Determine leadership/administrative structures	3ES					
CS	Determine overarching structure: small school, 9-12, 9 w/10-12, 9-10 and 11-12	3ES					
CS	Determine role of "elective" teachers	3ES					
CS	Determine role of Department Chairs	3ES					
CS	Determine role of guidance in each house/SLC/community	3ES					
CS	Determine role of special education	3ES					
CS	Address needs of ELL students	3ES					
CS	Determine summer planning time and needs	3ES					
CS	Develop business operation process for reformed school and individual SLC	3ES					
CS	Develop communications tools: newsletters, brochures, e-mails, Web page, building signs, SLC area signs, announcements	3ES					

(Continued)

The Punch List: Developing, Opening, and Evaluating a Smaller Learning Community (SLC) School

This copy used with permission by: Permission code:

To perform effective sorts, please position your cursor in cell A7 and then select the sort criteria through Data, then AZ Sort options.

Big 5 BIN	Task/Issue Category	Category	Priority Stage	Date Due	Person Committee	Date Done	Notes
CS	Develop coverage/substitute strategy for the team	3ES					
CS	Develop protocol for assessing committee structures, realigning, disbanding	3ES					
CS	Develop subcommittees to address key issues	3ES					
CS	Develop tardy/attendance policy that all can agree to support	3ES					
CS	Ensure alignment, meetings, discussions, communication of vendors, technical assistance providers, professional developers, reform models	3ES					
CS	Establish practice for "duty" coverage	3ES					
CS	Get copy of school calendar and ensure no conflicts for planning and implementation	3ES					
CS	Identify professional development needs [Teacher Readiness]	3ES					
CS	Identify space for SLC	3ES					
CS	Itemize union/vote issues	3ES					
CS	Plan differentiated professional development	3ES					
CS	Plan for "Moving Day(s)"	3ES					
CS	Schedule union/association votes	3ES					
CS	Secure dates and deadlines for scheduling, hiring, reviews, school improvement plans, requisitions, and budgets	3ES					

The Punch List: Developing, Opening, and Evaluating a Smaller Learning Community (SLC) School

This copy used with permission by: _____ Permission code: _____

To perform effective sorts, please position your cursor in cell A7 and then select the sort criteria through Data, then AZ Sort options.

Big 5 BIN	Task/Issue Category	Category	Priority Stage	Date Due	Person Committee	Date Done	Notes
P	Address summer orientation logistics	3ES					
P	Address transportation plan	3ES					
P	Create plan for student application and exit from SLC	3ES					
P	Decide/develop, conduct professional development around student advisories	3ES					
P	Design a process for placement of students in SLC	3ES					
P	Design a process for placement of students in teams	3ES					
P	Design a process for staff recruitment and placement in SLC and teams (GMS: Academy/SLC Selection)	3ES					
P	Determine % of time students will/must be in community/house/SLC	3ES					
P	Determine dress code/uniform policy	3ES					
P	Develop personal support plans for students	3ES					
P	Develop umbrella permission form	3ES					
P	Ensure common planning time and the effective use of it for team members	3ES					
P	Establish student leadership/governance council	3ES					
P	Establish student-led conferences	3ES					
P	Place staff in SLC and in SLC teams	3ES					
P	Plan schedule for Summer Orientation	3ES					
C	Determine plan for ELL success	3ES					

(Continued)

Tool Kit Snapshot 4.3 (Continued)

The Punch List: Developing, Opening, and Evaluating a Smaller Learning Community (SLC) School

This copy used with permission by: **Permission code:**

To perform effective sorts, please position your cursor in cell A7 and then select the sort criteria through Data, then AZ Sort options.

Big 5 BIN	Task/Issue Category	Category	Priority Stage	Date Due	Person Committee	Date Done	Notes
C	Ask partners to review, give input, design, coteach career-themed courses	4EC					
C	Establish college articulation agreements	4EC					
CP	Design a process for identifying current/possible SLC community partners	4EC					
CP	Design a process for ongoing teacher, student, family, and community engagement	4EC					
CP	Establish formal SLC partnerships	4EC					
CP	Establish partnership and articulation with middle/feeder schools	4EC					
CP	Meet with Community/Business for purpose of informing/engaging	4EC					
CS	Celebrate success!	4EC					
CS	Determine staffing needs and how they will be met	4EC					
CS	Hire needed faculty, plan for their orientation into the team	4EC					
P	Create community advisory board	4EC					
CS	Compare ninth grade data at mid and end of year around issues of demographics, academic gains and losses, and school climate [Data Tracking Tool]	5E					
CS	Compare whole-school data annually around issues of demographics, academic gains and losses, and school climate [Data Tracking Tool]	5E					

The Punch List: Developing, Opening, and Evaluating a Smaller Learning Community (SLC) School

This copy used with permission by: Permission code:

To perform effective sorts, please position your cursor in cell A7 and then select the sort criteria through Data, then AZ Sort options.

Big 5 BIN	Task/Issue Category	Category	Priority Stage	Date Due	Person Committee	Date Done	Notes
CS	Ensure SLC/reform plans are aligned with district/state efforts	5E					
CS	Have a regular system of checks and balances for monitoring implementation	5E					
D	Create exit survey for graduates, monitor 6 months, 1 year	5E					
D	Determine Student Evaluation/Assessment	5E					
D	Look at "repeater student" data	5E					
D	Run a "D and F" report by teacher, department, school. Determine strategy to coach teachers to success	5E					
D	Train others and then conduct peer review process	5E					
D	Gather a study team and engage in process of self-reflection geared at recommendations and next steps.	5E					

and those suggesting that you are already doing some of the items on the list. Affirm that the work ahead of you is indeed intense, and that some work is already being done. The focus now should be on what else is required to be done, what is being done well, and who will be responsible for leading and completing items.

After this initial review, teams will need to get much deeper into the discussion about the five bins of work. Using the Punch List cannot be approached as a simple checklist of actions to be completed. We have found the following procedure to works extraordinarily well. After the [4.2 SLC Punch List] has been reviewed in the possible sequence order, divide your group into those interested in thinking about and working on one of the five bins and present them with the [4.3 SLC Punch List 5 Bin Sort] file. Have them enter into a discussion about what is in place, what is working (as evidenced), what needs to be implemented, and what are they concerned about. With your Continuous Improvement Team, start making benchmark recommendations as to when things will be accomplished and who will accomplish them.

Some events, such as recruiting students or scheduling classes, are annual events; others are start-up practices. You will want to consider a minimum of one year of planning before you open an effective SLC. The guiding principles to consider will be: adequate time to engage faculty, students, families, and community; time for planned and ordered staff development; and the timely assignment of students to the SLC of their choice.

This Punch List then becomes the guiding document for the rest of your work. It is both guidepost and mile marker. It gets folded into all school improvement plans. It helps drive what grants and partnerships you will seek. It sets up the need for technical assistance and coaching support. Working through the document allows you to more narrowly define the elements you will include in your program and those you will delay or put aside. Having completed the initiative alignment and partnership pieces described earlier, you should be able to align some of the areas of responsibility more easily. Keeping the Punch List agreements and timelines at the forefront of your work will assist in all the critically important planning and implementation stages of your SLC.

You have begun the detailed work of *establishing structures.*

HOW MUCH WILL SLC IMPLEMENTATION COST?

Now that redesign elements are becoming clearer, getting a strong sense of the overall school budget will aid in your ability to plan for SLC activities. Knowing the budget and the budget cycle also provides you with another task on your "to do" list—ensuring, through grants and other resources, that SLC activities are addressed in the school budget.

Perhaps the most frequently asked question in relation to establishing SLC is "How much will it cost?" Unfortunately, there is no specific amount. The individual needs that you will have for funds will be determined, in part, by the specific initiatives you are undertaking, the skill set of the school staff, the complexity of the redesign initiative, directives from a model provider—if you are choosing one—and the availability of "in-kind" or donated resources. If you are an approved part of a federal or state reform, you may receive specific amounts of funding for SLC creation. In building an SLC budget, you will want to make sure that you keep track of all donated resources, both in terms of estimated dollars and in terms of contributed or in-kind services. This tracking can be used in grant applications as evidence of "matching funds."

Here is a partial list of the needs you will have in implementing SLC:

- Staff development, including the following topics: working as a team, understanding and working with data, serving as an advisor, effective meetings, curriculum integration, career-specific areas, extended-period day, teachers serving as advisors, and portfolio development
- Stipends for staff training time and funding for substitute/release time
- New student orientation
- Family involvement activities
- Curricular materials that reflect career integration
- Transportation funds for students to gain work-based experiences
- Work-based student materials
- Recognition of and incentives for faculty, staff, families, partners, and students
- Access to technology, computers, copiers, phone lines, phone expenses, and any related service contracts
- Office supplies, furniture, letterhead, brochures, and business cards for staff
- General operating costs for hosting/attending meetings (parking, cab fares, refreshments)
- Uniforms or "SLC dress" attire
- Summer training activities for staff and students
- Conference registration fees and related travel costs to share the best of your program and learn from others
- Yearly retreat for faculty and business partners and teams.

REALITY CHECK: STRENGTHS AND DEFICITS MAPPING

Once you have a general sense of how the school operates, have had a chance to establish the important relationships that will assist you in building SLC, and have arrived at the important first steps of establishing structures, you will need to perform an assessment of the existing strengths and deficits of your school(s) as they relate to what you are trying to accomplish. You have some initial baseline data from the tools we have already introduced. Your goal is to match this assessment to the specific efforts you will undertake as an SLC practitioner. The Tool Kit contains multiple tools that can be used to both conduct a quick reality check and dive deeper into discussions. Here we introduce [4.4 Strengths and Deficits Map]. You may choose instead to use [5.4 It Was the Best of Times] or [10.2 Prides, Pitfalls, and Priorities], all of which serve a similar purpose. Please refer to them now to choose the tool that best meets your needs and audience. The Strengths and Deficits Map shown in Tool Kit Snapshot 4.4 is a tool that you can use in every area of planning and implementation.

Tool Kit Snapshot 4.4	Strengths and Deficits Map

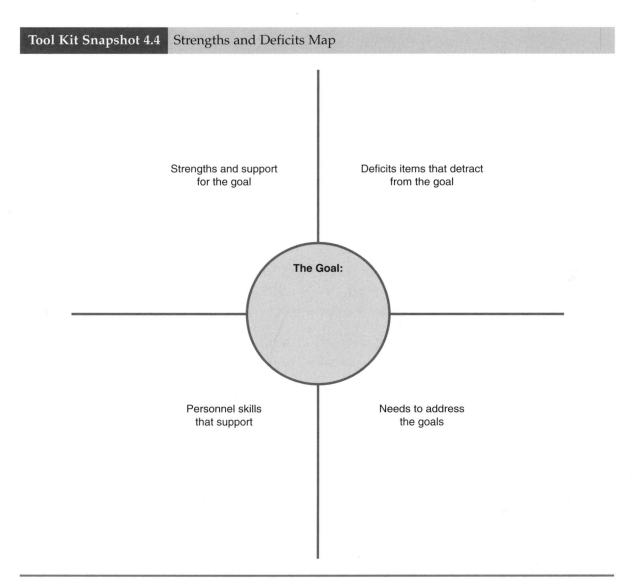

Strengths and support
for the goal

Deficits items that detract
from the goal

The Goal:

Personnel skills
that support

Needs to address
the goals

The technique for strengths and deficits mapping or "asset mapping" is simple, and a sample chart is provided for you. The idea is that you set a goal or objective to study, brainstorm, or plan for. In asset mapping, you want to capture the strengths—for example, a strong business advisory board, close relationships with FBO, a school building that is easily divided into team-specific SLC areas, or the staff skill base that is in place. You also need to address the deficits—such as new school administrative team with no experience in SLC, school designation as a school ready for reconstitution, or no faculty experience with interdisciplinary teaming skills. The last quadrant allows you to quickly capture what needs have to be in place to meet your goal.

It is a simple strategy, but one that allows you to focus your work quickly.

THE PLANNING STAGE

You now have a good picture of the school plan, the school staff, and the resources. You have overlaid that with the SLC formation initiative and have an idea of how far along the continuum you are with a whole-school redesign into SLC. Now it is time to get down to the hard work of building what is not there and fine-tuning what is already established.

Determining Themes and Numbers of SLC

Even if your school already has SLC, you will want to work through this section to ensure that the existing structures meet the district and school mission and are appropriately aligned to the objectives you have been outlining throughout this book. Later we will address the question of whether *whole-school reform means all-at-once reform*. For now, we are addressing the more basic question of "where are we going with SLC implementation?"

As we saw in Chapter 1, there are several designs in place across the country for SLC implementation. To recap, the vast majority of them fall into two general formations: the ninth grade academy coupled with upper-level SLC or career academies, and those that are configured for ninth to twelfth grade students. Regardless of design, students should enter by choice. If you are choosing a theme, it should be broad-based with individualized pathways reflecting student interest and, in the case of career academies, "all aspects of the industry."

While the "to do" list generated from the Punch List may seem like it is now never-ending, realize that a great deal has already been accomplished. Hopefully, you discovered during your meetings with the principal, teams, and other stakeholders that there has already been research and review of the nationally approved models on whole-school reform. Knowing the difference between a well-documented and prescriptive model, and developing a design in which you use proven practices targeted at your own school community, are essential. If you are choosing a prescriptive model, such as First Things First or Talent Development High Schools, you are committing to using their specified curriculum, a specific design structure, and a specified timeline for planning, implementation, staffing, and budget. You are gaining from their years of national experience and well-documented strengths. Going it alone or planning and partnering with a consulting organization that allows you to apply research and adapt best practices to your site-specific needs and cultural practices is another option. Knowing the different approaches of those with whom you seek to consult is essential and will help immensely with engaging others in your work.

If you are thinking of selecting career academies or career-focused magnets, the selection of the career theme programs you will house in your school(s) will be central to planning for your next steps. Please remember that, while career academies can lead to industry certifications and highly marketable skills for students, this only happens when it is planned for. Most career academies, by intent, focus on building relevance into the curriculum based on student interest. You will want to undertake a complete review of your local labor market research and speak to industry leaders, your local chamber of commerce, and, if applicable, your local Department of Employment Services and Workforce Investment Act Board. The list of possible career-focused programs should grow out of the work developed under the U.S.

Department of Education's former Building Linkages Project. The project identified sixteen industry clusters. Consortia of representatives from education, business, post-secondary institutions, and associations have defined the specific skills required for each of the sixteen areas. The consortia developed and promoted the standards and in some cases have created free tools and curricula for use in schools. This information is available at www.careerclusters.org; specific industry links for the clusters noted below are included in the Resources section.

The sixteen official industry career cluster areas are:

1. Agriculture, food, and natural resources

2. Architecture and construction

3. Arts, A/V technology, and communications

4. Business, management, and administration

5. Education and training

6. Finance

7. Government and public administration

8. Health science

9. Hospitality and tourism

10. Human services

11. Information technology

12. Law, public safety, corrections, and security

13. Manufacturing

14. Marketing, sales, and service

15. Science, technology, engineering, and mathematics (STEM)

16. Transportation, distribution, and logistics.

Lacking in most systems is a process for approval of themes—and in the case of career academies, the career theme—at each high school. Too often, principals and teaching teams determine what themes they would like to embrace based on past practice or personal interest, without reviewing what other programs are established or are being considered in their district. If you can encourage a blueprint for the approval procedure, you will have a significant impact on the SLC development process. Such a blueprint should include that the high school undergo an internal self-review; that a proposal for the implementation of the specific (career) themed programs be submitted to central administration; and that central administration approve the intended (career) theme or request revisions to the plan.

The number of SLC to be implemented depends in large measure on your decision about the design options you choose. Schools, and especially SLC, must be designed for student success. Many of our students are facing extraordinary challenges in their day-to-day lives. Even students who stay away from negative behaviors such as drugs, gangs, and violence can find themselves pulled between successful school behaviors and the demands and stresses of their family and community. Good students who have family demands to help out with younger siblings, less mature students, and students who find the ways of the streets more palatable than the ways of school hallways all may find themselves in danger of school failure and dropout. Putting in place school supports, or "safety nets," that address student needs is one approach to keeping students motivated and on track. In creating your small school design, it is essential to realize that there are students who will need, at some point in their high school career, additional targeted support. Researching models of alternative schooling and designing supports through such interventions as DuFour's "ladders of success" and "pyramid of interventions" (Eaker et al., 2002, p. 41), *prior* to needing them, will allow for delivery of a proactive, supportive program rather than one where students get a message of failure and punitive measures.

In many respects, it is simple number game—as we saw on the [1.1 Creating SLC Presentation] PowerPoint slide. You want your students and teachers in as small and diverse a grouping as your staffing numbers will allow—preferably in groups which don't exceed 400. Even within this group of 400, you will want to construct teams of approximately 150. Later on, we will look at staffing formulas and SLC purity. Here, let us concentrate simply on how we would distribute students across designs if we were seeking to create a personalized atmosphere for teaching and learning. Imagine a school of 2,530 students—with 780 freshman, 600 sophomores, 580 juniors, and 560 seniors. A quick look at the numbers tells us that, barring a demographic increase in population, this school is losing 180 of its students after the freshman year and an additional twenty students after the sophomore year. Looking at the data in this way highlights the need to intently address students' needs during the first two years. This can be done in any of the designs we have discussed—now is the time to determine your final structure. To help in that regard, we will again focus on the ninth grade and upper-level SLC experience.

THE NINTH GRADE EXPERIENCE

With an increased number of our ninth graders needing to consistently repeat ninth grade, and with even more alarming numbers of ninth grade dropouts, there is a clear need to pack the freshman experience with strategies for success. The objective is to create an atmosphere that continues the nurturing atmosphere many students experienced in earlier grades and eases the transition to high school. If you are considering a ninth grade–specific initiative, you will want to work with the principal(s) to organize a team of faculty members from across core disciplines (frequently called the MESS team—for math, English, social studies, and science), a special education teacher, a guidance counselor, and perhaps an English as a second language teacher as a core group committed to creating a certain structure and embodying a set of specific experiences that will address the special needs of these entering students. The ninth grade year will prove crucial in the real-time dropout rate of a school and in the atmosphere created by students who, although they continue to attend classes, have become disengaged from the educational process.

The ninth grade learning area should create a welcoming atmosphere for the students. Indeed, the Talent Development High School model calls for a completely separate ninth grade learning area with a separate entrance and isolated classes. The establishment of the ninth grade area sets the tone for class identity, and at the same time limits the interactions with upper-class students and physical movement throughout the building. This simple structural piece alone results in fewer referrals to the office and less tardiness to classes.

Exemplary programs, like that at Westgate High School in Iberia, Louisiana, showcase students working in teams and an extraordinary freshman transition course (FAME: Freshman Achievement, Motivation and Excellence) that introduces freshman students to the high school experience through academic skill building, tours, scavenger hunts, meetings, orientations, and self-esteem and academic esteem–building course work. Central to this program is the development of a high school plan that explains the need for graduation requirements, course sequences, and other activity options.

While there is a benefit to a separate treatment for ninth graders, and some models (as mentioned) call specifically for separate structures in the ninth grade academy, you will want to ensure that there is some appropriate bridging between the ninth grade and upper-level students. There are a number of researchers and practitioners, most notably First Things First and The Knowledge Works Foundation, who believe the creation of a separated ninth grade experience unnecessarily creates one more barrier to the road to young adulthood and school socialization. The ninth grade students will want to feel very much a part of the high school culture. As one student said to me, "I have waited my WHOLE life to get into high school. Being in the ninth grade academy is just like a continuation of middle school." Structured programs between freshmen and upper level-students—particularly in the areas of career exploration, in some social situations, in terms of community service, and in service learning—can benefit both sets of students. Ninth graders learn about the upper-level SLC and build relationships with upper class students. They begin a maturation process in negotiating how to deal with and work with older students. Upper-level students learn to give back to their younger schoolmates.

In staffing your ninth grade effort, regardless of design, be prepared for the fact that many teachers prefer not to work with ninth grade students. Those special ones who do will make a difference not only in the lives of the ninth graders but also in the whole-school experience. Schools across the country have large ninth grades that quickly pyramid to small graduation classes. The ninth grade experience sets the tone for a radically positive change in school climate. If we believe that our neediest students require our best teachers, and if we believe that small class sizes benefits these students, this is the time to begin an active recruitment process that attracts our best teachers to our ninth grade classrooms.

Teachers in all academies will need extensive staff development, and ninth grade teachers in particular will have a need for a common planning time to work on supports needed for ninth graders. They will need to determine which of the many supports proven to positively affect ninth grade outcomes they will embrace immediately and which they will incorporate later. The supports are listed below and captured for you in a separate MS Word document [4.5 Checklist for Ninth Grade] in the Tool Kit (see Tool Kit Snapshot 4.5) in order that you can use it to work with teams.

Tool Kit Snapshot 4.5   Checklist for Ninth Grade

	Checklist for Ninth Grade
	Collaborate with middle school.
	Review data.
	Actively recruit teachers of ninth grade.
	Decide on teams of teachers: math, English, social studies, science, special education, and limited English proficient.
	Engage guidance and support services; build them into the team.
	Develop a picture of an ideal graduate and an ideal ninth grader—build the structure of ninth grade to support the development of that student.
	Decide on strategy of supports for repeater students.
	Decide on a ninth grade–specific location and plan a "moving day" for faculty.
	Provide team time to develop protocols and practices: homework, discipline, tardiness, student supports, family contacts.
	Discuss and select best practices from past reforms.
	Create a working plan for effective ninth grade implementation.
	Determine ninth grade and whole-school leadership and administrative structure.
	Create summer bridge activities and lessons.
	Decide on teams for students.
	Determine bell schedule for ninth grade and understand implications for whole school.
	Commit to common planning time and its effective use around instruction and student support.
	Design a rigorous course of study where all classes meet or exceed college entrance requirements.
	Decide which "elective" courses are offered in ninth grade and whether elective teachers are part of teams.
	Design a meaningful freshman orientation.
	Design advisory.
	Decide on freshman orientation course.
	Hold a freshman fair for activities.
	Determine practices for students needing a double dose.
	Build in time for extra help.
	Build in credit recovery practices.
	Develop communication strategies for families: phone, newsletters, e-mail, blogs, handbook.
	Lead students toward student-led conferences.
	Commit to having students create a six-year plan.
	Look at strategies of instructional practice—commit to best practices.
	Determine the learning needs of teachers; create tailored professional development for their needs.
	Build a meaningful bridge to upper-level high school experience.
	Celebrate successes!

Upper-Level SLC

Regardless of your ninth grade design, you will also want to encourage the tenth through twelfth grade experiences to be rigorous and relevant. With recent studies pointing to the fact that most students drop out because their program of studies simply is not challenging, you have a basis for building these high-quality, high-standard SLC.

Begin this process by reviewing the [2.3 or 2.4 Data SLC Implementation Assessment] for strengths and weaknesses of existing SLC. Work with the Continuous Improvement Team to review the school plan to see what areas for improvement to existing programs are being undertaken, and what strategies are planned for developing additional (career) programs. Refer back to the just-completed work on career-focused clusters, make a decision about the commitment to this in your work, and plan on designing your upper-level SLC with themes that are broad-based and inclusive enough to attract students with varied academic abilities, interests, and backgrounds, regardless of gender identification. Then do the following.

- Determine what percentage of students is currently in SLC.
- Determine the number of academies or SLC that will be established at your school based on the number of students to be served. If you are serving a high at-risk population, you should keep in mind that, at least initially, freshman numbers will likely be double those of senior students.

Propose SLC themes based on the following:

- A survey of student's interests based on the Holland Interest Inventory or similar interest scan
- A survey of teachers' interests, skills, certifications, and avocations
- A review of the resources within the school (equipment, space, funding, location)
- A scan of other established like-minded programs throughout the district to determine audience served, aspects of industry, and feeder pattern enrollments
- A review of the labor market data and the industry growth areas
- A review of any state-directed or approved majors or career themes.

HOW FAST DO WE HAVE TO GO?

Determining whether you will go "wall to wall" immediately or focus on one or two "pocket" SLC will be a matter of resources, staff capabilities, and school culture. There are pros and cons to both strategies. Beginning with pocket SLC allows your school teams the leisure of developing skills and practices that can then be shared with the SLC developed later. If your school adopts a slow or incremental rollout for the establishment of these more individualized programs, beware of SLC rivalry! In almost every setting in which we have worked, establishing a practice of slow roll-out has also established the creation of a culture of "haves and have nots." Teachers and students in these individualized units, by design, have common planning time, more resources, more field experiences, and more partnerships. At times, non-SLC teachers begin to resent, and sometimes even undermine, the implantation process.

Based on your data, and district or state mandates, you will have a varied sense of urgency to move to the creation of SLC. As referenced earlier, you will want at least a year of planning before you open "wall to wall" with a comprehensive SLC for all students. Even then, you will want a staged approach for success that enables you to choose the things you can do well initially, take some risks, and build in a plan to incorporate many of the 100+ Punch List items into your design. What has proven to be the most difficult of implementations is one that is so staggered in sequence that you run the risk of fatiguing and disengaging faculty; losing momentum as changes in staff, administrations, and district mandates occur; or winding up with multiple small, disconnected SLC implementations that are difficult to manage in a whole-school design. Consult the school plan, the districtwide plan, and your work to date. Begin to propose a strategy for rolling out your whole-school, wall-to-wall reform.

We have worked with a school in Washington, DC, that weathered the storms of "pocket-by-pocket" academies and then decided to go "wall to wall" with the balance of the staff. The outcome was disastrous. Insufficient time and attention were paid to training staff, orienting families, or engaging new partners. Students were being placed in programs without consideration of their interests, but based only on balancing numbers. The results of a nonplanned implementation caused plunging graduation rates and triggered a staff and partner exodus.

South Grand Prairie High School in Texas took the dramatic step of deciding in June 1997 to go wall to wall in September of that same year. Common logic would have predicted almost inevitable failure for the school. Kim Brown, then principal of South, had extraordinary leadership and vision. She nurtured her staff to success and left a legacy of structures and commitments that ensured the staff could continue the reform. South was awarded the New American High School Award from the U.S. Department of Education in the spring of 2000.

Going wall to wall taps all the resources of the school and causes stress on schedules and staff. It does, however, even out the experiences for everyone, allow the faculty to grow as a team, and provide service to all students all at once. In short, done right, the school will reach the overall reform goals more quickly. SLC, by their very design, are intended to bring about success—not just student success but staff and school success—as measured both by school climate data and by test scores. Part of that success will be based on the "buy in," staff development, and agreements of the school staff. We worked with one school a few years ago that was proposing a more measured pace than we had initially suggested. Without casting any aspersions on any prescriptive model, this school had a bad experience. They were candid with us about why they thought more time was needed—"we need to recover from the past group's consulting strategy and their prescriptive directives that left our staff angry and disempowered." We listened, and two years later this school has a complete SLC design that is rich in all the SLC elements.

As you move toward the implementation phase, be realistic as to what can be accomplished and when. That is not to say that you can allow someone or something to derail the process. What it does mean is putting into place a strategic plan that sets you up for success. Select a range of elements that are immediately and easily doable and those that will be more challenging. The implementation has to take place, and all faculty and students should be included. The question is the timing. The Punch List should have allowed you to set reasonable and far-reaching goals. Your commitment is to making some big changes and working toward them, regardless of your goal for overall redesign.

At a Glance: Summing It Up and Next Steps

There is a lot to accomplish in creating a learning environment that is supportive of students, teachers, and families. Add to that the tasks associated with adjusting curriculum, addressing standards, involving partners, changing leadership and teaching styles, changing school structures and schedules, developing a means to effectively involve students in work-based experiences, and then integrating that experience back at school. That agenda demands a plan that reflects goals with associated timelines. It is the Continuous Improvement Team and the faculty as a whole that must set a clear mission and vision for SLC existence, and they must be able to communicate this vision to all stakeholders— especially families and students. Nothing will succeed like a strong plan that aligns the work to the overall mission of the school and district, keeps student and teacher success at its core, and remains focused on SLC designed for personalization and improved instructional practice. That plan includes having teachers imagine the school they have always dreamed of working in and then helping them create it! We tackle that in the next chapter.

5

Establishing SLC Teams

Developing the Mission, Culture, and Schedule

At every crossing on the road that leads to the future each progressive spirit is opposed by a thousand men appointed to guard the past.

—Maurice Maeterlink

Chapter 5 Road Map

Purpose	To provide the tools for engaging all staff in the SLC process by alignment of specific staff members to specific SLC, laying out teamwork mechanisms for teachers, addressing specific issues related to schedule and SLC practices.
Stage of Implementation	Establishing Structures, Engagement and Commitment—focus on personalization and climate for success.
Process and Action Steps	Identify academy teams. Provide time for team building and preliminary SLC planning. Make decisions about school schedules.
Tool Kit	5.1 Creating Teams—Roles and Responsibilities 5.2 SLC Staffing 5.3 Sample SLC Teacher Selection Interview Questions 5.4 It Was the Best of Times 5.5 Imagine That
Reflective Practice	What complement of teachers, administrators, and staff will best meet our *continuous improvement* goals? What schedule will help us in quality delivery of instruction? Are we on track with implementation as we laid out our plans in the Punch List? Is everyone involved? Who do I need to touch base with, have a hard conversation with, seek support and advice from?
Outcome	Each member of the teaching staff is assigned to an SLC. Preliminary details about practices within the SLC are established. A determination has been made about the schedule that will provide the best mechanism for what you want to accomplish.

The culture shift you are now creating is exhausting, exhilarating, and, for some, uncomfortable. It is becoming clear that the improvements you seek imply sweeping changes in practice—and we are not done yet! The Continuous Improvement Committee by this time has worked through its research and settled on design elements. It has also, using the Punch List, laid out a preliminary plan for ongoing work. Now, as a practitioner, you need to build on that momentum and inculcate in the whole faculty a restlessness for *continuous improvement*. This means, first and foremost, creating a true community of learners which understands that improvement means putting past practices on the table, looking at them through the lens of hard data, and holding discussions about how practice influences outcomes. The natural outgrowth of these discussions is that some practices should stay and others, including individual staff roles and specific job descriptions, must change. The details of answering the essential questions of who has to change, and to what, will be critical for making the nascent plan you have outlined from the last chapter begin to take shape.

Among the many questions that will arise about implementation are the very personal ones of what happens to "me" as an assistant principal, department chair, or classroom teacher. If you have not already done so, this would be a good time to revisit [3.1 FAQ Frequently Asked Questions] in the Tool Kit, adapting them to your system, and posting them. The more information available to educators, the more involved they will feel and the more they will trust the process that is transforming their school. Soon it will be time to designate SLC teams. District representatives and principals, in concert with all union and district guidelines, will determine who will have responsibility for an administrative and teaming structure to support a specified SLC. In many school districts, assistant principals take on the role of SLC principal, guidance counselors become affiliated with a single SLC rather than serving an "alpha-slice" of students, and teachers work collaboratively across disciplines more often than within the silo of their academic department. In these designs, SLC assistant principals shift from a sometimes single focus on facilities or discipline to one in which they handle all aspects of the SLC operations including staffing, instructional focus, scheduling, and discipline. It is also common for a program to appoint a "lead teacher," "coordinator," or "manager" to handle day-to-day operations which include staff meeting time, partner relations, activities, and classroom curricular issues. Teachers' roles change as well in an SLC design. Here, teachers are expected to work in interdisciplinary teams toward each student's success. They are asked to examine the difference between their role as a teacher of a specific discipline and that of an educator of a child. In effective SLC, as we will see in more detail in the next chapter, curricula are redefined and the practice of teaching takes on new attributes.

Perhaps one of the hottest debates in the establishment of the SLC structural and instructional improvements is the continuance of an allegiance to a department structure versus that of the SLC. In the intense twenty years or so of SLC implementation that has now occurred, we have seen a pendulum swing on this topic. Initial structures moved us fully away from departments in favor of interdisciplinary teams. Several years ago, most schools appeared to have struck a more balanced approach, allowing for departments and SLC meetings. At the moment, with the intense focus nationally on state tests as exit requirements for high school students, there is a shift away from the importance of SLC meetings in deference to department and grade level course instructional team meetings. As we will see, the balance between these meetings can be achieved through a common vision and a school schedule that commits to regular common planning time for both groups. Working in a school of wall-to-wall SLC does change the way teachers work together. It does not threaten the department structure, nor should holding on to a departmental structure be used as an excuse to hold on to old practices.

CREATING TEAMS

In the Tool Kit, we have provided a MS Word file [5.1 Creating Teams—Roles and Responsibilities] that lays out possible ways in which key roles, including those of guidance and special education, might be defined in an SLC structure (see Tool Kit Snapshot 5.1). Print it and use it in discussions with staff. You will see from the pages included here that the goal is to have each group engaged in the process of redefinition. As everyone's role begins to be reexamined and we move to a system of more shared decision making, you will want as much communication as possible about expectations and teaming.

Commit to transparency of process, and factor in the following steps for building teams:

- Use specific data to create a sense of urgency.
- Create an SLC mission, vision, and philosophy statement that is aligned with the overall mission of the school, but also highlights the uniqueness that each SLC offers students.
- Identify team space within the building and how it will be used.
- Set priorities and goals using the Punch List.
- Schedule team meetings and develop a team meeting calendar. Try to plan both formal and informal opportunities for the teams to get together.
- Establish SLC "norms" for running effective meetings and for working together. Set agendas with a clear purpose and with specific outcomes. To accomplish this, be on time, ensure everyone has a voice, take minutes, circulate announcements, and have everyone share responsibility for success.
- Discuss and designate shared team responsibilities.
- Develop subcommittees and outline specific needs and roles (e.g., student recognition and support, attendance, activities, academic support, family involvement, interdisciplinary curriculum, partnerships, scheduling, data collection, professional learning).
- Commit to a practice of continuous professional growth and learning. Survey team members on professional development needs and schedule appropriate in-service days.
- Discuss and design communication strategies (e.g., e-mail, blogs, Listservs, bulletins, newsletters, display case, summer updates).
- Develop and facilitate activities that highlight the SLC's works in progress and successes.

Tool Kit Snapshot 5.1	Creating Teams—Roles and Responsibilities

SLC Principal

The SLC principal plays a central role in the successful operation of a team. The principal serves as the head administrator of the smaller learning community and is responsible for the daily operation of the SLC. The SLC principal sets the tone for a shared vision, purpose, and mission for the SLC and for shared leadership and joint responsibility for the success of students within the SLC.

The SLC principal works with his or her faculty team on the areas central to creating effective SLC:

- An environment committed to **personalization** for faculty and students
- A **curriculum** that is of a high standard for all students
- A culture that works in close **partnership** with families, community organizations, and business/postsecondary partners
- A commitment to continuous improvement and **data-driven management**
- The creation of a **climate for success** that aligns and manages resources, provides effective professional development, and encourages shared responsibility by all members of the SLC.

Typically, SLC principals are certified administrators who possess strong leadership, interpersonal, and organizational skills and are drawn from the pool of assistant principals at the school. Some specific duties of an SLC principal may include:

- Setting a standard for instructional excellence
- Setting the tone for respect for students and their learning
- Managing daily operation of SLC
- Setting and monitoring short- and long-term goals
- Overseeing student recognition and discipline
- Overseeing schedules, teacher assignments, and evaluations
- Maintaining communication with whole-school principal
- Maintaining data and conducting teacher evaluations
- Overseeing student recognition and disciplinary issues.

SLC Teacher Leader or Coordinator

The SLC leader serves as the lead teacher in the SLC, taking on the role of guiding instructional practice. He or she shares responsibility with the SLC principal to work with the faculty team on the areas, noted above, that are central to creating effective SLC.

The SLC leader is sometimes, but not always, selected from the school's department chairs or leadership membership. Some specific duties of an SLC leader may include:

- Assisting in establishing the culture of the SLC and pathways
- Assisting faculty with classroom management issues
- Working with teachers on collecting and disaggregating classroom data
- Keeping the faculty informed of innovative instructional techniques
- Working with teachers to set and monitor professional goals
- Coordinating partnerships, work-based learning, and teacher externship programs.

SLC Teacher:

- Participate as a member of an interdisciplinary teaching team
- Attend team meetings held during common planning time for the purpose of student support, academic interventions, looking at student work, developing common assessments, and shared instructional practice
- Coordinate instruction and curriculum across subjects
- Commit to ongoing professional development and peer feedback for the purpose of improving teaching and learning
- Commit to participating in ongoing professional development and certification in specified content area through department and district meetings
- Function as an advocate/advisor for students
- Commit to students' academic success
- Commit to helping students recover from academic failure
- Conference with students and parents/families as a part of the team
- Work with the SLC team on evaluating and improving strategies for credit recovery and remediation
- Provide students with constructive support and in a united front on discipline and attendance, tardy policy, classroom rules
- Analyze data to assess student achievement, attendance, and behavior and to identify strategies and methods to address future goals
- Work with the SLC team to plan professional development
- Evaluate team performance.

Department Instructional Facilitator (DIF): The role of the Department Instructional Facilitator, formerly the department chair, is to foster the standards of excellence and instructional practices for his or her department in working across the school. The DIF takes the lead on integrated units, serving as a coach for increased instructional success and conducting departmental meetings that are focused and linked to the overall mission and vision of the school. He or she is responsible for fostering true professional learning communities (PLC) within the department based on study and inquiry. Each is expected to be a model for research-based instructional strategies and best practices in the classroom. Some specific duties of the DIF may include:

- Alignment of instruction around district literacy and instructional standards to improve teaching, learning, and quality of instruction, including research-based best practices, curriculum mapping, cross-disciplinary efforts, and common assessments, as demonstrated by a more collaborative approach to teaching and learning in all SLC
- Devising strategies for extra help and student success
- Coordination of literacy efforts with others tasked with instructional practice, such as literacy and data coaches and SLC Lead Teachers or Coordinators
- Adherence to data desegregation and item analysis regarding common assessments; individual reviews with teachers regarding their students' data and their strategies to ensure success for students
- Serving as a conduit for department-related information dissemination
- Managing departmental supplies and materials
- Facilitation of departmental budget requests in conjunction with the Business Manager.

The Role of Guidance in SLC

The School Counselor as Human Relations Specialist

School counselors facilitate systemic change by being a part of and/or leading:

- Community councils
- Cooperative learning groups
- Strategic planning efforts
- Shared decision-making teams
- Advisory committees
- School improvement teams.

The School Counselor as Facilitator of Team Building

Education reform or transformation models like Total Quality Management (TQM) stress the importance of team-building in the early stages of the change process. As trained group facilitators, school counselors are helpful in planning and conducting activities to promote cohesiveness, cooperation, and team identity.

The School Counselor as Resource Broker of Services

- School-based coordinator of integrated counseling services
- Coordinator of school-to-work transition programs
- Liaison from the educational system to business and industry.

The School Counselor as Promoter of Positive Student Outcomes

School counselors are the key players in the implementation of the recommendations from the U.S. Department of Labor SCANS (Secretary's Commission on Achieving Necessary Skills) report which identifies essential skills for successful employment:

- Communication skills
- Interpersonal skills
- Listening skills
- Problem-solving and decision-making skills
- Self-esteem and self-management
- Knowing how to learn.

The School Counselor as Change Agent

In their role as change agent, the professional school counselor facilitates change through prevention and intervention for all students. This new paradigm offers the school counselor the opportunity to be:

- Student advocate
- Catalyst
- Liaison with parents
- Systems thinker
- Provider of student services
- Transition consultant
- Policymaking facilitator
- Coordinator
- Team player
- Case manager
- Leader.

The School Counselor as Information Processor

One of the most important contributions to the success of any change effort is the feeling by all the "consumers" that they truly have been heard in the process. As trained listeners, school counselors are role models, summarizers, recorders, or facilitators of the listening process.

Their "consumers" include the following:

- Students
- Parents
- Teachers and colleagues
- Administrators
- Boards of education
- Community members
- Business and industry representatives.

(Continued)

Tool Kit Snapshot 5.1   (Continued)

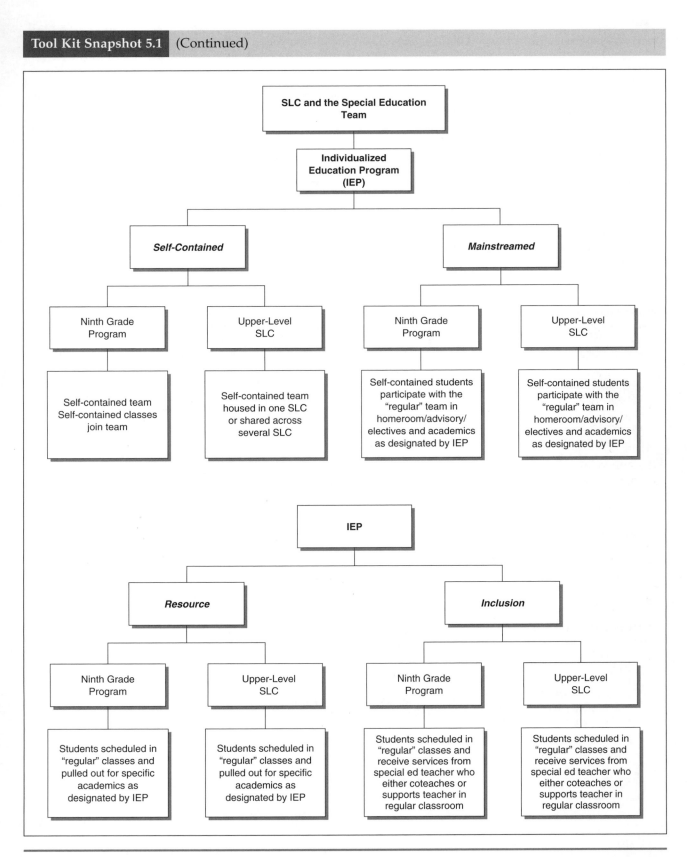

As teams are assembled and work through the regular process of forming, norming, storming, and performing, be on the lookout for signs that the team is struggling. Here are some examples of potential problem areas:

- Members cannot articulate the purpose of the team or the specific work in progress.
- Meetings are solely informational in nature.
- Meetings are held often but achieve little.
- People talk, yet there is no real communication.
- The "after meeting" is where disagreements are aired.
- The designated leader of the group makes decisions in isolation.
- Key resources and information required for effective decision making are not in evidence.
- The team does not assess its progress or process.
- The team does not have a protocol for sharing communication and working effectively.
- The team does not have a protocol for resolving conflict.
- The team members cannot articulate their individual roles and responsibilities on the team, and they do not have a sense of collective leadership.

CREATING SPECIFIC SLC TEAMS

Creating the teams that will staff each individual SLC is part math and part magic. The design you selected in the last chapter will in large part determine your staff needs, and the number of staff you have in each content area may indeed influence how many and what types of SLC you have chosen to implement. Depending on student numbers, staff ratios, vacancies, and other internal school issues, you will create small groups of teachers and support staff who will take on the very special responsibility of shepherding and challenging a cohort of students to success. Teachers in each SLC will need to develop a new skill set and must be able to blend their individual styles into a cohesive team that models best practices of teaching. Most SLC choose a staffing complement which ensures that math, English, social studies, and science as well as themed electives, guidance, and special needs are well represented. Without establishing a strong core of teachers, little substantive change in practice or results can be attained. For now, you want to ensure that each SLC has a core group which is committed to the SLC structure and, in the case of career academies, an interest in the designated career theme. But do not settle there.

Just as you want a diverse teaching core, you want to ensure that the student population within each SLC is heterogeneous. Well-designed SLC meet the needs of Advanced Placement (AP), Honors, "regular," and special needs students and speakers of languages other than English. Schools committed to success and high levels of teaching for all students do not create "smart kid" academies. AP students undoubtedly will take courses in multiple SLC as no single SLC should house all these course selections. Inclusion of special needs students can be a challenge for teachers who have not had extended experience with the range of varied abilities, challenges, legislation, and classifications of these students. Students with more severe challenges will still need to get all the supports they are due to receive under legislation and mandates. Students with less demanding needs will still require the extra supports to assist their learning styles.

In many schools, the answer to the delivery of services to special needs students has been addressed through teaming of services. Students who are excelling in one area can be teamed with students who are more challenged. We know that this simple educational strategy has a learning benefit for both parties and does not hold back the student who excels. Coteaching, the partnering of special needs teachers in classes with regular education teachers, has a wonderful effect on the entire class. Students who have special needs get the specific, timely services of the specialist they need, the regular education teacher learns more about serving this population of students, and regular education students benefit from having access to another adult role model and teacher.

In the last chapter, you made recommendations or decisions on the number and nature of your SLC. Having now laid the foundation for SLC that are fully staffed with a complement of cross disciplines, it is now time to gain a sense of which teachers want to be placed in the various SLC. In the Tool Kit, we have provided you with a two-tab/page MS Excel file [5.2 SLC Staffing] (see Tool Kit Snapshot 5.2). It is designed to allow you to capture teachers *and administrators* interested in working in a specific SLC. The process of teacher selection is critical to the SLC success. It is also a source of stress for teachers who are being asked to change the way they have taught and move into a new structure. Therefore, creating teams involves sensitivity to the interests and needs of the teachers and to the needs of the specific SLC programs you will create. Even if there are existing programs in your school, it is good to get a sense of interest and recommitment. Try to keep in mind that you not only want a content area balance but also one of personality, leadership, and skill sets. In creating a health-focused SLC, for example, a placement for an English teacher who might also have a first aid or CPR certification and has done volunteer work in a hospital may be a better match than an English teacher who sings in the church choir on weekends. That teacher might be a better match for a creative arts academy.

How It Works

Please open [5.2 SLC Staffing]. You will see two tabs at the bottom, one marked for "Interest and Avocation Sheet" and one "SLC Staffing." Create a simple questionnaire that contains the elements listed at the top of the interest tab. You want to know names, departments, certifications, avocations, and a ranked interest in the proposed, or decided on, SLC. If you have the technological capabilities to create this in a format such as MS Access or you have the capability of using technology to create a Web-based survey, you will be ahead of the game in terms of tallying responses. You could export that data to this Excel file or create queries within Access to match the sorts suggested below. Prior to distributing the survey, you will need to have ongoing communication with the whole faculty on the work of the Continuous Improvement Team. You will also want to share with staff as much detail as possible about decisions and expectations.

Once you have entered all the data fields for each faculty member in [5.2 SLC Staffing], you will be able to display the data in multiple ways, assuring that you get the clearest picture of your staffing options. Your goal is to make sure that each SLC is balanced with the most complete complement of faculty members who have both an interest and, in the case of career-themed SLC, a skill set that matches.

Tool Kit Snapshot 5.2 SLC Staffing

SLC STAFFING: Teacher, Administrator, and Staffing Interest Sheet

			Department	Certifications			Avocation		SLC Choice			
Staff ID #	First Name	Last Name	Position	1	2	3	1	2	name	ranking	name	ranking
X After all data is entered, place cursor in A5 to perform "sort," use *Data* dropdown menu, and select a specific primary column for sorting the data points you want to study.												

(Continued)

	SLC1	Room #	Ext. #	SLC2	Room #	Ext. #	SLC3	Room #	Ext. #	SLC4	Room #	Ext. #	SLC5	Room #	Ext. #
SLC Principal															
Counselor															
Clerk															
SLC Coordinator "Lead" Teacher															
MATH															
ENGLISH															
SCIENCE															
SOCIAL ST.															
CTE/CATE															
ROTC															
P.E.															
World Language															
Sociology/Psych.															
Special Education															
Fine Arts or Health															
Librarian															

Date: Date: Date:

Place your cursor in cell A5. Click. Then, *from the Tool Bar*, select Data, then Sort. You will be able to prioritize a column heading for the sort functions. Remember, to sort in any other manner in Excel prioritizes column data only, separating it from other information in the row. Sorts you will want to perform are on each of three separate "SLC Choice" columns. The document is set up for first, second, and third choices. This does not presuppose that you will only have three SLC—indeed, the second tab reveals that we have set you up to form at least five SLC. Providing educators with a first, second, and third choice, then performing the sorts, will lump the named programs together and provide you with a snapshot of your SLC teams. In sorting first in this manner, you will see whether you have the faculty you need to staff the individual SLC. Do not be surprised if this sort reveals a few challenges. Perhaps most of the English teachers have reported that their interest is to be in the arts and communication academy. Math and science teachers may have opted in disproportionate numbers for the "School of Engineering and Science." A closer look at the staff certifications and avocations will be the critical test for making the best choices for each program. Once the teachers make their initial selections, you and the principal will have the task of making SLC assignments.

Some schools determine that, prior to teacher assignment to an SLC, they want to conduct an interviewing process to determine the best staffing. This most often happens if a school has determined that it is starting with only a pilot program or, most importantly, when there is attrition and SLC openings and teams want to ensure that they select the best candidate from the available pool to match the SLC culture they have created. In the Tool Kit, we have included [5.3 Sample SLC Teacher Selection Interview Questions] should you determine to use such a process. Regardless of your decision to use the questions as part of a staff allocation process now, we strongly urge you to use these, or a similar set, as you interview new staff to be hired. A critical element of sustaining your work will be setting up a mechanism to attract staff who understand and support an SLC design. Appropriate questioning upon hiring helps.

Once the staffing assignments are complete, you can transfer the decisions to the second [5.2 SLC Staffing] tab, to develop a complete roster. The tool is set up for five SLC. You can add or delete columns and rename them as necessary. Now you are ready to announce the SLC staffing. This should be done in a personal and welcoming manner with sensitivity to the fact that not all teachers will get their first choice. Individual notifications are most effective. As soon as the teams are selected, there should be time to get together, celebrate, and begin work.

BUILDING THE TEAM

We now launch into the task list that teams have to adopt in order to begin the real process of transforming their schools. The amount of work and collaboration school transformation takes cannot be underestimated, undervalued, or minimized. If there are just two lessons we have taken away from our work across the country, in over 30 states and nearly two decades, it is the importance of understanding organizational change and the importance of team building. Unfortunately, it probably took most of the first decade to learn those lessons. Benefit from our learning experience. Take the time now to engage in team building.

Building a true team takes not only the initial identification of individuals with a variety of skills and abilities, but also working with those individuals in a systemic manner so that they learn to value and rely on each others' talents. It takes time and attention to detail. For many schools, time alone will be a real barrier. Go back to the commitments asked for in "building the definition." Time was on the list. A common time when faculty can work together, and can work together with other stakeholders, is imperative. If the school administration has not set schedules that allow for this time, and the team itself has not planned a strategy for them to meet, you will want to look at ways of working within union/association guidelines for "banking" or "buying back" time from within the union/association allotments. The staff of an SLC then needs to set its individual identity. Part of that identity will come from the very real challenge of developing the features of the SLC, but much of it will come from the shared time, trust, and commitment that develops with a team over a period of working together.

Team building will take more time than you imagine, and must be constantly addressed and revisited as team members leave and new members are brought on. Team-building workshops can be important. However, regardless of the type of team-building experience in which you engage, make sure that you take the time to prepare and debrief the team. For any experience to work effectively, it must have a purpose and an outcome. Sometimes the purpose is as simple as having fun together, but the real growth of the team comes when the members can point to measurable accomplishments. As members cycle on and off the team, invest in the time to orient new members to practices, traditions, and the SLC mission. Taking the time to really address these team issues will be worth the investment.

THE TEAM SETS THE AGENDA

Once the teams have been selected, *and they have done some team building*, they will need time together to accomplish a myriad of tasks and responsibilities. Have them review the SLC and academy definitions, the Punch List in both the sorted and non-sorted formats, and provide them with as much specific data as you can on the students they will serve. In many ways, this is your chance to share and model your own learning and that of the Continuous Improvement Team.

As part of getting the team focused, and partly to ascertain how much consensus there is in the group, use the [5.4 It Was the Best of Times] file located in the Tool Kit. It serves as a simple "prompt" for use in group discussions. Ask groups to simply chart what have been the best and worst of times, of strategies, and of implementation practices. These are displayed on the tool as pluses for the positives and "deltas" for areas that should be changed. Garnering these data will give you a valuable lens to look backward and forward for both process and programmatic changes. We have also used this tool at the "end" of a process to help understand whether we have made a difference. Used at this stage, groups will begin their work together focusing on positive aspects of their school at the same time as they note areas that should be improved (see Tool Kit Snapshot 5.3).

The team should be empowered to create and fine-tune many of the detailed elements related to their SLC. Only teams that are fully engaged can create an SLC that benefits from the individual team's expertise. Depending on what other structures are already in place (student and family groups, tutorials, student orientations,

| Tool Kit Snapshot 5.3 | It Was the Best of Times . . . |

It Was the Best of Times . . .	
Pluses	**Deltas**

faculty study groups, or existing business/community partners), other stakeholders should also be involved in this process.

Getting teams started on the right track by allowing them to make decisions about their own roles and the character of the SLC will make a positive difference in the start-up climate of your implementation. You can use the [5.5 Imagine That] tool, located in the Tool Kit and displayed in Tool Kit Snapshot 5.4, as either a planning tool to begin to define SLC within your building or after faculty has been assigned to a specific SLC. You may also refer back to the "what would an ideal SLC look like" form. Either way, the goal is to empower the teams to begin a process of envisioning a new way of supporting students to success and codifying their own interests and needs. By focusing on the need for additional training, partnerships, and necessary commitments from school administration, the message of a true partnership of stakeholders should be established.

The file [5.5 Imagine That] should be distributed to team members prior to the team meeting so that individuals can take time to think about and catalogue their input. Once that is accomplished, teams can come together to share their individual perspectives and hone a joint approach to the questions posed.

With time being always a constraint on teams, we have suggested a highly structured schedule for this early discussion. You may wish to allow more time for discussion and then give teams the time, noted parenthetically, to finalize their approach. Identify a timekeeper and a recorder to keep the discussion on task. This practice is a helpful one to adopt as a regular means of developing effective meetings. What we aim at establishing, right from the earliest of team meetings, is a format for meetings and discussions that focus on outcomes and cause efficacy of time spent together.

A possible agenda for the group meeting is shown in Box 5.1.

Tool Kit Snapshot 5.4	Imagine That!

Imagine That! Creating an SLC

Team Members: The process for restructuring, recreating, and revitalizing our school is underway. You have been asked to add your talents to the planning for a specific SLC team.

The SLC is now in your hands. Students and their families will need you to guide their decisions about the program that will best meet their needs and interests. This will require you to share and plan with your colleagues. There will be a lot of questions to answer, brainstorms to be had, tough decisions to be made, and excitement to be harnessed.

There is also, naturally, a timeline to be met. We have a master schedule of times and dates created from the Punch List (see Chapter 4).

"Imagine That!" is designed so that teams can come to some preliminary decisions and create an initial framework for their SLC.

1. What do I want my role to be (e.g., SLC principal, SLC leader, instructional coordinator, parent liaison, student internship coordinator, partner liaison, facilities development, steering committee, and recruitment)?

2. What skills do I bring to this SLC (e.g., subject area expertise, career-related expertise, grant writing, community experiences, publicity management, curriculum integration, and master teacher training)?

3. What do I need to know about this (new)(career-related) SLC implementation (e.g., research, labor market outlook, potential partners, skills used in industry, or technology used)?

4. What should the mission of this SLC be?

5. What do you think this SLC should offer students (e.g., rigorous curriculum, relevance of learning and adult role models and positive relationships, student internships, assistance with college placement, and portfolio development)? What will be different about this SLC versus other SLC?

6. What teaching strategies do I need additional training on (e.g., block scheduling, integration, working in teams)?

7. What courses should we offer; which should we require? What course subsets/pathways should be offered in the program, and how do existing courses match those pathways? What extracurricular activities, service, and work-based experiences should our students have?

8. What is in a name? Given the broad theme with which we are entrusted, what should the SLC name be? Is there an acronym we should consider?

9. What immediate goals should we set?

10. What commitments can we, individually and collectively, make to meet these goals? Who is interested in working in each of the five "bins" of work personalization, curriculum, partnerships, climate for success, data?

(Continued)

11.	What commitments do we need, individually and collectively, from the school or district to help this SLC succeed?
12.	What physical structures, signs, and equipment do we need to succeed and set the tone for our SLC?
13.	How will we promote the SLC (e.g., middle school articulation, working with guidance counselors, brochures, presentations, newsletters, recruitment, Web sites, and blogs)?
14.	How should we select our students in keeping with a commitment to heterogeneous groupings and equity?
15.	What types of business, community, and postsecondary partners do we have, should we involve, and can we attract to this SLC?

Box 5.1   SLC Start-Up Meeting: Imagine That!

Date and Time:

Location:

Purpose

To provide a forum for the SLC teachers to come together to "imagine" what their new program will look like and what they will need to accomplish in the creation of a highly personalized, high-standards environment for teaching and learning.

Expected Outcomes

- Staff will meet other members of their teaching and administrative teams.
- Staff will have crafted a brief mission statement.
- Staff will have identified an initial plan of action for SLC start up.

Agenda

General discussion of the academy theme and staff (10 minutes)

Setting the SLC/academy mission (15 minutes)

Goals: What will we want to offer students? (20 minutes)

Assessment: Punch List review (10 minutes); It was the best of times . . . (10 minutes)

Action Steps (15 minutes):

- Who will work on each of the five bins of work?
- Set a time for the team members to next meet and carry out the work suggested by their bin titles.

Summary comments

Adjourn

MISSION

In the last chapter, we touched on the importance of creating a powerful mission statement that captured the spirit of the SLC and was measurable. The mission you create should answer the questions: what function do we serve, who do we serve, how do we achieve our goals? Perhaps the best mission statement we have seen came from Ft. Wingate High School near Gallop, New Mexico (see Box 5.2). This Bureau of Indian Affairs school adopted a mission that could then be reflected and embraced in every dimension of the school culture. It appears here with permission.

As you can see, the school captured its commitment through a statement that embraced "TLC" at its core. Known to many of us as "tender, loving, care," the Wingate mission embraces teaching, learning, and caring. This TLC theme was incorporated into each area, becoming a mantra as evidenced by the library's transforming into *The Learning Center*, and the Athletics Department having adopted "*Think Like Champions*" as a motto for all students.

Box 5.2   Wingate High School Mission

The mission and vision for Wingate High School is to produce literate, problem-solving, critical thinkers who are responsible citizens and assets to their communities.

Wingate High School graduates will be prepared to function successfully within family, society, and career in our modern world while maintaining traditional and cultural values.

The mission of Wingate High School is to develop a positive, accepting, nurturing, and challenging environment by:

Teaching

- Having high expectations for all students, and believing that all students can learn
- Working cooperatively in providing opportunities that utilize staff, student, and community strengths
- Equipping students with knowledge, values, and skills that will enrich their lives and enable them to become responsible, contributing citizens of a changing global community

Learning

- Creating rich, varied experiences in curricular offerings
- Enhancing the academic and social skills necessary for all students to be productive in society
- Recognizing that cognitive, social, emotional, and physical growth emerges and is taught at different times, rates of speed, and through a variety of avenues, places, and people

Caring

- Fostering enthusiasm in every member of our school community
- Acknowledging that the responsibility for all of our students is shared by the entire staff
- Appreciating this multicultural community

SOURCE: Used with permission from Wingate High School. Mary Ann Sherman, Principal.

Push yourselves to create a mission statement that can be embraced and will "come off the page" in the way it translates into how you operate. Ask what it means to have a mission statement come to life. What would it mean and how would it be measured if the mission statement were met? Remember, SLC are designed so that everyone succeeds—students, teachers, and schools. Set goals that combine reachable objectives with those driven by the urgent needs of your particular school. Write mission statements, review them, commit to them, and communicate them.

COMMITMENT TO STUDENTS AND FAMILIES

Equal to setting in place a mission statement should be the establishment of a specific commitment to supporting students' success. In most instances, this will be reflected in the mission statement. Crafting a special credo or statement of commitment to students and their families can help keep teams focused on why they are undergoing such demanding work. As you work through these, keep in mind the creation of a commitment statement that asks teachers and administrators to commit to specific measures that help ensure that no child is left behind, and that all children are promoted toward success. Find many ways to involve families in the life of the SLC through student-led conferences, course registrations, and workshops aimed at skill building and understanding the high school experience. Regardless of the community of learners you serve today, it is safe to say that the families of these students will be largely unfamiliar with course and testing requirements, portfolios, work-based learning, and school schedules. Research has demonstrated that, just as students feel more at home in an SLC, so do families. Having them involved in the process of educating their child is a much-desired asset and should be cultivated.

SCHEDULING

Getting it "right" in SLC, of course, includes the myriad activities and curriculum pieces that will make the SLC true to the definition you crafted for your design. These are the subtle, but essential, school practices that make the SLC a home and safe haven for students. These practices help address the SLC mission, develop a framework for community involvement and shared leadership, and provide a forum for role modeling. Each requires a mechanism that makes it work—more often than not, that mechanism is a creative school schedule. The schedule needs to reflect time together and the flexibility to adjust the schedule for extended learning activities such as in-depth science experiments, field research, in-school tutoring, or job shadowing. The schedule *must* also allow for common planning time for teachers across disciplines and within the SLC.

Without engaging in a debate about the pros and cons of any one of the countless possibilities for school schedules, let it suffice to say that there is no convergent research on one type of schedule being better than another in addressing academic gains. What matters in this regard is what happens in each individual classroom, bell-to-bell. What we do know, however, is that the best laid plans for creating wall-to-wall SLC fall flat without a schedule that supports it. Involve, at the very beginning of your thinking process, the school master scheduler. Their asking of the hard questions and their understanding of what you are trying to accomplish will save many hours in the spring of each year as schools build their schedules. Understand, too, that the best scheduling is now done by a committee representing each SLC.

Over the last decade, we have seen a shift from traditional six-to-eight period days to block schedules of approximately ninety minutes offered in either semester-long or alternate-day formats. In the last few years, we have begun to see a shift back to traditional scheduling. The type of schedule a school selects should be one of form follows function. What is it you are trying to accomplish, and what schedule makes that happen? Below we have outlined some scheduling options and concerns, and displayed some sample schedules.

Teacher Assignment and Course Loads

Depending on your state and district union agreements or historical practices, teachers are usually tasked with only a certain number of class preparations per semester, have specified lunch and planning periods, and have set times for which they are contracted to arrive and complete their school duties. It is likely that there is also a teacher-to-student ratio that sets the number of students that teachers may have in their classes and a maximum number of students for which they are responsible in any given semester.

The contract issues and the individual needs of the school will have a definitive impact on how you schedule teachers for SLC. The goal is that you have enough teachers to cover all your classes and that teachers and students stay together in all, or at least key, subject areas over a period of their SLC years. The reality is that, with the addition of NCLB's highly qualified teacher certification issues, the inclusion of state test prep classes as part of the school day, and a national teacher shortage—coupled with whatever specific shortages there may be within your district—it is extremely difficult to obtain the perfect complement of teachers in wall-to-wall designs. It is even more difficult to schedule students and teachers together in schools that have a very broad range of student needs and talents. That said, the goal should still be a complete teaching and guidance team. What occurs is that teachers have, as my colleague Peggy Silva, author of *Standards of Mind and Heart: Creating the Good High School* (Silva & Mackin, 2002), pointed out, "rings of membership." They belong primarily to a core SLC team, then a department, and then perhaps a grade-level team.

Student Schedules, "Purity," and "SLC Only" Classes

A commitment to effective SLC requires that students are scheduled together in their coursework and are known well by their teachers. A schedule that works just for teachers to have common planning without common students, or one in which students travel together but do not have teachers connected by common planning, defeats the core purpose of SLC. Scheduling allows for the "family-like" atmosphere reported as important by many students, but it is also *essential* to the ability of teachers to address student needs, focus on quality instruction, and work to integrate lessons.

The discussion of "purity" of SLC—the concept that students and teachers within an SLC are intrinsically linked for all learning—has gone on since the late 1960s. The goal of creating SLC was *not* to create autonomous small schools but rather to create semiautonomous learning environments that keep students together for as much of the school day as possible to achieve the purpose stated above. It was *never* the intent—nor have schools found it possible—to provide all things to all children within one SLC. Some systems mandate a specific amount of time students must spend in SLC. Indeed, prior to a move to block schedules, the California

Department of Education only awarded state SLC grants to schools that kept students together six out of eight periods per day. Other systems have started with small teams of teachers working together rather than a full faculty complement. Certain model providers create teams of core, noncore, or "planning lane" teachers. These teachers receive students from the SLC while "core" teachers meet. This provides a greater ease in scheduling; however, it divides the thematic courses from the academic core. Early SLC designs worked to move fully away from departments; more recently, research has proven that the departments, when focused on instructional practice, are essential to the continuous improvement goals for teaching and learning. This "who is in, who is out" of SLC has deep implications for the quality of the learning environment. That said, a discussion on purity, and a commitment to basic tenets, are critical at the outset of the SLC design process. The results of this discussion will make the entire process of creating effective SLC clear for everyone from students to families to teachers and master schedulers. That discussion begins with considerations and establishing a set of agreements.

Each item you consider must be based on a set of common beliefs and agreements. This is a good time to do a reality check with your administrators and teaching teams about the purpose of SLC. Do you agree that the purpose of creating and sustaining SLC is to establish the best possible climate for highly personalized and rigorous, career-focused teaching and learning for all students? Do you agree that the expected outcomes of a "pure" SLC should be:

- Schedules that support autonomy of practice and time for teachers to work and plan together
- Teacher placements that foster a focus on best practices, data, student support, and reflective inquiry
- Administrator assignments that encourage leadership of a small group of faculty and students for the purposes of a focus on instruction, personalization, and creating positive learning environments
- A supportive guidance system that includes a guidance counselor's alignment with a specific SLC
- A curriculum and system of instructional delivery, based on state standards, that encourages thematic and integrated lessons, work-based learning, speakers, partnerships, and senior projects
- A support system for students where each is known well by a group of adults and is nurtured toward success
- A safe and more orderly school environment?

Once you have confirmed the purpose, you are ready for deeper considerations and a process of committing to scheduling agreements. You are about to explore and agree upon criteria that will have specific implications for the student experience, for teacher professional practice, and for creating a schedule that supports your agreements. As you enter into the discussion, consider how to make your mission come off the page, and make a note of any and all implications for the teacher and the teacher contract, such as certifications, teaching out of area, multiple preparations, and use of common planning time. The agreements you make will have direct implications on the schedules, as you will most likely want to preserve departmental planning time to ensure common planning time for designated SLC teams. The agreements reached here (see Box 5.3) will have implications for how the school day is structured, how planning time is set, and whether there needs to be a consideration

Box 5.3 Agreements for Discussion

Agreements

The purpose stated above for creating SLC is our purpose.	Y	N
Students are part of their SLC and part of the whole school.	Y	N
Students should receive the majority of their instruction within their SLC.	Y	N
Students should have access to courses and activities outside their SLC.	Y	N
Ninth and tenth grade students are most in need of closely knit SLC teams.	Y	N
Math, English, social studies, and science (MESS teams) must be in SLC for Grades 9 and 10.	Y	N
Themed electives/majors (both content and career) must be in SLC.	Y	N
Academic support in reading/math must be in SLC.	Y	N
Students should receive appropriate special education support in SLC.	Y	N
Students should receive appropriate second language support in SLC.	Y	N
Advisory must be in SLC.	Y	N
Honors must be in SLC.	Y	N
Advanced Placement may be out of SLC.	Y	N
When not part of a student's core SLC area, other electives may be outside of SLC.	Y	N

In regard to common planning time for faculty, we believe:

• Only MESS teams need to share a common time	Y	N
• MESS plus content/career teachers must share a common time	Y	N
• All members of the SLC must share a common plan	Y	N
• There is a difference between PLC and common planning	Y	N

PLC takes place:

• By department	Y	N
• By grade level	Y	N
• By subject	Y	N
• By SLC	Y	N

We believe in limiting the number of electives available to ninth graders	Y	N

What areas need to be in place for eleventh and twelfth grade? In what percentages?

• _____	Y	N
• _____	Y	N
• _____	Y	N
• _____	Y	N
• Senior project _____	Y	N

Other Agreements

• _____	Y	N
• _____	Y	N
• _____	Y	N
• _____	Y	N
• _____	Y	N

for early releases and late starts as a regular part of the school day. In addition, the agreements you make will have implications for professional development as teachers learn new ways to work together as teams, in interdisciplinary settings, and in close partnership with special needs and limited English teachers.

If scheduling all your students together is not possible, make a determination regarding which courses will be scheduled back to back so that they are tacitly SLC-only classes. An immediately reachable goal should be the establishment of a core group of "SLC only" classes. These classes are the nonnegotiables. They are taken within the SLC and serve only students in that cohort. This may necessitate designating course numbers for both core and elective/career themed classes that flag the course as SLC only. One solution, in a school with a traditional school schedule, was to have all nonacademy classes scheduled for the first two periods of the day (in this case, it was physical education and foreign language) and all academy classes scheduled together for the balance of the day.

A further goal should be that the teaching team has as much control of the student and class schedules as possible. Creative teachers can look at the district course offerings and their students and arrive at solutions, in conjunction with the principal and school master scheduler, that can set high standards, create course options, and not overburden faculty.

Advanced Placement and Other "Special" Courses

There are always exceptions (and sometimes excuses) to keeping students together or apart from each other. The most notable is in Advanced Placement (AP) and upper-level math and science courses. With limited numbers of students enrolling in these classes, having SLC-specific classes is in many cases impractical. However, the integrity of the SLC can be preserved if the special course teacher has students from specific SLC scheduled together, can develop project-based assignments that are tied to the student's program theme, and is supplied with enough support materials from the core teaching team to reference appropriate skills and standards.

Extended Period

This is a term used for courses that are not offered in the traditional approximately forty-five-minute period of time. The extended period, usually ninety minutes in duration, is embraced across the country as both a school management tool and a student engagement strategy. The extended period, by design, means that there are fewer period changes during the school day and fewer times when a student can be in the halls or in the wrong place. It makes for quieter buildings with fewer disruptions. Teaching in these extended periods allows for a more substantive look at subject matter, more time for student interactions, and more time to apply a variety of teaching techniques to varied learning styles in the classroom. The extended-period day has immediate implications for staff training needs and on the availability of certain course offerings as fewer classes are scheduled in any given semester. At the same time, however, the intensified period of instruction enables students to earn more credits toward graduation and allows for what some programs call "double dosing" on developmental coursework, especially in the ninth and tenth grades. Double dosing means that students can take extra English and math, particularly, to improve their skills and better their chances of succeeding at both higher course level offerings and on the all-important standardized tests. While moving to extended period schedules may be desirable, it should not be done without the understanding of the impact on electives and a student's overall development. And it cannot be undertaken without a focus on instruction and the practices that are required for quality teaching.

Block, A/B Block, Modified Block, and Fats and Skinnies

Once there is a clear goal of what you want to accomplish in the school day, and you have also built an understanding that it is only the prescribed hours of instruction that need to be met not in what format in which those hours are to be delivered, the rest of the bell schedule is as flexible as the imagination allows and should be as varied and flexible as you need. The type of schedule that your school or schools adopt will have an obvious impact on the number of courses offered. But more germane to SLC, and specifically to career academy formation, is the effect of the schedule on common planning time, professional development, and out-visit and work-based experiences.

Beyond the traditional multiperiod day, there are three general ways schools are using time to accomplish their mission:

- *Block.* Sometimes called 4 × 4, this approach has students enrolled in four classes that meet each day, with full-course credit being earned in one semester. A benefit of this type of schedule is that it is the option that allows for the maximum credits to be earned toward graduation for students. It also allows for students who need additional academic support to take a "double dose" of reading or math in subsequent semesters and still stay on track for graduation. A caution here: AP courses taken in a fall term will need refresher support in the spring, prior to the national tests. Students who are "on the bubble" of needing extra supports, but are not on a double-dose schedule, run the risk of large gaps in instruction on, for example, a Spanish I placement in the fall of the freshman year and Spanish II placement not appearing on the same student's schedule until the spring term of the sophomore year.
- *A/B Block.* Also called alternating block, this schedule still has students taking only four courses per day (but these alternate every other day), resulting in alternate weeks where the courses meet either two or three times.
- *Modified Block—Fats, Skinnies, and Wacky Wednesdays.* Many schools have discovered that there are ways to get everything they want in a schedule—extended periods of time for classes that benefit from longer instructional periods, traditional forty-five to fifty-minute classes in place when it is important for teachers and students to meet every day, common planning by SLC and by department, time for advisory meetings, and time for whole-school professional development. These schools employ any of a variety of techniques known as a modified or flexible block. "Fats" are the extended-period timeframes, usually of ninety minutes. "Skinnies" are the traditional forty-five-minute classes. Obviously, you can have two skinnies for every fat. "Wacky Wednesdays," "Manic Mondays," and "Freaky Fridays" provide students with four classes on two of the week days, four different classes on an alternating two days, and on the Wednesday, Monday, or Friday, all the classes meet for a forty-five-minute period.

One Lunch or More?

In the scheduling discussion, even the traditional number of lunches scheduled within the day comes into play. One long lunch for faculty and staff may seem daunting, with potentially thousands of students free to be around the building. But it also allows for students to take advantage of extra help and work on projects. It provides teachers with opportunities to plan and participate in student supports. Because school cafeterias cannot for the most part accommodate the entire school population at the same time, they utilize portable kiosks located throughout the building. As everyone is at lunch at the same time, noise in the halls is not an issue. Student safety, of course, is of primary concern, and each school has to define a plan for minimizing dangerous activity.

Late Start/Early Release

To put all the desired common planning and professional development activity in place for schools that understand more time is indeed needed if they are going to improve instructional practice, many schools seek waivers from their districts for either a late start or an early release that allows for teachers to meet anywhere from weekly to monthly. This extra meeting time does not affect the contracted time, but does impact instructional time unless, as you will see below with the Milby High School schedule, you take other activities into consideration. There are pros and cons in opting for either the early release or the late starts, including student safety and what we know about adolescent development. Late starts have teachers arriving at the normal start of the school day and students arriving later. Early releases may include a shortened bell schedule and students leaving early for the day. Here, however, faculty are frequently not at their peak performance times and those staff members who coach are frequently not able to participate in the meetings.

While there are many excellent examples of schedules, I am most impressed with what Principal Richard Barajas has accomplished at Milby High School in Houston, Texas. I asked Mr. Barajas to explain how his schedule worked (see Box 5.4).

The resulting schedule met each of Mr. Barajas' requirements (see Figure 5.1 on page 107).

The schedule worked well for Milby; however, being restless for improvement, school administrators continued to tweak the schedule and are now poised to implement a schedule that includes fats and skinnies—thus providing a continuity of instruction for classes that needed more time throughout the year. It is shown in Figure 5.2 on page 108.

Chavez High School, also in Houston, has also crafted time for teachers to meet "in" SLC and in departments. They too have had the deep discussions and made some hard choices about the use of time to improve instruction. Chavez students no longer take physical education (PE) classes until the eleventh grade. This was decided based on the evidence that PE and algebra are the most frequently failed classes in the nation. Loading a freshman schedule with both those classes—which is also a national norm—places some students at a greater risk of being retained in ninth grade. Moving the PE class to the eleventh grade allows the Chavez schedule to offer all ninth graders one of three academic support options: a keystone transitions course, Advancement Via Individual Determination (AVID), or Junior Reserve Officer Training Corps (JROTC) leadership. The schedule is shown in Figure 5.3 on page 109.

There is no question that devising the schedule to meet your goal is a complex process. However, with the goal in mind, a committee and a skilled master scheduler can fit in everything. For scheduling support, you may want to research CASN's and NWREL's Web sites, both noted in the Resources section.

Box 5.4   Milby High School Schedule

___

Overview

- Students in an A/B block, with an additional forty-five-minute period four days per week for advisory
- Built-in forty-five-minute grade level and department meetings weekly
- Built-in forty-five-minute SLC meeting time, weekly
- Built-in professional development, forty-five minutes every other week—led by literacy coach and lead teachers

Accomplished By

- Respect for teacher agreement/contract
- Providing teachers with a thirty-minute duty-free lunch and forty-five minutes of personal planning time each day
- Research on the importance of extended period time
- A belief that fewer transitions make for increased focus on instruction and a safer and more focused learning environment
- Adherence to required minutes of instruction
- A search for wasted minutes in existing schedule
- Core teachers and academics driving the schedule; elective teachers are the "surround"

The Search for Time—places where minutes were picked up

- Reduced class passing time from eight to five minutes (pick up nine minutes)
- Eliminate passing time for lunch (pick up twenty minutes)
- Redesign the ten-minute daily homeroom (recapturing those minutes for other purposes)

Considerations

- Could not work in a multiperiod day format
- Opted for multiperiod lunch. Three periods cycle A/B/C lunch by zone of building to further improve school climate (quiet in hallways, etc.), traffic flow and passing time
- A commitment to this may result in an imbalance of class size
- With few exceptions, all teachers are grade level teachers

SCHOOL PRACTICES

Once the broad strokes of themes and schedules are worked out, it will be the little things that build the SLC identity and make it a home for positive experiences and increased expectations. Encourage and empower teams to create an atmosphere for positive teaching and learning. Discourage conversations that begin with "what about hats and gum"—focusing on discipline and deficits first, rather than beginning with respect for students and creating a high-expectations environment based on positive support, undermines the spirit of the SLC. Safety is absolutely at the center of our assurances to students and families, but this commitment does not translate to how we are going to handle hat wearing, untucked shirts, missing ID tags, gum

Figure 5.1   Milby High School Schedule—Version A

MON "A" (A/B alternates each week)	TUES "B"	WED "A"	THURS "B"	FRI "A" Alternates: the next week is FRI "B" with periods 5, 6, 7, 8
(1) 8:20–9:50 Students in class **All English and Language on plan** *Department meeting*	(5) 8:20–9:50 Students in class **All ninth grade teachers on plan** *Grade level meeting*	(1) 8:20–9:50 Students in class **All English and World Language on plan** *Professional development **every other week***	(5) 8:20–9:50 Students in class **All ninth grade teachers on plan**	(1) 8:20–9:50 Students in class **All English and World Language on plan**
9:55–10:35 45 minute **9–12 Advocacy**	9:55–10:35 45 minute **grade level homeroom and interventions**	9:55–10:35 45 minute **grade level homeroom and interventions**	9:55–10:35 45 minute **grade level homeroom and interventions**	(2) 9:55–11:35 **(lunches)** Students in class
(2) 10:40–12:10 Students in class **All Science on plan** *Department meeting*	(6) 10:40–12:10 Students in class **all tenth grade and Special Ed teachers on plan** *Grade level meeting*	(2) 10:40–12:10 Students in class **All Science on plan** *Professional development **every other week***	(6) 10:40–12:10 Students in class **All tenth grade and Special Ed teachers on plan**	(3) 12:00–1:25 Students in class **All Science on plan**
(3) 12:15–2:10 A/B/C LUNCH Students in class **All Math on plan** *Department meeting*	(7) 12:15–2:10 A/B/C LUNCH Students in class **all eleventh grade teachers on plan** *Grade level meeting*	(3) 12:15–2:10 A/B/C LUNCH Students in class **All Math on plan** *Professional development **every other week***	(7) 12:15–2:10 A/B/C LUNCH Students in class **All eleventh grade teachers on plan**	(4) 1:30–3:00 Students in class **All Social Studies on plan**
(4) 2:15–3:45 Students in class **All Social Studies on plan** *Department meeting*	(8) 2:15–3:45 Students in class **all twelfth grade and CTE/CATE teachers on plan** *Grade level meeting*	(4) 2:15–3:45 Students in class **All Social Studies on plan** *Professional development **every other week***	(8) 2:15–3:45 Students in class **All twelfth grade and CATE teachers on plan**	3:00 **Early RELEASE for students** *45 minute SLC meeting—includes all elective teachers* **Teachers out at 3:45**

chewing, cell phones, and the myriad of violations to the code of conduct regulations in the student handbook. Encourage teams to operate out of a strengths, not a deficit, mode in building their community culture. That said, with the exception of the final item, the following list is presented alphabetically for later ease of reference. It is decidedly *not* displayed in the order in which the points may need to be addressed.

Advisory and Teacher Guides

As guidance counselors' loads grow to over 300 students, and the challenges faced by our students also grow each year, it should be clear that students need more than one counselor can provide. They need a positive role model, a confidant, and a guide to help them through the high school transition period. Many faculty teams are agreeing to serve as special mentors or guides for a small group of students during their years in the SLC. As Marilyn Raby, formerly of the CASN (considered by many to be

Figure 5.2   Milby High School Schedule—Version B

MON	TUES	WED	THUR	FRI
(1) 8:20–9:50 FAT of 90 minutes, meets four days per week	(1) FAT of 90 minutes, meets four days per week	(1) FAT of 90 minutes, meets four days per week	(1) FAT of 90 minutes, meets four days per week	All classes meet in skinnies
9:55–10:35 45 minute advocacy, extra help, supports	45 minutes advocacy, extra help, supports	45 minutes advocacy, extra help, supports	45 minutes advocacy, extra help, supports	
(2) Skinnies	(5) Skinnies	(2) Skinnies	(5) Skinnies	
(3) Skinnies	(6) Skinnies	(3) Skinnies	(6) Skinnies	
(4) Skinnies	(7) Skinnies	(4) Skinnies	(7) Skinnies	
(8) 2:15–3:45 FAT of 90 minutes, meets four times per week	(8) FAT of 90 minutes	Meets four days per week	(8) FAT of 90 minutes	3:00 **Early RELEASE for students** *45 minute SLC meeting—includes all elective teachers* **Teachers out at 3:45**

the "godmother of academies"), states, "If you work with a student for a year they are on your mind. If you work with them over three years they are on your conscience." Indeed, it is the commitment of teachers to specific supportive strategies, such as greeting students by name at the start of each class, or committing to making regular phone calls home to students, and serving as a guide, that begins the real transformation of schools into a "caring environment" for students. There are many questions to be answered about advisory—should it be a formal process with a specified curriculum, who should serve as advisors, does it count as an additional "prep" for a teacher? These are all important to address, and we will cover some of the ways schools have answered them in Chapter 9.

Absenteeism

While research shows that participation in SLC does result in increased attendance rates, attendance is still a major issue in many schools. The attendance rate has an obvious impact on the individual student's academic success, but it also has an effect on the overall learning experience in the SLC, and on the opportunity to succeed at project-based learning or out-visits and work-based experiences. Low attendance impacts on budgets for buses hired but not needed for field trips, public transportation fares purchased and not needed, and tickets to events that go unused. It impacts on work-based hosts who set aside time to plan and engage a student in a shadows or internship placement only to have wasted that time for a student who does not attend. Increasing student attendance is critically important, and it is the responsibility of everyone.

The SLC team will need to establish a practice for following up on absenteeism. Staff, families, and the students themselves can all be involved in phone calls home (as long as confidentiality and legal issues are considered). As important as calls

Figure 5.3   Chavez High School Schedule

Time	Monday	Tuesday	Wednesday	Thursday	Time	Friday
8:15 First bell						Alternating Schedule for Fridays—one week 1–4 , next week 5–8
8:25 Tardy bell						
8:25–10:05	1st Period Foreign Language common planning	5th Period Special Education common planning ROTC common planning	1st Period Foreign Language common planning	5th Period Special Education common planning ROTC common planning	8:25–9:25	1st/5th
10:10–11:50	2nd period Math common planning	6th period Science common planning	2nd period Math common planning	6th period Science common planning	9:30–10:15	**Advocacy**
11:55–2:10	3rd period/ lunches Social Studies common planning	7th period/ lunches English Language Arts (ELA) common planning	3rd period/ lunches Social Studies common planning	7th period/ lunches ELA common planning	10:20–11:20	2nd/6th
2:15–3:55	4th period Fine Arts common planning	8th period	4th period Fine Arts common planning	8th period	11:25–12:25	3rd/7th
					12:30–1:30	4th/8th
					1:30–2:00	Dismissal or lunch
Lunch Schedule: A Lunch: 11:55–12:25 (House A, Halls F and H) B Lunch: 12:30–1:00 (House B, Hall K) C Lunch: 1:05–1:35 (House C, House E) D Lunch: 1:40–2:10 (House D, Hall G, Gym, Field House)					2:10–4:00	3 x per month Academy Team mtgs 1 x per month Faculty (2:10–3:00) Dept. (3:05–4:00)

home and documenting attendance are, the need is equally great to welcome students back to school and communicate to them that their presence in the community is needed and desired.

Contracting for Success

To further support the tenet that all students in SLC can and should succeed, many schools are beginning to contract with students to establish practices that act as "safety nets" for their success. For students who evidence consistently tardy or truant attendance, or for those with failing grades, meetings are held to try to identify and target the specific issues causing the behaviors. Once identified, a plan of action and support is put in place. Students are part of the planning and agree to the plan, enter into a contract, and understand the direct consequences of their not complying with the supportive practices.

Forms and "Stuff"

As soon as you begin developing your SLC practices, you will find a massive need for "stuff"—form letters to advisory board members and forms for students, notices, and scheduling guides, for example. An excellent resource for *free* downloadable material is the CASN Web site, previously noted and listed in the Resources section.

Hall Representation

Teachers' presence in the hallways during class changes is a school climate and management issue. Although block schedules and SLC-only classes minimize hallway disruptions, the presence of a faculty member in the hall between classes increases the possibility of smooth class transitions and positive interactions between students and staff. It also allows a forum for teachers to welcome students into their classrooms. While this is clearly a safety and supervision issue, teachers in SLC should truly use the hall representation opportunity to catch up with students and to touch base with colleagues on instructional practices, student needs, and schedules. This reinforces that in *this* SLC—even if in no other part of the school—students are welcome, respected, and challenged to success and colleagues work together.

Handbooks

Create SLC handbooks that catalogue all practices, policies, and procedures to include everything from "hats" to "habits" to "hallways" in your manual. It is the little things like saying what practices are in place for hats off in school and hallway passes as well as the more substantive issues such as testing and classroom participation that will create a positive environment. As always, consistency of practice by the adults is what meets with the consistent actions of students. As with the "hats and gum" reference, please work to ensure that your handbook reflects the climate in which you want students to learn and in which you wish to teach. Too often I find that practices and expectations for students do not have to be followed for teachers (e.g., a teacher may bring a beverage into the classroom or have an untucked shirt but a student may not). There are even practices that *appear* to help teaching and learning but in fact inhibit it. In one school, each child is greeted at the door, not for a welcome but for a check on ID, textbooks, and the like. If the student is unprepared, they are sent to their principal, who then writes them up and sends them back to class with a pass that says they were unprepared. The student has lost instructional time, the teacher's class is interrupted, and we have reinforced nothing positive about a student's ability to learn or a teacher's ability to teach. Be creative, be positive, and create a handbook that reflects a high standard of practice for all.

Student Governance, Councils, and Town Meetings

Because of the individualized nature of the SLC, it is very common for students to seek to establish their own student government, and for students and teachers together to hold regularly scheduled "town" meetings to address issues such as senior projects, student-led conferences, discipline, special events, and grades. In the case of career academies, these forums should mirror the career theme's industry structure and be encouraged whenever possible. For example, a health academy might institute an ethics review board, a law academy might establish a teen court, and a business academy might opt to cast their meetings as those of a board of directors. The tie to the industry theme provides one more vehicle for learning.

Celebrations and Traditions!

Take every opportunity to celebrate as a community. Welcome new staff members, welcome new students and families, hold orientations, make "back to school nights" events of importance and celebration. Hold awards ceremonies for students and partners. Send seniors off with a special recognition ceremony. Welcome recent graduates and alumni back. Hold an annual "academy" awards to highlight achievements and thank partners. Traditions are those occasions that are looked forward to and looked back on: they help us honor who we are in the SLC.

At a Glance: Summing It Up and Next Steps

This chapter began by asking that roles and responsibilities shift from those of a traditional school to practices that will support a school committed to *continuous improvement* through an SLC. Here we looked at changed schedules and changes in approach to school policies and practices. The challenge for principals, practitioners, and faculties is to push past the "tried and true" practices of the past. As a body of work, they no longer reap the results we need for all students and they are ineffective in an educational climate which requires that we now must meet with success.

Our work to date has teachers and administrators in new roles as they have been assigned to new academy groupings. We have also asked that they let go of some old practices—perhaps even the schedule with which they are most comfortable. Along the way, we have also empowered them to make choices and recommendations. The work of the full faculty has begun, and we are standing on the threshold of a newly configured school where the very sacred cows of curriculum, instruction, and professional practice get deep scrutiny as we stay committed to a plan for *continuous improvement.*

6

Curriculum for College and Careers

Education is not the filling of a pail, but the lighting of a fire.

—William Butler Yeats

Chapter 6 Road Map

Purpose	To ensure the establishment of a high-standards curriculum for both college and careers.
Stage of Implementation	Study and Assessment, Engagement and Commitment, Establishing Structures—focus on curriculum and instruction, data, partnerships, and a climate for success.
Process and Action Steps	Teams build and align their SLC-specific sequence of courses, make determinations about integration and infusion strategies, identify places to connect business and community partners to curriculum development.
Tool Kit	6.1 SLC Pathways Course and Experience Planning 6.2 Curriculum Planning Templates 6.3 Brief-Cases Teacher Sheet 6.4 DBL Experience Log
Reflective Practice	What is our focus on curriculum, instruction and quality teaching? What is the specific curriculum mandate of each SLC? What does rigor look like? What expectation should we set for curriculum integration? Is there a way our partners can help influence and assist our curriculum work?
Outcome	Each SLC has a program of study outlined, and they have determined what curriculum framework is necessary to meet high expectations for student success. Teachers have improved their skills in building an integrated, standards-based curriculum that reflects higher-order thinking skills.

The changing face of schools is also changing the way we think of curriculum. As school and districts focus on whole-school reform versus pockets of excellence, curriculum and instruction become the focal point of the educational experience. In an increasingly complex, knowledge-based, global society, it is becoming increasingly apparent that our students must experience an education that leaves them college-ready *and* workplace skilled. Many students who choose college as an immediate postsecondary option will still need to work to meet the growing costs. Students who do not attend college immediately, or at all, need a complex series of skills in order to succeed. A recent ACT report compared 476,000 high school juniors across two exams: the ACT for college entrance and WorkKeys, an employability assessment instrument. The report determined that the reading and math skills required to succeed in the first year of college were similar to those needed to succeed in entry-level employment. It further concluded that

> the expectations of students who choose to enter work force training programs for jobs that are likely to offer both a wage sufficient to support a small family and potential career advancement should be no different from students who choose to enter college after high school graduation. There is this impression that all students cannot take the same courses. That certainly isn't true. We can't afford to educate kids to a lesser standard based on misassumptions. (ACT, 2006)

This understanding of college and career readiness is reflected in many states, including Indiana and Louisiana's rigorous career majors and options programs legislation, which is at the core of their secondary education systems. In spring 2006, the state of Florida passed, with an astonishingly wide margin in both the Senate and the House, Governor Bush's A++ legislation that will require an extra year of math classes for high school seniors. In addition, the legislation calls for all high school students—even those with special needs—to have the opportunity to select a major and minor concentration of studies. Students in seventh and eighth grades would be required to take a course in career planning. This legislation, and a growing body of similar work in other states, seeks to both improve postsecondary outcomes for students and better align the high school curriculum with college entrance expectations. College- *and* career-ready students are becoming a national priority.

In SLC, teachers and students learn together and continually "connect the dots" between classroom instruction and the multitude of experiences that reinforce such learning. This practice brings the factors of *rigor, relevance, and relationships* to bear on the *results* we seek—highly successful students and schools that are continually improving. It is this connecting of the dots which makes for a high school education that is more than the checking off of accomplished graduation requirements but rather the lighting of a fire that truly positions students to be ready and to learn more as the lifelong learners our mission statements suggest they should become.

CURRICULUM DEFINED

Curriculum components of successful SLC are likely to include traditional classroom academics, transition coursework, extra help classes and supports, project-based learning, performance-based measures of assessment, cross-disciplinary integration, inclusion of academic and industry skill standards, advisory programs, student-led conferences, senior projects, participation in a career and technical student organization (CTSO), work-based learning experiences, and the inclusion of service learning and community service. Such a comprehensive connection between school and community experiences begs a comprehensive definition of curriculum and a thoughtful approach to addressing the multiple opportunities we have to focus student learning. In the schools in which we work, we introduce the following as a working definition. Curriculum is:

- Focused on what students need to know and be able to do to succeed in high school and in the postsecondary worlds of work and education
- Integrated across disciplines and across other school-based and community-based activities
- Content rich, thematic, student centered, multiple assessments based, standards driven, inclusive of multiple intelligence, technology linked, career focused, rigorous, college prep, gender/race sensitive, and . . .

The additional "to be continued or extended" dots above are intentionally left there. In our work with schools, as in your own, there will always be additions made to the curriculum definition. "State test-centered" is one obvious addition. Curriculum is "the what." Here we will focus on the elements that comprise curriculum in an SLC as well as look at some ways of connecting across disciplines while supporting academic achievement and success.

UNDERSTANDING AND ADDRESSING ACADEMIC AND INDUSTRY SKILLS STANDARDS

In every state, there are specified tests administered to students throughout their K–12 academic careers which are aimed at raising the standard of academic achievement and stopping the phenomenon of "social promotion." Indeed, these tests are now rites of passage, determining a student's ability to graduate high school. It is not just students who are measured by the results. In aggregate, teachers and schools are all measured on the basis of the results of students' tests. In many states, NCLB—with its emphasis on the state tests—has created a sense of teachers "teaching to the test" in an effort to increase student scores, their own performance ratings, and the rating assigned their school and their district. While the ultimate result of education is to increase students' knowledge, and their ability to perform in society, the standardized test movement has increased the focus on test scores in an era where, increasingly, the research shows us that "performance-based" measures are a better indicator of student knowledge and understanding.

The research has not significantly demonstrated that SLC positively or negatively impact test scores. What it does show is that the diversity of experiences offered through them has kept students engaged, interested, and committed to their education, and that the activities build in a rigor and relevance not present in traditional high school programs.

Of critical importance to SLC teams and to practitioners will be referencing the specific academic standards set for each academic discipline as outlined in your school's and state's standards for teaching and learning. Academic skill standards are *not just about tests.* The standards for teaching and learning will describe a curriculum and its commitment to rigorous content standards that set high expectations for all students. The standards represent important developmental skills for children and are taught systemwide to ensure that students are indeed reaching the standards. The content standards are usually supported by performance standards for each grade level and each course. Teachers are expected to use standard-based curriculum documents to guide instruction in their classrooms. SLC teams will need information on the items bulleted below, much of which should be readily available from your district office.

- Information on concepts, skills, scope, and sequence of courses, standards-based instruction, and performance-based education
- Techniques and strategies to apply the standard
- Benchmarks at predetermined academic grade levels
- Resources, innovations, and core assignments.

We cannot put enough emphasis on the move to raise and incorporate an array of standards in schools. Over the next few pages, we will highlight the work of industry and academic standards. The intangibles in this discussion, however, are the very real concerns of teachers who find their courses now driven not by what they believe are best practices but by test scores. When states like Florida rank their schools as "F" schools when high percentages of students do not meet state standards, and when Massachusetts and others mark their schools "ready for reconstitution," and when states are paying cash awards to students and teachers who meet the state standards, the pressures become crystal clear. Something drastic must happen in order for children to succeed not only at the standardized tests but in life.

Rigor has become the buzzword for a high-standards curriculum. Yet, when teachers are asked to describe what rigor looks like, they quickly cite the number of Advanced Placement (AP) or Honors (H) courses their buildings offer. Rigor, by definition, is adherence to a strict standard. This would beg a definition of a standard for teaching and learning that seems illusive to most educators. Rigor is not measured by the AP or H indication on a transcript, nor is it measured by the number of books you read or pages you write. It must be measured by the quality of the work you do. That quality must be looked at both in terms of the quality of what you teach and the quality of what your students produce. Are they utilizing higher-order thinking skills? Are they engaged in provocative, engaging, complex work that is challenging? The question of what good teaching looks like, and thus what is rigorous, is addressed in the next chapter.

FROM GOALS 2000 TO SCANS: WHAT WORK REQUIRES OF SCHOOLS

The first major attempt to move American educators toward embracing skills standards was begun under the U.S. Department of Education initiative, Goals 2000. The two major objectives of that initiative set the goal for *every educator to ensure* that, by the year 2000:

- Students, when measured in Grades 4, 8, and 12, would be able to demonstrate competency in *challenging* course work, and be able to use their minds to be responsible citizens, engage in further learning, and undertake productive employment

- Every adult in America would be literate and have skills to compete in a global economy.

Six years after the anticipated benchmark of reaching this goal, we would be hard pressed, as a nation, to say we have succeeded. Yet it is more important than ever to achieve this goal. To continue to work toward it, we can refer back to the supports that were put in place for educators in 1991. To ensure that these goals were met, and in support of them, the U.S. Secretary of Labor convened SCANS in June 1991. The work of the Commission was to determine what we, as a nation, should expect people *"to know and be able to do"* as a result of their education and training and in their entry-level employment. The tasks before the Commission were as follows:

- Define the skills needed for job entry and future planning
- Propose acceptable levels of proficiency
- Suggest ways to assess proficiency
- Develop a dissemination strategy of their report for schools, businesses, and homes.

The Commission was able to demonstrate that globalization and technology were having little, if any, impact on the way educators were preparing youth to take their places in a postsecondary world. Indeed, SCANS found that fewer than one half of all young people had achieved a reading and writing minimum level of competency and that even fewer could handle the math basics. It also found that schools only minimally addressed critically important listening and speaking skills. The impact was profound. Almost every major piece of legislation and newly applied teaching strategy can be tied to the implications of SCANS. To deal with these deficits, the Commission set specific proficiency skill levels. An essential part of your work as a practitioner will be to communicate the importance and the information contained in SCANS to teams working on improvement. It is now uniformly accepted as a baseline by those working with education and skill standards. As you review the competencies and foundations outlined by SCANS, you can see several clear implications for your work in creating SLC, addressing student and teacher skills and interests, and for having a very real impact on curriculum.

The expectation that students be able to perform at skill standards levels calls for a change in the way we deliver education. As outlined by SCANS, these competencies and foundations continue to support a rationale for a move to SLC and they set in place a framework where the results are real improvements for students. SCANS demands that real learning:

- Takes place in context
- Should be judged through alternate/authentic assessment
- Should be matched to national standards
- Sets a series of benchmarks or gateways
- Includes portfolio development and work-based experiences
- Is competency based.

KNOWLEDGE, SKILLS, AND ABILITIES

The competencies and foundations set by SCANS address an individual's knowledge, skills, and abilities in *five* competency or attribute areas and in *three* skills and personal foundation areas:

The Competencies

- *Resources:* the ability to identify, organize, plan, and allocate resources in such areas as:
  - Time
  - Money
  - Materials and facilities
  - Human resources.

- *Interpersonal:* the ability to work with others:
  - Participates as a member of a team
  - Teaches others new skills
  - Serves clients and customers
  - Exercises leadership
  - Negotiates
  - Works with diversity.

- *Information:* the ability to use and manage information:
  - Acquires and uses information
  - Acquires and evaluates information
  - Organizes and maintains information
  - Interprets and communicates information
  - Uses computers to process information.

- *Systems:* the ability to understand complex interrelationships:
  - Understands systems
  - Monitors and corrects performance
  - Improves or designs systems.

- *Technology:* can work with a variety of technologies:
  - Selects technology
  - Applies technology to task
  - Maintains and troubleshoots equipment.

The Skills and Personal Foundations

- *Basic Skills:* has mastery:
  - Reading
  - Writing
  - Arithmetic/math
  - Listening
  - Speaking.

- *Thinking:* can demonstrate:
  - Creative thinking
  - Decision making

- – Problem solving
- – Seeing things through in the "mind's eye"
- – Knowing how to learn
- – Reasoning.

- *Personal Qualities:* demonstrates:
  - – Responsibility
  - – Self-esteem
  - – Sociability
  - – Self-management
  - – Integrity/honesty.

Career-Focused Standards

Partly in reaction to SCANS, the nation now has industry skill standards developed that support career integration strategies in classrooms. These impact student outcomes as they seek employment and appropriate postsecondary educational opportunities. Every SLC practitioner and every career-focused program, academy, or SLC must be aware of the industry standards that relate to their particular industries. Like academic skill standards, industry skill standards address what a person should *know and be able to do* to effectively perform within that industry. Based on both Goals 2000 and SCANS, some of the standards categories transcend industries and, like academic standards, can be taught in a variety of settings. "Oral and Written Communication Skills," for instance, is a central element of any industry. The industry skill standard, however, defines the specific application of that skill. In health, for example, that specific skill is applied as the ability to "read and write well, clarify information, use technology to input and access data, be culturally sensitive, and be able to communicate highly complex and sensitive information to a wide audience." Over the years, a great deal of work has been done to expand and keep the sixteen identified career clusters we noted in Chapter 4 up to date. Information on standards and practices for each cluster is located in the Resources section.

IDENTIFYING AND HONING THE SLC CURRICULUM: PATHWAYS, COURSES, AND INTEGRATION

As the teams continue to study and become aware of the standards and elements that compose a good SLC, they should have general oversight for developing a curriculum, as defined earlier, which meets those standards. This requires an integrated system of educational delivery. Perhaps the most frequently asked question in all SLC planning is "How can we accomplish teaming, themed curriculum, and integration of careers and work-based practices, while still meeting the demands, pressures and realities that loom with the standardized tests?" It is an honest and worthy question that will, in some respects, not be answerable until teachers begin to work together. Teams also will not do this work in isolation. Partnerships with postsecondary institutions, business, and community organizations will be essential. There are also multiple resources available on the Internet and in other forums that can give teachers a leg up in tackling the balance between the academic and industry standards that build relevance into a curriculum. It is the relevance that in so many cases serves as the "hook" for engaging student interest.

When teams begin to focus on the career or themed pathways, they immediately see that this is where the benefit of having guidance counselors and elective teachers as members of each team begins to pay off. The SLC core team works closely with school guidance staff and teachers from other disciplines to determine what courses will best prepare students for what they need to know and be able to do at the end of a course or sequence of courses. An excellent way to begin this process is to create a focus group that can help the team determine what expectations the community would have of a student graduating from a specific theme- or career-focused program. Employers will insist that, first and foremost, they are eager to have students develop a positive work ethic and the ability to interact with others, perform basic math, and demonstrate effective English and communications skills. There is also, however, a certain expectation of what students should have accomplished as a result of their SLC.

Use the focus group to identify knowledge, skills, and abilities and then match those skills to your district's course offerings and graduation requirements. Push in the discussions for high standards and be on the alert for any indication that a different standard of practice or outcome is being set for any one group of students. A little later in this chapter, we provide a curriculum-planning tool that will include some sample focus questions. The skills you are looking to identify will vary from one SLC to another. Let us take the example of Travel and Tourism. An initial list of expectations for students in these programs would likely include: the ability to communicate well with others; have a positive, welcoming demeanor; have an understanding of customer relations and customer service; and have computer skills in one of the major reservation systems (e.g., SABRE or Apollo). A more in-depth list would undoubtedly highlight a need for excellent geography knowledge and an understanding of government regulation of travel industries. These areas of understanding have a direct bearing on what types of courses and work-based experiences should be developed for the program and how courses will be taught.

Career Pathways

If you have selected a career academy approach to your SLC, you will want to address a special set of sequencing concerns in order for your students and your faculty to qualify for certifications and possible federal funding. You will recall that, in Chapter 1, we defined *pathways* and addressed the NSTWOA requirement that all students have the opportunity to be involved in school-to-work and that all aspects of the industry should be available for inclusion in the learning experience. You will also recall that the research points to SLC being most effective if they are defined in size by having fewer than 400 students. These two factors have pushed the development of career pathways programs in all major school systems.

In large SLC you will want to be able to offer students a more defined program of study by creating pathway themes and individualized course work and work experience. By creating multiple pathways in large SLC, you continue the sense of an SLC by providing one more nucleus where a student can find a center of caring and commitment. Here, pathways can be both broad and specific, depending on the size of the school and the size of the SLC. For example, students can follow a "health" pathway as part of a larger "health and human services" academy, while others in this same academy may be following a sequence that is more closely aligned to the human services. Similarly, a student may have a major or pathway in the area of "voice" in the larger "creative arts" SLC. Pathways not only allow for students to follow their specific area of career and academic interest, but they also continue the SLC approach by further dividing a large group of students into smaller groups.

Once it has been determined what the educational goals are for the students, the teaching team meets with the guidance staff to determine which courses match the themes. Needless to say, there should be an upward progression of complex coursework that refines the elective and required courses into a course sequence that develops the students' understanding and skills. These should be matched to post-secondary course articulation agreements with the high expectations goal of having students graduating from high school already having earned college credit.

You may need to be creative in bringing the depth of experience you want to a course of study. If you are interested in your students taking robotics, for example, there may be two similar course listings in both the Engineering section and in the Science section of your school district's master course book. By making the effort to find these similarities, you enable students to increase the number of science courses that support their career theme.

Work-based offerings are addressed in Chapter 9; however, here we want to make a note that, especially for career academy teams, a curricular cross-reference to work-based experiences is important for three reasons:

1. Teams need to include and value the work-based activities in their planning of the whole educational experience.

2. Work-based experiences should be linked, whenever possible, to specific course outcomes and academic/Carnegie unit credit.

3. Many programs call for work-based experiences to be included in the school/educational plan for all students, and addressing them here reaffirms that commitment and requirement.

Once teams have agreed on the nature and scope of their curriculum, it will be important to capture the specific elements of their program. This capturing serves several vital purposes in the SLC implementation. First, it defines the nature of the program. Second, it states what is expected of student experiences and shows students and their families an array of options, pathways, and related experiences. Third, it sets up a cycle of courses for scheduling. The first step in defining the scope of the curriculum is to have the team, or the committee designated with handling curriculum, meet and list every experience that may have a bearing or impact on the SLC theme. Every system has "the book" that lists all the approved district course offerings. Cull this resource and determine all courses that have a relationship to the SLC under consideration. Do not stop there: consider *all* the experiences that can potentially impact student success and get at deeper levels of their understanding. For example, participation in CTSO adds great depth to student learning. CTSO develop citizenship, technical, leadership, and teamwork skills essential for students who are preparing for the workforce and further education. They provide a unique instructional method for attaining the competency goals and objectives identified in each course. The U.S. Department of Education has information on each of the CTSO noted below on the Web site noted in the Resources section:

- Business Professionals of America
- Distributive Education Clubs of America (DECA; Marketing)
- Future Business Leaders of America—Phi Beta Lambda
- Family, Career and Community Leaders of America
- Health Occupations Students of America
- National Future Farmers of America (FFA; Agriculture)
- National Postsecondary Agricultural Student Organization
- National Young Farmer Educational Association
- SkillsUSA-VICA (Vocational Industrial Clubs of America)
- Technology Student Association (TSA).

To assist teams in their planning of the scope and sequence for their SLC, we have provided you with [6.1 SLC Pathways Course and Experience Planning] in the Tool Kit. It is a two-page MS Word file and is shown in Tool Kit Snapshot 6.1. The first page is designed to help teams capture all the courses and the related experiences that can positively impact a student's SLC educational experience. In planning and identifying key elements, you will also want to pay special attention to the particular "culture" of your community. Certain states have made commitments to football, cheerleading, chorus or band as central points of their schedule. Still others have made a senior experience that includes extensive time off campus as a rite of passage. If there is something that pushes your scheduling, please make sure you capture it here and share with the master scheduler or scheduling committee as soon as possible to maintain the integrity of the scheduling discussion from the last chapter.

Once the course and experience determinations have been made, you can fit them into the second page of the file, Planning 2, by grade and pathway. By charting out a sequence of course offerings, you have now set in place the important process of communicating the specific nature of your SLC to families and partners. It is now time to make some initial determinations about how you will teach.

Courses

The pathways noted above must comprise courses that reflect high standards. Consider eliminating from your pathways list any course that is regarded as remedial in nature. Students who are expected to perform at low levels do just that. By eliminating courses traditionally set for tracking and lower expectations, and by providing additional academic supports, the faculty makes a statement and embraces a philosophy that says all children can learn to a high standard with our help. In a like manner, you will want to make accommodations in your planning and scheduling for students enrolled in Advanced Placement (AP) classes. The importance of addressing AP issues is also discussed in other sections of this book.

Increasingly, we are seeing that schools do not necessarily have the programmatic depth they seek in order to prepare students for college and careers. This has necessitated either the total revision of courses that are on the books or the creation of entirely new courses. This specific curriculum planning requires extended amounts of time for teams. To make that work easier we have supplied you with the MS Word Tool Kit file [6.2 Curriculum Planning Templates] (see Tool Kit Snapshot 6.2).

(Text continues on page 131)

Tool Kit Snapshot 6.1   SLC Pathways Course and Experience Planning

SLC PATHWAYS, COURSE, AND EXPERIENCE PLANNING "1"					SLC/ACADEMY NAME:			
First cut at course and experience offerings. List all courses and experience you feel apply to this SLC/Academy.								
English	Math	Social Studies	Science	Other Required Courses	Electives	Extra-curricular, CTSO, and Service Activities	Work-Based Experiences, Portfolio, Certifications

SLC PATHWAYS, COURSE, AND EXPERIENCE PLANNING "2"   SLC/ACADEMY NAME:

Pathway One: _____

Arrange all courses and experiences from "1" in a chronological planning sequence.

	English	Math	Social Studies	Science	Other Required Courses	Electives	Extra-curricular, CTSO, and Service Activities	Work-Based Experiences, Projects, Portfolio
Ninth								
Tenth								
Eleventh								
Twelfth								
Dual Enrollment/ Articulation/Certifications								

Tool Kit Snapshot 6.2	Curriculum Planning Templates

Criminal Justice/Law Enforcement Course

Curriculum Planning

Course Title: *Introduction to Criminal Justice*

Start Date: September 1995

Sites: Calvert High School with video link to Northern High

Proposed Text: *The American System of Criminal Justice,* 7th Edition, Cole.

Course Description:

This course provides an overview of the structures and jurisdictions of the police, courts, and corrections. It describes the roles of various officials (e.g., police officer, prosecuting attorney, public defender, probation and parole officers) and actively involves students in the interrelated activities of the various components of the criminal justice system. This course will be taught by actively involving students, educators, and members of the criminal justice systems in units that are integrated across academic discipline.

Goals:

1. Develop career awareness and experience.

2. Establish a foundation for understanding the criminal justice system and its effects on students.

3. Build citizenship, civil rights understanding, and life skills (with a strong understanding of a commitment to public/community service).

4. Create portfolios of work that document student understanding and competencies (to include a résumé which reflects job shadowing; informational interviews, certificates of diversity and conflict resolution training, student-generated business correspondence which reflects career-specific vocabulary, business cards collected through the year, articles on current events, videotapes, mock trial materials, etc.).

Possible Course Sequence for Career Pathway:

Ninth grade: Civics

Tenth grade: Introduction to Criminal Justice (Civics prerequisite)

Eleventh grade: Youth and the Law (with a strong underpinning of psychology and sociology)

Twelfth grade: Criminal Law/Evidence and Procedure

Curriculum Planning Sheet One: Start-Up Questions

Course Title/#:_____

What content should be included in this unit/course?

_____

_____

_____

_____

What resources are available to augment the unit? Consider sites, personnel, materials . . .

_____

_____

_____

_____

_____

_____

_____

What type of staff training might be necessary for the teacher(s) to effectively communicate and lead this unit?

_____

_____

_____

What supports are available to the teacher(s) for this unit?

_____

_____

_____

What are natural outgrowths or career pathway links from this unit (e.g., for a law course: Street Law, Report Writing, Conflict Resolution, Business Law)?

_____

_____

_____

(Continued)

Tool Kit Snapshot 6.2   (Continued)

Curriculum Planning Sheet Two: Identify Knowledge, Skills, and Abilities

What are the careers related to this unit/course/experience?

_____

_____

What are the top five skills needed by successful people in these professions?

1. _____

2. _____

3. _____

4. _____

5. _____

What do you consider the critical steps a student would have to take to be successful in these professions?

_____

_____

_____

What skills or knowledge would you expect a student to have mastered in this unit/course/experience?

_____

_____

_____

_____

What site visits or resources do you think should be closely linked to successful delivery of this course?

_____

_____

_____

_____

Curriculum Planning Sheet: Identify Knowledge, Skills, and Abilities

Course: Criminal Justice/Law Enforcement Course

Planning Results

What are the top skills needed by successful people in your profession?

Communications: written, oral, technical (specifically computer applications)

Analytic: reason, problem solving

Organizational: time management, crisis management

Interpersonal

Ethics/values

Research

Cultural diversity/multiculturalism

What do you consider the critical steps a student would have to take to be successful in your profession?

Commit to the profession

Understand the impact of current behaviors on future goals

Understand and commit to community/public service

Know the 3 R's

What skills or knowledge would you expect a student to have mastered in this course?

Role of law enforcement in a free society

The role of police officer as "peace" officer

Problem solving

Understanding of the Constitution

Understanding of the structure of the courts, police, corrections, and legislature *and* the interaction between the areas

Computer skills

Understanding of educational, age, and physical ability requirements for various careers

Conflict management

Crisis management (understand and solve)

(Continued)

Tool Kit Snapshot 6.2 (Continued)

Criminal Justice/Law Enforcement Course   Planning Sheet 3: CRIMINAL JUSTICE

Overview/Unit Outline	Competency Skills	Performance Objectives	Suggested Activities	Evaluation	Resources/Supplements
I. Law-Making Process a) Legislative b) Case	• Teleconferencing skills • Portfolio development • Memorization • Critical thinking • Public speaking, debate • Know the steps for making and changing a law	Beginning portfolio development Define "Law" As a class, chart the law-making process Interpret a law Distinguish between legislative and case law	Law-making process sheet Steps in changing a law review "Senseless statutes"—repealing a law/referendum repeal	• Exhibit understanding of group processes • Successful/cogent argument of repeal	***The development of an Advisory Board is deemed essential to the delivery of the site-visit and school-visit components of this course. In each resource citation, it is hoped that an Advisory Board member will be able to assist.**
II. Components of the Criminal Justice System a) Police b) Courts c) Corrections	• Critical thinking • Research skills • Public speaking • Writing skills • Career awareness	Define "system" Define "criminal justice" Determine whether the criminal justice system is a system List the primary agencies of criminal justice Identify available career pathways	Discussion: Is the criminal justice a system or a non-system? Why/why not? Site visit: police dept., courts, corrections Discussion: What happens when a person is found guilty?	• Class participation • Effective use and development of debate • Debrief site visit • Writing activity: Discuss observed occupations; detail/outline career paths	Book: *Crazy Laws* Police station Courts Corrections facility
III. Understanding Criminal Behavior and the Law	• Critical thinking • Analysis • Interpretive skills • Teamwork and collaboration • Technology • Identify academic links with math	Define components of a crime Distinguish between substantive, procedural, and case law Distinguish between types of crime Describe criminal behavior Identify elements and flaws in the law	Review criminal code Analyze U.S. Constitution and Bill of Rights Distinguish between regulatory and criminal law (Code of Student Conduct; Rights and Responsibilities) Develop a profile of a criminal Develop a list of crimes Compare and contrast crime in Calvert Co. with the state	• Class participation • Exhibit cooperative group dynamics	Code of Law/MD Police Training Site Police Dept. Psychiatrist/Sociology teacher Court psychologist Cpl. Titus

Criminal Justice/Law Enforcement Course

Planning Sheet 6: CORRECTIONS Continued

Overview/Unit Outline	Competency Skills	Performance Objectives	Suggested Activities	Evaluation	Resources/Supplements
IV. Prison Society	• Career awareness • Business writing skills • Research skills • Interpersonal	Describe prison society	Student-run panel discussion with prison workers	• Effective development and use of informational interviews for panel discussion	Prison officers and officials
V. Release and Supervision	• Career awareness • Writing skills • Research skills • Interpersonal	Explain the parole and supervision process	Guest speaker: Parole officer	• Effective development and use of informational interview • Prisons posttest *PORTFOLIO FINAL SUBMISSION will include résumé, business cards of shadow hosts and visiting speakers, copies of informational interviews, certificates of diversity and conflict resolution training, student-generated business correspondence, articles on current criminal issues, video of mock trial*	Parole officer

(Continued)

129

Course Title: _____

Text (if appropriate): _____

Planning Sheet: _____

Topic: _____

Overview/Unit Outline	Competency Skills	Performance Objectives	Suggested Activities	Evaluation	Resources/Supplementary

It is frequently used with teaching teams *and their partners* as they begin the very real challenge of working toward adding depth and curricular integration to their programs. Before you begin using it, however, please check with your district-level secondary curriculum department to ensure it meets the specifications and planning needs of the district. It worked for us several years ago when we were faced with the problem—or, rather, given the opportunity—of outlining an integrated, year-long course for Calvert County Public Schools in southern Maryland. The challenge was that we had just two days to complete the task. We quickly discovered that the planning tool moved the team quickly through a process that resulted in the desired course outline.

How It Works

- In our example, the course title and textbook were already approved. The challenge was to develop a course that reflected careers, met standards, reflected multiple forms of assessment, and had ties with other curricular areas. The course was "Introduction to Criminal Justice"; the text was *The American System of Criminal Justice*.
- We created a template with key questions and another to organize course specifics.
- We assembled a teaching team made up of the business, English, industrial arts, and social studies teachers. We invited a police officer and a lawyer to join us for half a day to provide real-world relevance to our plan.
- The social studies teacher outlined the goals for the course, and we set to work.
- We looked at what courses already offered in the school were related to this course and noted them with the idea of creating a pathway course sequence.
- We posed the "start-up" questions about course content and staff training. We acknowledged that it would be beneficial to get the course teacher out into police cars, jails, and court rooms and made arrangements for that.
- We then *listened* very carefully to the lawyer and the police officer, who outlined what they believed a student should really know and be able to do as a result of taking a course with this title.
- We documented those points, and you can see the result here.
- During our attentive listening, we also received offers of help for field trips, speakers, periodicals, etc.
- We *listened* some more as the industrial arts teacher offered to build a mock court room inside the classroom with his students and the English teacher volunteered to help with writing briefs. Although we had a goal, we were without a predesigned plan; however, we saw linkages, partnerships, and wonderful possibilities for learning emerge.
- We then got down to the very real task of determining what the course would look like. Chapter by chapter, we went through the text, noting the chapter headings in the Overview/Unit column of the template. We then worked our way across the columns to determine what competency skills could be linked to this unit, what types of performance-based objectives could be set, what activities should be included in the unit, how the competencies objectives could be measured and evaluated, and, finally, what resources, supplements, or field experiences could be incorporated into the unit.

- Once we hit our stride, the planning went quickly and the course took flight. The results of that planning for the first and final chapters of the text are included here in order that you can model the planning framework. The blank templates for this work, as noted above, are included in the Tool Kit.

"QUICK WINS" CURRICULUM TOOLS

The purpose of integration is to build relevance into the curriculum and to ensure those deeper connections to and across content areas that help students apply and remember the lessons learned. Integration of curriculum is at the heart of a great deal of the conversation around school reform, and is certainly at the heart of SLC. True integration takes staff planning time, skill, supportive texts, and a commitment to plan and deliver instruction across the curriculum. In addressing issues of curriculum integration, you will need to take an honest look at the school staffing structure and resources available. You will also need to review the texts and materials currently being utilized in course delivery. Finally, you will want to determine how and whether they lend themselves to an integrated approach to SLC.

It is probably not realistic for your SLC to achieve true integration across the curriculum in the first years; however, you will want to agree on an expectation for this work and at least work with individual teachers to *infuse* the curriculum with elements of other courses and career-related information. Below we have provided you with a "quick wins" strategies building from the general to the specific. We identify them as quick wins because they take little planning or preparation time on the part of individuals or teams of teachers. These can be used to help infuse elements of cross-curricular and career-related information into your classes. They are the strategies that lead to feelings of success for faculty teams which are wrestling with getting multiple events and meaningful learning objectives met; more importantly, they reap tangible results. We have also provided you with materials, both in print and in the Tool Kit, that you can use to develop more expanded approaches to curriculum integration. Let us be very clear: these strategies are useful in energizing faculty and students. They are helpful in bringing focus to the need for further integration and infusion. They do not, however, an integrated curriculum make. True integration requires adherence to curriculum standards and attention to detail. You will see evidence of this in the activities and tools below.

Curriculum on the Wall (COW)

While many curriculum mapping and alignment tools are now available electronically, in our experience teachers often do not take advantage of them. This is regrettable in that, when teachers—especially those on teams—know when a colleague is teaching a specific unit or a specific standard, others on the team can reinforce the learning in their own classes, reinforce standards, and work toward common assessments. A simple example of this would be that if the French Revolution were being taught in a certain week in World History and several weeks later *A Tale of Two Cities* were being read in World Literature, students would benefit from teachers connecting the two events and perhaps aligning their sequence of delivery. A very simple way to accomplish this is to post a nine-week (or the duration of your grading period) chart on the wall and ask each member of the SLC team to post their objective for the days and weeks in the grids. Using Post-it notes, teachers can then move their objectives to be aligned with those of other teachers. This is a small step in adding depth to students' understanding of the curriculum, begun simply by posting it on the wall.

Brief-Cases: Exercise in Employability

This is perhaps our favorite "quick win." It is easy to organize, meets the needs of many students at the same time, is highly interactive, and involves partners and the whole SLC staff. It costs nothing, can be accomplished in a ninety-minute or double block period, and has an immediate impact on students' and staff's understanding of integration and infusion. Here is how it works. Review your educational objectives for what you want your students to know and be able to do. Invite a business/community partner in to work with a group of students and express these. Ask them to open their discussion with what their job is, how they found their way to their profession, what they do on a daily basis, what is the most interesting part of the work they do, and what is the most boring. Ask them to talk about what curricular skills they use in their job—for example, math, writing, or experimentation. Then ask them to present a "brief-case" from their experience that the students can dissect and engage in. The idea is that, presented with a situation from the partner's experience, both faculty and students can learn more about a particular career field and also build curricular links.

We have had great examples of this, from FBI agents posing drug raid problems to transportation workers positing inventory control situations. The individual "case" is for the partner to design. You simply set it up and coach him or her through it. Here is a clear example and a real outcome.

A lawyer came to work with a group of ninety students in a ninth grade law academy. He presented all the basic information covered above and then presented his case. He personalized it for the class by substituting the names of the principal and lead teacher in the position of "Person A" and "Person B." This is what he described. Person A and B were involved in a car accident on a Friday night in January in front of the high school. Person A has a history of drunk driving. Person B has no driver's license. The case given to the students was to decide who was at fault. Their further task was to try to resolve the matter through arbitration or negotiation and without going to court.

The class was divided in half, with half of the class trying to find for Person A and half for Person B. They were presented with copies of the police reports, medical records, and insurance rate information.

Very quickly, the students became engaged in active dialogue about the meaning of arbitration and mediation. They were calculating insurance rates and deciphering police reports. English, social studies, and math teachers rapidly saw the links to vocabulary, report writing, formulas and calculations, and laws governing events. In this one example, there was one teacher—it happened to be the science teacher—who remained uninvolved, grading papers. After about twenty minutes of sitting next to a group of students who were trying in vain to understand the extent of the injuries incurred by Person B, something permeated the teacher's concentration. He exploded with "if you had only listened when we were doing anatomy you . . . "

then stopped midsentence. In that instant the light bulb went off *for the teacher*. He understood why a science teacher belonged in a law academy. He asked immediately for field experiences to crime labs and forensic sites and saw many connections for how he could apply his science teaching to the career theme.

Brief-cases are easy to arrange and provide multilevels of learning for all. Even though they are partner delivered, they are teacher planned and reinforced. We have provided [6.3 Brief-Cases Teacher Sheet] in the Tool Kit as an organizer to use as students observe and participate in the sessions and also to use later in planning sessions with their team (see Tool Kit Snapshot 6.3). Brief-cases also reinforce the critical elements that we want to see in SLC—mainly partnership, teaming, and integration.

Assignments

A simple approach to getting students making the all-important cross-curricular, "why does this have meaning" connections is simply to create assignments that can be accomplished individually or in teams and need little direction from teachers. Asking students to find, for example, job placement advertisements for jobs within their themed area quickly builds a bridge to what they need to know and must be able to do in certain professions. It also expands their understanding of the job market, salaries, hiring practices, the impact of education on career options, and the full range of jobs within their discipline.

Another approach is to assign students to find articles related to the SLC theme, either in print or through the Internet media. This assignment builds linkages and addresses multiple teaching standards simultaneously. It encourages a sense of inquiry and allows for students to also identify what they do not know and learn about it. Have students read an article and then document all the curricular and career links they are able to identify. This takes some expansion and guided discussion for some students. If they, for example, picked an article on the new stadium for a sports academy, were they able to identify the city zoning issues, construction jobs, or the environmental or economic impact issues connected to the event?

A team in Maryland took yet another approach. A business teacher, an art teacher, and an Engilsh teacher, lacking time to commonly plan integrated lessons, opted instead to design projects that could be jointly assessed. Striking the balance between each teacher's objectives was not always easy but common planning discussions helped them get it right. This teaching team recast the typical biographical report writing that was a standard part of the curriculum. Students still had to read a biography; however, rather than creating long reports, teachers asked students to develop a résumé for the person they were studying. Like all résumés, it had to capture where the person lived, his or her educational background, what positions the person held, and his or her accomplishments. The results were wonderfully interesting works, easily read by the teachers and shared with other students. It reinforced the importance of career preparation and boiled down key elements of the character's life into salient focal points. Rather than simply taking a quick stab at putting something together, most students engaged in an in-depth study and became very creative in their approach. Students created résumés for an array of famous individuals, citing their accomplishments. Some even included a references section in their person's résumé. When the art teacher received one student's résumé for Claude Monet, with a section

Tool Kit Snapshot 6.3 | Brief-Cases Teacher Sheet

Brief-Cases: Exercises in Employability   **Teacher Reflection and Connection Sheet**
Brief-case session, date, contact information:
Brief summary of presentation:
Relevance to real-world learning and careers:
Ah-ha! I didn't know that!
Skills I can teach my students:
Habits I need to encourage in my students:
Vocabulary and English language arts connections:
Math and science connections:
Social studies and humanities connections:
State test relevance and connections:
Other:
Notes:

Relevance to my class:	Relevance to our SLC:	My commitment to follow up:
☐ High	☐ High	☐ High
☐ Medium	☐ Medium	☐ Medium
☐ Low	☐ Low	☐ Low

for references that listed the rest of the Impressionists, the point of cross-curricular connections and successful learning came through.

Discovery-Based Learning

This is a curricular approach we first piloted with middle schools and quickly adapted for use with teaching teams and high school students. The idea is to get individuals and teams to see the task before them as an opportunity for discovery. In truth, it is our spin on "problem-based learning." We have recast the problem approach to make it one of discovery, with the idea that most of us do not like having problems. We do, however, welcome an adventure. Looked on as a challenge—or perhaps an opportunity—the same event takes on a new light.

Here (see Tool Kit Snapshot 6.4) and in the Tool Kit is our planning sheet for Discovery-Based Learning (DBL) [6.4 DBL Experience Log] helps you go a bit deeper than simple assignments as you apply the skills evident in problem-based learning. You goal is to form student teams, have them synthesize their challenge,

Tool Kit Snapshot 6.4	DBL Experience Log

Explorer Team	What needs to be discovered?	DISCOVERY-BASED LEARNING (DBL)	Supply the links and the missing links	Ah-ha! I didn't know that!
1			What school subject knowledge applies here?	Facts you learned
2				
3				
4				
5		QUEST!		
Explorer Skills— Specialties				
				Careers and Service Links
	How and where can these things be discovered?	The task, challenge, problem, or opportunity is…		
			What subject area might be missing? Current events? Technology? Outside resources?	Log what you learned about yourself, your team…your learning style.
What teams are you collaborating with? What teams are you competing against?				
		5 W's / P.A.C.E.S		
		Who / Plan		
		What / Act		
		Where / Create/Catalogue		
		When / Evaluate		
		Why / Sustain		

What Will We Create?	Who Will Do What?	DISCOVERY-BASED LEARNING (DBL)	When Is What Due?	My Responsibilities Are...
		Our discovery will be documented and shared by...		
		We will be successful if...		
Does it need to be sustained? If yes, how?				

identify their individual talents, decide on an approach to completing the project, and document the lessons learned.

How It Works

Teams are formed and presented with a "quest." It could be something as central to "academics" as researching and presenting a project on World War II and the Great Depression, or a more experiential and career-focused project such as creating a student-run business or increasing organ donation registration.

On side one, the quest is written in the dark, black-rimmed box. On side two, the final product, test, project, or portfolio piece is noted, as is a rubric for successful completion of the assigned discovery.

Team members' names go in the Explorer Team listing. This is preset for teams of five because that number tends to work well, but there is no magic to that number.

Teams then take some time to talk about the various tasks before them. There are two sides to the DBL form, one for documenting and one for planning. There is no specific order to how they should address the topic areas. There are spaces, among other things, for:

- Synthesizing the "problem" or quest: "What needs to be discovered?"
- Deciding where research, materials, interviews, etc. can be discovered
- Assessing who is best at what
- Determining who should do what
- Thinking about whether this is a competitive challenge or a collaborative one
- Guideline reminders to make sure the project is planned effectively
- Cataloguing new learning
- Building connections between courses and careers
- Describing the specific plans and rubric expectations
- Detailing deadlines and itemizing individual responsibilities.

The result should be a fun, interactive, useful exercise to get teams working together and being very focused on what has to be accomplished, by whom, and by when. We have cited an example—"discover how to increase organ donation registration." DBL could be a good match to move that effort forward. It promotes teamwork and helps catalogue an individual team member's learning and contribution to a project. When we use it, we generally provide a minimum of information to the students. We give them a framework. It is exciting, but may seem obvious when read here, that in order to even begin this quest they must first discover the current rate of organ donation. It is the type of activity that promotes their higher-order thinking skills. In its simplicity, it also forces students to make the often-missed critical connections to what they are learning in school in one course with what they are learning and doing in another. The cataloguing of new skills—whether the learning of an Excel spreadsheet or being able to present comfortably in front of a group—builds student self-esteem and provides material that can then be placed on résumés and in portfolios.

In developing this particular discovery, we were reminded of two very different but important lessons. In working with student teams on this activity, we uncovered that their greatest resource for success was not the science or health teachers, as we had assumed. Rather, students quickly determined that the driver education teacher, having ready access to students getting their driver's licenses—the very place most people register as donors—was their best asset. In a very different vein, we were reminded of the need to always be cognizant and respectful of the cultures in which we work. When working on Native American lands, this activity fell flat in a culture that respects the sanctity of a whole human body upon death. Inclusion and adaptation of these "quick wins" leads to substantive changes in instructional practice and to a different approach to classroom instruction.

Model Lessons

Even without the benefit of in-depth common planning time, teachers can share their expertise and reinforce specific skills across disciplinary lines through sharing of model lessons. I learned this from master teacher Cindy Fairbanks from Sharpstown High School in Houston, Texas. In a very quick twenty minutes, she taught all of us how to address content, skills, and the ever-looming state test—Texas

Box 6.1   Model Lesson—Louis XIV: Successful or Not?

(Since this was a model lesson, teachers took on all student roles.)
This lesson involves reading, paired discussion, analysis, writing, and a self-check. The *only* part of the lesson that is graded is the writing exercise.

Getting Started

- Pair students.
- Provide or assign a reading. In this example, we were assigned five pages of the *World History* text.
- With their partners, students have ten seconds to decide whether they will research/ read the assignment through the lens of noting successes or failures (pros/cons or strengths/deficits). In this case, we had to decide whether we were reading for the successes or failures of Louis XIV of France. Students are allowed ten minutes to do the reading and fill in the list below:

SUCCESSES   FAILURES

1.

2.

3.

After ten minutes, all the "successes" gather in one area of the room and the "failures" gather in another. Each grouping quickly cross-checks the other's lists.

Great Debates!

Pairs regroup to determine whether Louis XIV was a successful monarch or an unsuccessful one. First, students rank order their list and any extensions they have made in their like-pair discussion. Students then have fifteen seconds to convince their counterpart of their position, using the list they compiled and any extensions of that they made from their same-group colleagues. *Each person then gives their partner feedback on what was the most convincing argument—fifteen seconds each.*

Writing Project

(This serves as scaffolding.) Students must write a five-sentence paragraph that explains their position.

1. Louis XIV (was/was not) a successful monarch.
2. Give one reason/CD (concrete detail) supporting your statement.
3. Give another reason.
4. This proves . . .
5. Louis XIV . . . (restates the topic sentence).

Self-Check

Have students review their writing for the following:

- Underline the subject in the topic sentence.
- Circle the opinion in the topic sentence.
- Make sure they have written in complete sentences, no phrases.
- Cross out extraneous words, NO formulaic writing! (Apparently, TAKS penalizes for this writing style. For instance, the following sentence, "For example, Louis XIV depleted the national treasury" would receive a higher point score on TAKS if it read: "Louis XIV depleted the national treasury." Teachers can train their students for this.

Assessment of Knowledge and Skills (TAKS). She also made recommendations on modifications for special education students and those who were English language learners. The lesson, described in Box 6.1, was powerful. What made the *teachers' learning* powerful was the follow-up discussion when each teacher reflected on how to ensure higher-order thinking skills and how to adapt the lesson to their specific class and discipline. In essence, students would be building the same skills over multiple classes.

Every teacher in the SLC was able to easily see ways to deliver and adapt this lesson. We all saw that multiple standards from across disciplines were being taught. Each teacher could see their ability to impact student and school results on TAKS. In a simple model lesson, each team member was energized to look beyond the stated curriculum and engage in a process of changed professional practice.

At a Glance: Summing It Up and Next Steps

Creating effective curriculum is a complex process that can be supported by fellow faculty and partners. It goes well beyond the approved textbook or a set of standards and is certainly more complex than a bag of tricks to engage student interest. At the core, the curriculum must meet high standards for *all* students. As the research shows, our graduates must be taught to the same standard and given the same opportunity to meet with success, regardless of their immediate postsecondary choice of work or college. Each SLC should now be well on its way to having a scope and sequence of courses as well as plans for integration. The next challenge is to take a hard look at professional practice and determine how SLC can best excite and engage their students to be active learners.

7

Professional Practice

Quality is never an accident; it is always the result of high intention, sincere effort, intelligent direction and skillful execution; it represents the wise choice of many alternatives.

—William A. Foster

Chapter 7 Road Map

Purpose	To provide the practitioner with the tools to move into a deep data-driven discussion on instruction, roles, and responsibilities of stakeholders; the use of time of administrators; and professional practices—including professional development—that lead to improved outcomes for students.
Stage of Implementation	Study and Assessment, Establishing Structures—focus on personalization, instruction and curriculum, and data.
Process and Action Steps	Utilize the tools to gather specific data. Engage the faculty in a discussion on what grade distributions tell about instructional and school practice. Engage in specific discussion with department chairs and other school leaders, focusing on their roles and responsibilities in a school working in SLC and committed to *continuous improvement.* Implement a plan to align all professional and instructional practices, including work done while attending conferences.
Tool Kit	7.1 Department Instructional Facilitator Roles and Self-Assessment 7.2 Instructional Leadership Team Roles and Self-Assessment 7.3 Data Table 7.3 Whole-School Data 7.4 Data Table 7.4 Content Area Data 7.5 Data Table 7.5 Classroom Course Data 7.6 Use of Time 7.7 Lessons Shared
Reflective Practice	Do we know our data? Do we know how to find it, use it, and hold hard discussions? Do we use data to support individual classroom practice? Do we do this in a way that supports teachers to success? Is reflective practice a part of our school culture, should it be, how can we move toward that? Does everyone's role need to change in a redesigned school—how, to what, and with what supports?
Outcome	Data are increasingly at the core of discussions about school improvement. Roles and responsibilities have been reviewed, recommitted to, or redesigned. A plan for professional practice is in place. Teams are using data to inform and guide instruction.

The past decade of education reform has laid the concerns of parents and communities, as well as those of public officials, postsecondary institutions, and the business community firmly at the school house door. There is little question that this has placed an unprecedented focus on improving teaching and learning in our nation's schools. And there is little question that in SLC, as in every educational setting, the focus is on professional practice. In many cases, it will be the practitioner who supports the school in a honing of practice that leads to the real gains schools seek to make. It is the practitioner who will create an atmosphere in which data, professional practice, and policy are looked at in a reflective manner for positive growth rather than through one that seeks to document, intimidate, or alienate.

The national outcry—that we need to increase students' capability to succeed in school, as lifelong learners, and as contributing citizens—has brought teachers and principals under intense pressure. They must show that their students can understand the content of school subjects and can use that knowledge in performance-based situations and on standardized tests. The standards and accountability movement has also been accompanied by a move to change the culture of schools. That culture—increasingly one with a focus on literacy—must reflect the new responsibilities of school staff to account for students' learning. Continuing demands exist for teachers to adapt their teaching styles to include meeting the needs of students' multiple intelligences, vastly diverse cultural backgrounds, and varying abilities and challenges. While we are seeing a sea change in isolated pockets of the educational community, it is still the norm that—especially at the high school level—teachers operate in isolation. Too often, teachers see little correlation between their teaching styles and the failures met by their students. They share even less of a sense of responsibility for these same failures. Sharing instructional practice, while on the rise, is rare. Even when formal evaluation is absent in the equation, high school teachers are uncomfortable, as a rule, about sharing their work and receiving feedback from their colleagues. The pace of our lives, and the running of school buildings, has left us little time for reflection on how we work. The questioning of teachers' instructional practice by administrators or colleagues is rarely seen as an opportunity to improve practice. Too often it is seen as an affront to our professionalism at best, and at worst it quickly turns into grievances, reports to the union, or cries of a violation of academic freedom. This lack of reflection, responsibility, and accountability flies in the face of good business and professional practice across occupations and industries. More importantly, it flies in the face of what all good teachers want and should be held accountable for—namely, children succeeding.

I recently had the benefit of listening to Jane Lozano, School Improvement Facilitator at Sharpstown High School in Houston, Texas. She was sharing with me the Toyota example she learned from Dr. Kelly Trlica, Assistant Superintendent for Secondary School Reform. Jane and Kelly made strong connections to the standards that Toyota sets for itself in terms of meeting with success—success in design, success in sales, success in operations. In design and function, Toyota puts its most highly skilled engineers on the engine, the critical element in the car's operation. In sales they carefully monitor exactly how many cars they produce, how many they sell, how many are left on the lot. They are continually responsive to what their clients want and need. The analogy Lozano shared was that the best teachers (engineers) have to be working with the ninth grade, the most important part of the school in changing student outcomes. She continued that we have to start thinking of our students in terms of hard numbers. It would be unacceptable to build a car that was not responsive to the wants or needs of the client (students and families). It would never be acceptable for Toyota to have a year in which they made 2,000 cars (students) but left a significant proportion languishing on car lots (to eventually drop out of school).

A change in outcomes requires reflection, assessment, and a honing of practice. How odd it is that, in a system that by design is based on making the most minute distinctions in a student's performance (between say a 3.9 and a 4.0 GPA), there is so little tolerance for self-scrutiny. It is no surprise to those who can be very honest about how we have worked in high schools that we know something has to change—but preferably not in "my" classroom. This is where the practitioner plays a critical role in creating a climate of reflective practice.

The federal government has become an instrument of change for helping schools and teachers move from where they are to where they need to go—to become higher functioning schools with a more competent teacher corps. Currently, there are national efforts to improve reading and math proficiency, to lower class size, and to create smaller learning environments. These efforts also aim to extend the traditional time set for learning to better encompass the expanded resources of communities and to provide reinforcing opportunities. Schools may now select from a number of national initiatives, school reform models, and recognized methodologies. Many of these initiatives contain their own professional development or technical assistance components designed to support teachers and to change the culture and structure of the school to support learning. Many are based on particular strategies and are ingrained in philosophies of learning in which faculties must be steeped. As a result, staff development calendars are crowded with a range of "must-have" topics such as literacy, numeracy, leadership, cultural competency, state standards, alternative assessments, data analysis, and an array of instructional strategies. Teaching staffs are confronted with a plethora of resources and opportunities for training and expanding their skills from a variety of sources. This seeming abundance of opportunities and supports nevertheless does not go far enough to rectify the general misalignment of teacher professional development opportunities with the skills needed to perform effectively in the actual day-to-day conditions and challenges of today's classrooms.

Amid this flurry of activity, what has been missing from many staff development efforts is the commitment to a *strategic approach* between principals and central administrations to *systematically* develop a faculty that not only understands and is ready to change or augment its teaching methodologies but is also able to take responsibility for shared vision, leadership, and management of the school community. These roles are not optional, nor should they be approached tepidly. They represent the bottom line of what has to be accomplished if the gains in student achievement are to be met and sustained, and if our schools are to continue to improve.

A *strategic approach* requires clear communication and leadership from the school district's central administration on current educational reform priorities. It requires principals who are equipped with the knowledge, training, tools, and resources to identify their own staff's talents and abilities and to provide *job embedded* training and coaching support to teachers. Just as we design student learning with the aim of "meeting them where they are and taking them where they need to be," we need to design staff development opportunities for teachers that recognize their individual talents and experiences and build from that base. Staff training must be individualized to the extent that it builds on the strength of each teacher's experience and expertise while also providing the basic knowledge that developing teachers need to succeed.

MOVING INTO DATA-DRIVEN DISCUSSIONS

Many curricular and assessment discussions begin with the question, "What do we want our students to know and be able to do as a result of this experience?" Likewise, discussions on professional practice should start with the same query, "What knowledge, skills, and abilities do we want our teachers to be able to *demonstrate* in a school committed to *continuous improvement?" What evidence will we have?*

As a baseline, we know the nation looks to—or in some cases requires teachers to:

- Be knowledgeable about the standards endorsed by their state department of education, as well as those endorsed by their respective professional associations
- Extend their subject area knowledge to include higher-order thinking skills
- Improve their own instructional strategies to ensure that every student can reach the standards
- Work collegially with parents, community members, and other teachers in realizing the goals for student learning
- Participate in building the school structures necessary to support new standards, new accountability tools, new teaching strategies, and new professional development needs.

Does this list get us closer to "the Toyota approach"? Does it reflect what students want and need in good teachers? In Chapter 2 we suggested that you conduct a focus group of students and have them create the ideal teacher using [2.1 What Should a Graduate—Teacher—SLC Look Like?]. If you have not done that yet, you might seek to do it now. The results can be a powerful vehicle for teacher reflection. Here is a sample list designed by students in one Washington State school.

This list brings us much closer to what the client—our students and their families—wants and needs to succeed. It is a great list, but how do we expect teachers to embody these characteristics? How do we encourage this personalized list while also setting a high standard for teachers' capacity to deliver good instruction? The first part of the answer comes in the understanding that creating this ideal teacher is at the very core of why we are seeing so much interest in SLC. It is extremely difficult to change a whole school culture. It is much less difficult to take a small group of teachers, let them create their ideal learning environment, empower them with the opportunity to focus on a specific cohort of students, provide them with the resources they need, have them agree on instructional and personalization practices to which they will hold themselves accountable, monitor their data, and watch them meet with success. The second part of the answer comes in developing a culture of literacy.

A CULTURE OF LITERACY

Literacy is often thought of as simply the ability to read, which entails a complex set of skills and the ability to construct, extend, and examine meaning from text. However, literacy is much more than this. Literate adults need to be able to more than meet that baseline expectation. They need to be able to communicate fluently in both the oral and written word, and they need to have mastery of problem-solving and numeracy skills. It is generally agreed that a true literacy framework is comprehensive and addresses the complete needs of the student to read, write, think, and compute. Our definition of literacy, then, results in a student who possesses the ability to read, write, compute, and communicate at college-ready levels. In other words, students leaving high school must have the ability to enter credit-bearing college courses without need of remediation. Regardless of their intention to attend a postsecondary institution, to be a literate adult, and to be able to contribute to and gain from society, students need to leave our high schools literate. A decade ago, we would have believed this was the norm for all our students. Research evidence abounds, however, that this is far from the truth for many of our nation's youth.

Moving to a school culture that demands literacy is therefore not an option. It requires the creation of a framework that is firmly rooted in research on instructional practice and an unwavering commitment to establishing practices that execute that plan.

While this book does not deal in depth with instructional practice, the true heart of school improvement, we will talk about creating a culture of literacy and a focus on instruction. We will address the structures and practices that help move the *continuous improvement* agenda forward. Committing to a focus on professional practice is the distinguishing feature of SLC that are successful and those that stop at the structural elements. Establishing a broadly defined culture of literacy is the critical piece that links a successful SLC structure with their intended result—student achievement.

A school focused on literacy must commit to *model, coach, provide feedback,* and *be accountable for good instruction.* For most schools, this will mean a culture shift away from independent silos of work in their classrooms to shared instructional practice, common lessons and assessments, looking at data, examining student work and teacher assignments, and a climate where teachers are *regularly* in and out of each other's classes—not for the purpose of assessment but for the purpose of focusing on improved practice.

Creating a culture of literacy also demands that what you teach is as important as how you teach it. Becoming a literacy-focused school cannot be done in a climate of "gotcha"—or catching someone doing something bad. It has to be nurtured in professional development targeted at teacher success. It also demands that you begin to support teachers in meaningful ways. As hard as it might be to accept, most faculties cannot agree on what good teaching looks like. Groups can gain consensus on the theoretical components of good teaching but they have little success at establishing a shared rubric for instructional excellence. This is why the work of Bloom, Marzano, Wagner, and others is critical to a discussion on instructional practice.

As a practitioner, your job must entail creating a shared vision of what good teaching looks like. We address this in the final chapter which, again with a nod to the nonlinear process of improving schools, is in very many ways a companion to this chapter. Be prepared for the many questions that will arise. Among them will be the following: What does good teaching look like? How is it assessed? How are students engaged? What is the classroom environment? What strategies are in evidence? How do we agree on a rubric for self-assessment? How do we demonstrate consistency of grading—understanding that an A or a D from one teacher is the same as an A or a D from another? How do we really have literacy embraced and taught by all teachers? How do we integrate literacy into daily lessons? How do we create intervention plans for students significantly below standards (2+ grade level)? And how do I, as a classroom teacher, open my door and invite scrutiny that will not result in a negative evaluation? You do not need to have the answers right now. You will have to create a structure and an atmosphere in which they can be answered.

We believe that literacy and numeracy coaches are the single best strategy for ensuring that the instructional agenda stays at the core of any school redesign or improvement effort. These individuals may be full-time staff or serve as classroom teachers who may teach a class or two and "coach" (not evaluate) an assigned/ selected group of teachers. They often create and model demonstration lessons, videotape others, and provide supportive feedback. They engage teachers in learning around standards and strategies to improve the quality of teacher assignments and student work. They do their coaching in the classroom, reflecting a commitment to job-embedded professional development. At times, they may introduce then model a skill or strategy to small groups. Really good literacy and numeracy coaches have their own professional developer, who is responsible for "quality control" and supporting the coaches.

In tandem with a commitment to a literacy coach goes the hard work that must happen in departments. While early SLC structures put little emphasis on departments, we now understand the instructional and critical-specific work that must be done here. This is why the bell schedules referenced in an early chapter ensure that departmental planning time is guaranteed. Each department will want to target strategies that help students meet with positive results. With this in mind, the position of Department Chair is transformed into DIF with concrete responsibilities for leading a department instructional agenda as we will see in the coming pages.

We originally pioneered this transformation at Waltrip High School in Houston, Texas, with profound and rather immediate results. The first step was understanding that the traditional role of a department head had to change if we were going to move the instructional agenda. The second was asking for the current chairs to create a position description for themselves in a school that was serious about looking at improvement—what stayed the same, what changed. Engaging the current chairs in the process, rather than dictating one, was critical for success. Box 7.1 presents the description that they created for the DIFs.

After the position description was honed, the current chairs participated in a self-assessment, indicating on every criterion what they felt they were doing well, not doing well, or barely doing. They were asked to supply *evidence* of their accomplishment or struggle. They also had the opportunity to state what coaching or support they would need to become adept at meeting and exceeding the expectations set in this new description. The entire process was conducted in a "hold harmless" framework. No department chair could have been held responsible for not doing some of these criteria well. The expectation for them to do so had not been set. The result was significant buy-in on the part of the chairs, a changed name to the position, and a year-long coaching plan. The coaching plan supported each DIF in conducting classroom walk-throughs, looking at student work, assessing data, and focusing on classroom instruction. This process is now being followed at other schools. The Tool Kit contains [7.1 Department Instructional Facilitator Roles and Self-Assessment] (see Tool Kit Snapshot 7.1). It is the tool created by the Waltrip team, which is now used as a benchmark for their own annual assessment.

Literacy coaches and department chairs (now DIF) need not be islands in a sea of instructional change. They can, however, be the foundation upon which is built an expectation for the collaborative roles and responsibilities of assistant principals, department chairs/DIF, and SLC coordinators/lead teachers to serve as part of an *Instructional Improvement Team* you build in the scaffolding that supports an

| Tool Kit Snapshot 7.1 | Department Instructional Facilitator Roles and Self-Assessment |

Department Instructional Facilitator Roles and Self-Assessment

Please review, reflect on, and assess your work in these areas.	Doing well	Barely doing	Not doing	What evidence do you see related to how you rated this area?	Need to do
Roles					
Fostering the standards of excellence and instructional practice across the school—for example, serving as a coach to teachers for increased instructional success.					
Fostering true professional learning communities within your department based on study and inquiry.					
Conducting departmental meetings that are focused and linked to the overall mission and vision of our school.					
Modeling research-based instructional strategies and best practices in the classroom.					
Responsibilities					
Aligning instruction with state tests to improve teaching and learning and quality of instruction, including research-based best practices.					
Using specific formats for a more collaborative approach to teaching/learning in all academies.					
Devising strategies for extra help, student success, and teacher support during tutorials.					
Coordinating literacy efforts with Literacy Coach and SLC Coordinator as demonstrated by a plan for regularly scheduled meetings.					
Supporting and participating in the reform initiatives.					
Conduit for department-related information dissemination.					
Management of departmental supplies/materials.					
Facilitation of departmental budget requests in conjunction with the Business Manager.					

Need to have: please list what you need to have to accomplish the "need to dos":

SOURCE: Created in collaboration with Grace Sammon and Waltrip High School, Houston, Texas.

instructional agenda. This team coordinates and supports strategies for improving instruction and achieving academic success for all students. In developing these teams, we follow much the same process as described for the Waltrip DIF. The goal is to reinforce, at every level, a focus on instruction. These teams move the process away from evaluation and focus on professional practice, especially in the case of assistant principals who so often have evaluative responsibilities. The Tool Kit file [7.2 Instructional Leadership Team Roles and Self-Assessment] (see Tool Kit Snapshot 7.2) was crafted by Sharpstown High School, also in Houston. It expands the work begun by Waltrip.

In a layout similar to the DIF Self-Assessment file, this team inserted a mission statement at the top to continually guide its work. Simply stated, this team is "committed to nurturing a positive climate for continuous instructional improvement." Members laid out their responsibilities as follows:

- As you will see on that template, shown here, this team chose to build an action plan into its assessment.
- The entire process for DIF and Instructional Teams needs to be data driven with close adherence to standards and standards of practice. There are several pieces of primary evidence that need to be incorporated into data analysis:
  - Agreement on a definition of what good teaching and learning looks like and a rubric to match it
  - Agreement on the roles and responsibilities of coaches, DIF, Instructional Improvement Team
  - Conducting an initial "Data in a Day" process and committing to renewing the evaluation annually (discussed in Chapter 9)

Box 7.1   The Department Instructional Facilitator (DIF)

The DIF will:

- Foster the standards of excellence and instructional practice across the school (e.g., serving as a coach to teachers for increased instructional success)
- Foster true professional learning communities within their department based on study and inquiry
- Conduct departmental meetings that are focused and linked to the overall mission and vision of our school
- Model research-based instructional strategies and best practices in the classroom
- Align instruction with state tests to improve teaching and learning and quality of instruction, including research-based best practices
- Use specific formats for a more collaborative approach to teaching/learning in all SLC
- Devise strategies for extra help, student success, and teacher support during tutorials
- Coordinate literacy efforts with the Literacy Coach and SLC Coordinator as demonstrated by a plan for regularly scheduled meetings
- Support and participate in the reform initiatives
- Serve as a conduit for department-related information dissemination
- Manage departmental supplies/materials
- Facilitate departmental budget requests in conjunction with the Business Manager.

Tool Kit Snapshot 7.2	Instructional Leadership Team Roles and Self-Assessment

Instructional Leadership Team Roles and Self-Assessment
Committed to nurturing a positive climate for continuous instructional improvement

Please review and reflect on your practice.	Doing	Doing well	Not doing	What evidence will we have/do we have of effectiveness? What does "doing well" look like?	Action plan	Date
Fostering the standards of excellence and instructional practice across the school—for example, as a coach to teachers for increased instructional success.						
Fostering true professional learning communities (PLC) within your department and SLC based on study and inquiry.						
Conducting departmental and SLC meetings that are focused on data, policy, and practice and are linked to the overall mission and vision of our school.						
Modeling research-based instructional strategies and best practices in the classroom.						
Aligning instruction with state tests to improve teaching and learning and quality of instruction, including research-based best practices.						
Using specific formats for a more collaborative approach to teaching/ learning in all academies.						
Devising strategies for extra help, student success, tutorials, interventions, and teacher support.						
Coordinating literacy efforts with the Literacy Coach and SLC Coordinators, as demonstrated by a plan for regularly scheduled meetings.						
Supporting and participating in the continuous improvement initiatives.						
Coordinating and planning with assistant principals to focus and support a positive climate for success.						
Nurturing a positive climate of inquiry, exploration, use of data, and teaching and learning.						

Notes: Please indicate here perceived challenges in order that we can, together, address resources, support, training, incentives, coaching support, etc.

SOURCE: Created in collaboration with Grace Sammon and Waltrip High School, Houston, Texas.

- Monitoring D and F student data at every progress reporting (not report card) period. Looking at this data by school, department, teacher, and student and committing to a strategy of support for teachers and students
- Monitoring the array of standardized tests
- Addressing deficits, celebrating strengths!

DATA, DATA EVERYWHERE

Most educators have little exposure to or experience with using data to understand instructional practice. They are either inundated with massive amounts of data through e-mails that have little bearing on their specific classroom practice or they are not taught how data can be a powerful not a threatening tool for school improvement. While the state test is the big indicator for most schools, with the advent of NCLB, there are many more personal indicators that attract teachers' attention. Run a "D and F" report. If you do not know what one is, that is not surprising, since many schools do not run them, or, if they do, they stay within the sight of a few in administration. A "D and F" report is a simple computer run for those specific grade allocations. See if you can run it in two ways: first, by number of students receiving D's and F's, and second, for grade distribution by teacher. Depending on your school, the numbers will be both staggering and alarming. On the student side of the equation, we know that students who receive a D in one subject—for example, Algebra 1—have little chance of performing very well in a related subject—say, Geometry. In terms of the numbers of F's reported, we know (at least from the Chicago study) that students earning even one F in the freshman year have only a 60 percent chance of graduating from high school (Roderick, 2005). In looking at the students receiving D's and F's, several approaches present themselves. Moving to data-driven discussions must be approached in a thoughtful manner and based on respect for the individual teacher. Teachers in SLC need to be supported and taught how to monitor data regularly, as mentioned above. We also have to find meaningful ways to involve students in the discussion. We know from our sample Ideal Teacher description that students want teachers to let them know how they are doing. Yet even in SLC we must modulate our approach on how best to intervene. A typical response to a student receiving a D or F would be to assign them to tutorials. However, we are learning that tutorials meet with success for only some students. There are students who certainly need the extra academic assistance to build their skills and understanding as they struggle with subject matter. There are others, however, who are not succeeding because of a myriad of challenges they face at home or in other settings. These students do not necessarily benefit from tutorials; they need mentors and guides who can help them get back on track. Absent the SLC approach of teachers dedicated to looking at data and supporting students to success, and struggling students receive the same "treatment" and meet with uneven success.

Now we come to the potentially far more uncomfortable position of looking at D's and F's through several lenses, which gets us closer and closer to the classroom instruction. We will move from macro to micro levels and see what assumptions we can make about the data and pose some ways of utilizing these reports. These are real data for a real school of 1,202 students, but let us call it "Our High School." When we get to the specifics of classrooms, we have omitted names and simply listed the course title.

Tool Kit Snapshot 7.3	Whole-School Data

Number and Percent of Students Receiving Grades D and F, by Content Area, "Our High School"			
Subject	**D's** **Number (%)**	**F's** **Number (%)**	**Total** **Number**
Language arts	15 (4.7)	29 (9.1)	316
Math	41 (12.0)	69 (20.2)	340
Social studies	24 (8.0)	30 (10.0)	298
Science	24 (7.0)	69 (20.2)	340

As you begin your data discussions, you may find it helpful to take what I call a "first blush" approach. Here, you take a broad look at the data without making specific decisions or judgments. What are the things we might first assume before we dig deeper to get at the right answer? What are the assumptions that occur to us in looking at this data? In the data table in Tool Kit Snapshot 7.3, the D and F data for core subjects in "Our High School" are presented. The numbers in parentheses indicate percentages, the other number is the actual number of students receiving either a D or an F. The total numbers of students enrolled in the core areas is in the final column.

The first-blush approach shows that significantly fewer students are enrolled in social studies than in the other core areas, most likely because of state requirements. We can also see that the D and F rate is higher in this distribution than for language arts. We can see that there is a significant challenge in math with 32.2 percent of all students enrolled in this course receiving D's or F's. The comparable figure for science is 27.2 percent. This presents an opportunity for interventions, but of what type? Do the students need the support or do the teachers? How do we account for that unknown of "what does it mean to earn a D from one teacher versus an F from another?"

Now, let us go a bit deeper and look at the data by content area (see Tool Kit Snapshot 7.4).

Please keep using the first-blush approach. A review of the course listings indicates that many remedial courses are offered. However, many researchers would note that this practice does not call all students to reach high standards. So this is an area we will want to study further. What are the trends within departments and across departments? Where are students meeting with success, and where are they in most need of support? Which departments have the greatest work ahead of them if they are truly committed to *continuous improvement*?

A look at the English I "D and F" distributions shows us that this is where most students struggle in English. This mirrors the national trend. It is understandable, but is it acceptable? As you review the data, what else occurs to you? Look at the number of students who are struggling even in courses noted as "H" for Honors. What might this tell us about appropriate placement of students? Does it open the opportunity for a discussion about what rigor looks like in a classroom? Is Honors

Tool Kit Snapshot 7.4	Content Area Data

Number and Percent of Students Receiving Grades D and F, by Course, "Our High School"		
Course	**D's** Number (%)	**F's** Number (%)	**Total** Number
English I	11 (10.0)	20 (18.0)	109
English II	2 (3.0)	5 (4.0)	78
English II H		2 (7)	29
English III	3 (4.0)	10 (12.8)	78
English III H	2 (4.0)	2 (4.0)	47
English IV	5 (7.0)	3 (4.0)	67
PreGED ELA	3 (6.0)	23 (44.0)	52
Geometry	17 (17.7)	22 (22.9)	96
Algebra I	9 (13.6)	20 (30.0)	66
Alg I Part I	17 (9.9)	36 (21.0)	171
Algebra II	4 (9.0)	9 (20.9)	43
Algebra II H	3 (9.0)	0	32
Gen Math	2 (6.0)	6 (19.3)	31
Trans Math	1 (7.0)	5 (35.7)	14
Financial Math	1 (3.0)	0	30
PreGED Math	1 (4)	9 (37.5)	24
Free Enterprise	3 (4.0)	11 (15.0)	72
American History	10 (13.6)	16 (21.9)	73
Geography H	1 (2.5)	1 (2.5)	40
Geography	4 (4.7)	16 (18.8)	85
Civics	5 (8.6)	4 (6.9)	58
World History H	1 (5.0)	1 (5)	19
World History	6 (10.0)	6 (10)	59
Biology	9 (12.0)	16 (21.9)	73
Biology H	3 (4.0)	4 (5.8)	68
Envir Sci	2 (5.0)	6 (16)	37
Physical Sci	13 (8.0)	48 (30)	159
Physics H	0	1 (2.9)	35
Exploring Sci	1 (11.0)	7 (77.8)	9
Chemistry	1 (5.0)	3 (15.7)	19

just more work, as we alluded to in the previous chapter in the discussion on rigor, or is it a different quality of work? If the answer is the latter, do we need courses designated as Honors or should all students have the opportunity to achieve at Honors standard? Using data in this first-blush and hold-harmless manner helps teachers begin a process of assessing instructional practice and enables departments to set goals for reducing the number of D's and F's. Yet there is still at least one more level—the classroom teacher. Let us look at Tool Kit Snapshot 7.5.

Tool Kit Snapshot 7.5 Classroom Course Data

Number and Percent of Students Receiving Grades D and F, by Class, "Our High School"		
Course	D's Number (%)	F's Number (%)	Total Number
Eng GED	0	5 (35.7)	14
Eng GED	0	4 (44.4)	9
Eng GED	3 (10.3)	14 (48.2)	29
Eng I	1 (5.8)	5 (29.4)	17
Eng I	3 (12.5)	4 (16.6)	24
Eng I	3 (18.7)	3 (18.7)	16
Eng I	1 (5.2)	2 (10.5)	19
Eng I	3 (15.0)	3 (15.0)	20
Eng I	0	3 (23.0)	13
Eng I H	0	0	26
Eng II	0	1 (4.0)	25
Eng II	1 (4.0)	2 (8.0)	25
Eng II	1 (3.5)	1 (3.5)	28
Eng II G	0	0	5
Eng II H	0	2 (6.8)	29
Eng III	0	1 (3.5)	28
Eng III	1 (4.0)	2 (8.0)	25
Eng III	2 (8.0)	7 (28.0)	25
Eng III H	2 (6.8)	2 (6.8)	29
Eng III H	0	0	18
Eng IIIG	0	0	8
Eng IV	4 (15.3)	1 (3.8)	26
Eng IV	0	1 (4.7)	21
Eng IV	1 (5.0)	1 (5.0)	20
Eng IV H	0	0	34
P-Calc H	0	0	16
Adv Math H	1 (4.1)	0	24
Geometry	2 (16.6)	6 (50.0)	12
Gen Math	0	2 (66.6)	3
Geometry	1 (5.8)	7 (41.1)	17
Algebra	6 (24.0)	10 (40.0)	25
Alg I P1	2 (8.0)	6 (24.0)	25
Alg I P1	2 (12.5)	4 (25.0)	16
Gen Math	0	2 (15.3)	13
Finan Math	1 (5.0)	0	20
Finan Math	0	0	10
Alg II	1 (9.0)	0	11
Geometry	6 (35.2)	3 (17.6)	17
Geometry	4 (30.7)	1 (7.6)	13
Alg I P1	6 (27.2)	2 (9.0)	22
Pre GED math	1 (11.1)	3 (33.3)	9
Pre GED math	0	6 (42.8)	14
Alg I	2 (9.0)	5 (22.7)	22
Alg I	1 (5.2)	5 (26.3)	19
Alg I P1	2 (13.3)	6 (40.0)	15
Trans Math	1 (7.1)	5 (35.7)	14
Alg I P1	1 (5.2)	5 (26.3)	19
Alg I H	0	1 (3.3)	30
Gen Math	0	0	5
Gen Math	2 (20.0)	2 (20.0)	10
Alg II	0	4 (40.0)	10

(Continued)

Tool Kit Snapshot 7.5 (Continued)

Course	D's Number (%)	F's Number (%)	Total Number
	Number and Percent of Students Receiving Grades D and F, by Class, "Our High School"		
Geometry	1 (10.0)	0	10
Alg II H	3 (9.3)	0	32
Alg II	3 (13.6)	5 (22.7)	22
Alg I P1	3 (12.5)	9 (37.5)	24
Alg I P1	1 (5.0)	12 (60.0)	20
Geometry	3 (11.1)	5 (18.5)	27
Geometry G	0	0	7
Adv Math II G	0	0	5
PreGED Math	0	0	1
Free Ent	0	0	32
Free Ent	2 (8.3)	7 (29.1)	24
Free Ent	1 (6.2)	4 (25)	16
Am Hist	1 (5)	11 (55)	20
World Hist H	1 (5.2)	1 (5.2)	19
Am Hist	1 (7.6)	4 (30.7)	13
Geo H	1 (5.0)	1 (5.0)	20
Geo H	0	0	20
Am Hist	7 (33.3)	0	21
Civics	2 (13.3)	2 (13.3)	15
Civics	2 (14.0)	0	14
Geo	0	4 (25.0)	16
World Hist	3 (21.4)	5 (35.7)	14
Geo	0	6 (28.5)	21
World Hist	3 (10.7)	0	28
World Hist	0	1 (5.8)	17
Geo	3 (12.5)	3 (12.5)	24
Civics	1 (3.4)	2 (6.8)	29
Geo	1 (4.1)	3 (12.5)	24
Biology	2 (8.0)	5 (20.0)	25
Envi Sci	2 (10.5)	3 (15.7)	19
Envi Sci	0	3 (16.6)	18
Biology	2 (14.2)	2 (14.2)	14
Phys Sci	0	3 (25.0)	12
Phys Sci	3 (14.2)	8 (38.0)	21
Physics H	0	0	22
Expl Sci	1 (11.1)	7 (77.7)	9
Physics H	0	1 (7.6)	13
Biology H	0	1 (3.7)	27
Biology	0	5 (41.6)	12
Biology	5 (22.7)	4 (18.1)	22
Phys Sci	2 (6.6)	2 (6.6)	30
Phys Sci	0	9 (56.2)	16
Phys Sci	1 (6.2)	10 (62.5)	16
Phys Sci	0	6 (33.3)	18
Phys Sci	2 (9.5)	6 (28.5)	21
Phys Sci	5 (20.0)	4 (16.0)	25
Chemistry	1 (5.2)	3 (15.7)	19
Biology H	0	1 (5.8)	17
Biology H	3 (12.5)	2 (8.3)	24
Chemistry H	0	0	26

Here there are many first-blush assumptions to be worried and wondered about. Look at the differences in class size. Does this seem to make a difference in student achievement? Is the level of instruction—or the success of students—different, for example, with each of the teachers teaching Honors biology? Even if you could assume that it is the students' "fault" for not attending class or being recalcitrant, is it acceptable to have 44.4 percent of students in Pre GED Math, a course of just *nine* students, receiving either a D or an F? This is the time for both departmental and individual teacher intervention; however, without the availability of a "D and F" report to launch the conversation, you will not get there. These reports provide the on-ramp for discussions about specific students and specific teachers. They are much more personal than the student results on the state test. Use these reports to open a dialogue that focuses on what students need in order to succeed and what teachers need to help them succeed. Engage teachers as part of the solution. There may be one thousand reasons why Johnny cannot read—he may be placed in the wrong class, he may need a vision assessment, he may have issues at home and in the community that keep him from participating, he may have met with so many incidences of past school failure that he is unmotivated. There may also be scheduling indicators that have led to certain class "D and F" reports. Was a new teacher given a large class of ninth graders? Was the assistant principal so mired in discipline issues that he or she was unable to support that teacher? Did the team not look at data at progress reporting periods, thus missing the opportunity to provide interventions? Did class size, teacher certifications, the adoption of a new curriculum, or a shift in instructional focus affect achievement? Regardless, it is still the teacher's responsibility to teach Johnny. Are the D's and F's the result of poor teaching? It is a serious question, and we cannot assume the answer is "yes" or "no." This is something we have to face in each and every one of our schools, and we can only do this through a process of inspection and reflection coupled with good coaching.

We have bundled all three of these tables in the Tool Kit in order that you can replicate this activity with your teams. It will be much more powerful and useful, however, if you run your own specific data reports that allow you to get to a personal level of discussion. In making it even more personal, you may want to follow the lead of Adlai Stevenson High School in Michigan. When staff first engaged in the "D and F" reporting process, they posted the names of every student receiving those grades. They then asked themselves the question "which one of these students' names can we erase because we will not or cannot teach them?" Their answer was none. Instead, they erased the students' names only when they had created the appropriate tutorials and support mechanisms that removed the student from the "D and F" listing. Like Toyota, they knew what quality meant. It did not mean leaving these students behind.

USE OF TIME

The pace of schools and districts is daunting. Both classroom teachers and school and district administrators need to work more efficiently and use time to their advantage. Classroom teachers will need support in the use of common planning time. Initial moves in this direction have been uneven at best. Not all teachers have made the shift to realizing that this is not the time for them to prepare their classes in isolation. Common planning time has specific anticipated outcomes for looking at data, student work, teacher assignments, curriculum integration, professional practice, student interventions, and personalization—this is new to high school teachers. Schedules will need to reflect the negotiated agreement that supports classroom preparation. They will also need to reflect common time when teachers can work to examine student work and teacher assignments, study data, discuss support strategies, and model and practice instructional strategies. Many teams will need help in getting started; this is where the DIF and Instructional Improvement Team come into play. Protocols and strategies for thinking about, talking about, and solving problems or opportunities can be particularly helpful to group development. Here, we would refer you to the NSRF and Critical Friends Group training noted in the Resources section.

Although non-classroom teachers have a much more flexible—albeit no less demanding—school day, they too have to ensure that their schedule of activities reflects adherence to their mission as instructional leaders: striking the balance between classroom visits, instructional practice, meeting with parents and community members, and managing the school. For many of these individuals, the day gets whittled away by tasks that never seem to lead them to the results they hope for: a focus on instruction, strategic planning, classroom observations, and effective leadership. Building on the work of the National Association of Secondary School Principals (NASSP), we have developed the MS Excel [7.6 Use of Time] file contained in the Tool Kit (see Tool Kit Snapshot 7.6). For school and district leaders, the most precious commodity is their vision and ability to shape and change organizations. The biggest challenge to accomplishing this is frequently time. The [7.6 Use of Time] file contains five tabs/pages. The first reflects the text in this section. The three immediately following it are three "Sample Day" charts, followed by a summary sheet that calculates how you spend your time.

How It Works

Please pick three days over a two-week period that reflect how you regularly and typically spend your time. Fill in the chart on tabs 2–4 by cataloguing your activity and placing a number between one and four, correlating with the quadrant descriptions, next to that activity. Each activity can reside in only one quadrant. Ranking an activity in multiple quadrants will give you a score of over 100 percent of your time. You can certainly do this by hand as you walk through your days—but taking the time to enter your data directly in the Excel file provides you with specific calculations based on embedded formulas. Using the tool in this manner gives you specific targets to shoot for and adjust your practice, helping you use your time in the quadrant areas that are most important to school success. If you have a half-hour segment with multiple activities, you must determine where you will rank that half hour. If, however, you spend two hours in a meeting, you can determine where certain aspects of the meeting fall based on the quadrants. We have also provided space for you to make notes about possible adjustments to your work. The summary sheet tallies your three days and prompts you to strategize about a more effective and efficient use of time.

In *Battling the Hamster Wheel* (Sammon, 2006, p. 34), I identified seven habits of highly effective schools regarding time:

1. Demonstrate high expectations and a vision that matches it.

2. Build capacity and create a true climate for success.

3. Think small and dream big.

(Text continues on page 162)

Tool Kit Snapshot 7.6 | Use of Time

Use of Time Leadership Matrix

Fill in the chart on each sheet by cataloguing your activity and placing a number between 1 and 4, according to the quadrants below, next to that activity. Each activity can reside in only one quadrant. Ranking an activity in multiple quadrants will give you a score of over 100 percent of your time. The Excel formulas embedded in the sheets summarize your activity for the day. If you have a half-hour segment with multiple activities, you must determine where you will rank that half hour. If, however, you spend two hours in a meeting, you can determine where certain aspects of the meeting fall based on the quadrants. We have also provided space for you to make notes about possible adjustments to your work. The summary sheet tallies your three days and prompts you to strategize about a more effective and efficient use of time.

I	**Urgent and Important** Crisis Pressing problems Deadline-driven projects Meeting preparation	**II**	**Not Urgent and Important** Prevention Values clarification Planning Relationship building Empowerment
III	**Urgent and Unimportant** Interruptions *Some* mail, reports, meetings Popular activities Pressing matters	**IV**	**Neither Urgent nor Important** Busy work Junk mail *Some* phone calls Escape activities

- *Quadrant I*: represents tasks that are both "urgent" and "important." This is where we deal with an irate parent, meet a deadline, or handle an emergency. We cannot avoid spending time in Quadrant I. This is the Quadrant of Management, where we bring our experience and judgment together to respond to many challenges. If we ignore the tasks in this quadrant, they typically escalate into hard-to-solve challenges.

- *Quadrant II*: represents tasks that are "important" but not "urgent." This is the Quadrant of Quality. Here is where we conduct long-range planning, anticipate and prevent problems, empower others, and increase our skills through effective professional development. Increasing time in this quadrant increases our ability to effectively lead. Investing in this quadrant shrinks Quadrant I tasks. Planning, preparation, and prevention keep many things from becoming urgent. Ignoring this quadrant enlarges the tasks in Quadrant I, creating stress, burnout, and deeper crises. Quadrant II empowers you to look at the best use of your time with the thought of importance rather than urgency

- *Quadrant III:* is the shadow of Quadrant I. It includes tasks that are "urgent" but not "important." This is the Quadrant of Deception. The feelings of urgency create the illusion of importance. The actual activities, if they are important at all, are only important to someone else. Many phone calls, meetings, and drop-in visitors fall in this Quadrant. We typically spend a lot of time dealing with Quadrant III tasks, meeting other people's priorities and thinking we are really in Quadrant I. A quick way to distinguish between Quadrants I and III is to ask yourself whether the urgent task contributes to an important objective.

- *Quadrant IV:* contains those tasks that are neither "urgent" nor "important." This is the Quadrant of Waste. We really should not be in this quadrant at all but we sometimes seek relief from the tasks of Quadrants I and III. Such things as reviewing junk mail, escape activities, and some phone calls reside in this quadrant.

(Continued)

Tool Kit Snapshot 7.6	(Continued)

Use of Time—Day 1

Date						

Time	Activity	Quadrant				"Adjustment"
	Please place the number 1, 2, 3, or 4 in the appropriate Quadrant columns to ensure accurate calculations.	I	II	III	IV	
7:30						
8:00						
8:30						
9:00						
9:30						
10:30						
11:00						
12:00						
12:30						
1:00						
1:30						
2:00						
2:30						
3:00						
3:30						
4:00						
4:30						
5:00						
5:30						
6:00						
6:30						
7:00						
8:00						
	Totals	0%	0%	0%	0%	

Notes on the day:

Use of Time—Day 2

Date						
Time	**Activity**	**Quadrant**				**"Adjustment"**
Please place the number 1, 2, 3, or 4 in the appropriate Quadrant columns to ensure accurate calculations.		I	II	III	IV	
7:30						
8:00						
8:30						
9:00						
9:30						
10:30						
11:00						
12:00						
12:30						
1:00						
1:30						
2:00						
2:30						
3:00						
3:30						
4:00						
4:30						
5:00						
5:30						
6:00						
6:30						
7:00						
8:00						
	Totals	0%	0%	0%	0%	

Notes on the day:

(Continued)

Tool Kit Snapshot 7.6   (Continued)

Use of Time—Day 3

Date						
Time	**Activity**	**Quadrant**				**"Adjustment"**
	Please place the number 1, 2, 3, or 4 in the appropriate Quadrant columns to ensure accurate calculations.	**I**	**II**	**III**	**IV**	
7:30						
8:00						
8:30						
9:00						
9:30						
10:30						
11:00						
12:00						
12:30						
1:00						
1:30						
2:00						
2:30						
3:00						
3:30						
4:00						
4:30						
5:00						
5:30						
6:00						
6:30						
7:00						
8:00						
Totals		**0%**	**0%**	**0%**	**0%**	

Notes on the day:

Use of Time Leadership Summary Matrix

I	Urgent and Important MANAGEMENT		II	Not Urgent and Important QUALITY
Day 1	0%		Day 1	0%
Day 2	0%		Day 2	0%
Day 3	0%		Day 3	0%
Overall	**0%**		**Overall**	**0%**
III	Urgent & Unimportant DECEPTION		IV	Neither Urgent nor Important WASTE
Day 1	0%		Day 1	0%
Day 2	0%		Day 2	0%
Day 3	0%		Day 3	0%
Overall	**0%**		**Overall**	**0%**

Your strategies to increase your effectiveness:

1	
2	
3	
4	
5	
6	
7	
8	

4. Engage in legitimate community support.

5. Thrive with strong, sustained, and shared leadership.

6. Effectively align and manage resources.

7. Understand time.

Each of these is essential to the work you undertake in creating effective SLC. Specific here is understanding that the effective use of time is the deciding factor in developing the other habits.

PROFESSIONAL DEVELOPMENT

The amount of staff development needed by your school and within each SLC team will vary depending on their previous experiences. You have already documented this in Chapter 3 with the [3.2 Teacher Readiness] tool. Revisit that work now. The staff development strategy for each team, and for the school, will also need to be tied to your district's staff development office. Each year, that office will likely provide a list of staff training offerings and will have a central theme and goal for its teachers. You will want to honor these at the same time as you are fighting for the specific needs of your faculty, based on its skills and the mission you are trying to meet. Those working in SLC have a specific set of needs that ensure the teachers have the appropriate administrative supports to succeed and that they have capacity in the following areas:

- Working as a team. When the teachers can begin to work as a team, trust each other, learn to plan together, and learn to rely on the balance of their talents, the entire SLC will succeed in ways you can only imagine.
- Using time and meeting times effectively
- Visiting sites within their district and beyond that are working in the SLC/academy structure
- Teaching strategies for the extended-period day, for those who you are working in any variation of block scheduling
- Creating advisories
- Participating in externships associated with their SLC industry theme
- Working with partners and community organizations
- Strategic planning.

Like Wiggins and McTighe (2006), "we are advocating for something more than the professional learning communities that DuFour and others have so eloquently described." We believe that "School leaders need to create job requirements that make learning *about learning* mandatory" (Wiggins & McTighe, 2006). The DIF and Instructional Improvement Team assessments noted above move us in that direction. In a like manner, teachers should be invited into a process that has them develop for themselves a standard and rubric for which they agree they can be measured. As we did with the other groups, this process should be one of engagement and not of dictation. Based on the individualized experiences and practices of your faculty members, the [3.2 Teacher Readiness] tool has automatically calculated, on a 4.0 scale, their readiness for change, their knowledge of SLC, approach to curricula, and involvement in partnerships. At a meeting in Tennessee one assistant principal commented,

It's a very useful tool. It allowed us to see quickly that we, as a staff, are stronger in business and community partnerships than we believed we were and that our small learning community structures and faculty were pretty well established. Where we needed to put our emphasis for this year was not in those areas but in getting teachers to work more closely at integrating career and academic and industry standards into our classrooms. [Teacher Readiness] helped us design our staff development. In addition, we can measure our success by revisiting and recalculating our staff's growth based on shifting priorities and staff turnover.

What also becomes apparent once a scan of the faculty is performed is that there are individuals who do not need certain staff development activities but, of course, need to be involved in others. Recognizing and valuing staff skill sets and previous training, encouraging staff to lead certain aspects of a staff development, or giving them the freedom to design and carry out their own professional development all have a positive effect on every aspect of the school. Such actions build morale and self-esteem, add depth to the overall expertise of the faculty, and encourage the types of leadership skills required in schools today.

WILL THIS IMPACT STUDENT ACHIEVEMENT?

In the end, it comes down to the fundamental question of student success. Are teachers meeting the needs of the students by effectively preparing them to take their places in the workplace and in higher education across the globe? Do they leave school with the knowledge, skills, and abilities to do this? Regardless of educational initiatives, that will always be the job and the challenge of good teaching. If we approach professional practice and staff development with the same sound educational principles we know work with our students, and follow a systematic approach, we will be able to meet our goals. We will sustain our successes and operate from a position of continued growth and development, not one of continually redefining and retooling. That formula can only have a positive impact on student achievement.

PULLING THE PIECES TOGETHER

If there is one role that falls over and over again to the practitioner, it is coordinating priorities. You have learned this already as you balance multiple meetings, the myriad of "Punch List" tasks, and now instructional practice, the use of time, and professional development. Here are some critically important points for you to consider in assessing where you are and build momentum.

Planning Staff Development

Planning appropriate staff development means assessing the school's financial and programmatic resources. Many schools have access to multiple grants, consultants, and implementation strategies. However, there is rarely any effort to coordinate these resources or to have the various consulting teams jointly discuss the overall mission and status of each other's work. It is an extremely useful exercise for school leaders, and those tasked with training and technical assistance, to approach staff development and school reform efforts in a coordinated manner. We touched on this before with the [4.1 Initiative and Partnership Identification and Alignment] tool. If you did not use the tool then, you may wish to revisit it in light of staff development needs. This entails laying out the mission, the skills of the faculty, the specific training/consulting activities of the variety of consultants/trainers, and a discussion of timelines, methodologies, deliverables, tools, and objectives.

Attending conferences can be an important part of staff development. Travel to new sites, engaging with new colleagues, and attending workshop sessions all do a great deal to boost morale and expand awareness. However, these experiences are extremely expensive and need to be woven into a *strategic* plan for staff development. In reviewing potential conferences, determine how specifically they fit your mission. Who on your school team(s) may be ready to be a conference presenter, who should be there to learn? What is the specific outcome you want from the conference? Ask the conference coordinators to send a detailed agenda *before* you register. Review the sessions and their descriptions, and then assign team members to specific sessions. Spread the team among sessions, highlighting what lesson you want learned from that session. Have your teams "de-brief" at the end of each day so they can use this as a working session and capture the best practices. We have developed [7.7 Lessons Shared] in the Tool Kit specifically for this purpose (see Tool Kit Snapshot 7.7). In addition, have attendees build in a time when they can develop a plan for integrating the lessons learned into their school plan. Have those who attend report back to the whole team and the school at large on what was learned and how the lessons learned can be used to further improvement goals. An effective way to do this is to dedicate staff development days as miniconferences where teachers have multiple options to learn from each other.

At a Glance: Summing It Up and Next Steps

Coordination of school resources makes for not only a coherent, systematic, supportive staff development strategy, but one where the multiple objectives can be supported by an array of sequenced training and the time to work in a manner which enables those skills to be *evidenced and demonstrated* in practices. The essence of why a school or system moves to SLC is to create an environment in which quality teaching and attention to professional practice can flourish. The practitioner has to serve as the person who facilitates data-driven discussions in a manner that enables educators to learn and apply that learning to their work. This commitment to data and reflection has not been the norm in most of our high schools. It is the norm in organizations that seek to continually improve on the quality of their work. In the next chapter, we will reach out to our community partners to learn from them, seek their support, involve them in meaningful ways with our staff and students, and continue to push on further in our commitment to creating or enhancing a quality school.

Tool Kit Snapshot 7.7 Lessons Shared

Lessons Shared

Workshop Name _____   Presenter _____

Contact Information _____   Person Attending _____

Key Practices   **Key Points**

1. _____   1. _____

2. _____   2. _____

3. _____   3. _____

4. _____   4. _____

5. _____   5. _____

Pitfalls to Be Avoided: **How We Should Apply This:**

_____   _____

_____   _____

_____   _____

_____   _____

_____   _____

_____   _____

Lessons Learned:

_____

_____

_____

_____

_____

_____

8

Powerful Partnerships

Teamwork is the ability to work together toward a common vision. The ability to direct individual accomplishments toward organizational objectives. It is the fuel that allows common people to attain uncommon results.

—Andrew Carnegie

Chapter 8 Road Map

Purpose	To expand the circle of those that can positively impact the school's direction toward school improvement and industry-specific development.
Stage of Implementation	Establishing Structures, Commitment and Engagement—focus on partnerships and personalization.
Process and Action Steps	Review partnership audit from Chapter 4. Check on your Punch List progress. Discuss with Continuous Improvement Committee the role of partnerships in the school and in each SLC. Determine role of various partner organizations. Determine whether you are going to establish schoolwide and/or SLC-specific partnership boards.
Tool Kit	*None*; however, please refer back to [4.1 Initiative and Partnership Identification and Alignment].
Reflective Practice	What role is played by partnerships in our *continuous improvement* goals for students *and* teachers? Is the inclusion of partnerships "just" about relevance or is it also about skill standards? Do we have a strategy to include partners in meaningful ways? Is our strategy focused on true partnerships? What does our current school culture reflect about the importance we place on work-based experiences compared with "academic" work?
Outcome	Areas for need and support, as well as ways to give back to partners, will be defined. Partnership strategy will be developed. Student work-based learning will be defined and planned.

W e are coming down the home stretch in addressing the elements that, when thoughtfully implemented and continually assessed, lead to effective and sustainable SLC. Two critical pieces, however, have not yet been addressed: partnerships—essential to any design—and personalization—the defining piece of SLC educational delivery. As you will see here and in the next chapter, these two pieces are closely intertwined and play key roles in achieving student success. Establishing and tapping into business and community partnerships invites the opportunity to bring resources and expertise into the school to enhance every aspect of the school's structure. Seeking community and business partners can make the critical difference not only in terms of real resources, but also in the relevance of the academy education to the students.

PARTNERSHIP DEFINED

At the outset, let us be clear about what partnership means. It means a *collective commitment and a sense of accountability to a shared vision.* Partnerships are two-way streets. In education, all too often we have made them one-way streets. We have not sought partnerships but rather simple *relationships* that have left us largely on the asking and receiving end. We have traditionally used partners to provide us with some missing element that a budget did not cover. We have erred in making them more about money than about the partners' expertise or interest. We have rarely invited partners to the table as colleagues and as true and equal partners in a process that creates a vision, reflects on and assesses whether we are meeting that vision, and as the ones who help strategize how we can move the vision to success. Indeed, Reverend Bill Byron, former president of Catholic University in Washington, DC, has a valuable lesson for those seeking to work with partners: "first you friend raise, *then* you fund raise." Once you capture the hearts and minds of your partners, and directly engage them with your students and teachers, everything else becomes possible.

PARTNERSHIP POSSIBILITIES

The list of what is possible is quite extensive, as you will see throughout this chapter. Keep in mind that *partnerships,* rather than *relationships,* are more about a commitment to a shared vision and accountability for it than about money and resources.

Here is a sample of desirable targets for your partnerships:

- Creating success for students through in-school lectures, work-based experiences, and serving as mentors and role models
- Creating success for teachers through providing teacher work-based experiences and teacher mentorships
- Increasingly effective use of school funds and resources through a review of spending practices by the board
- Dealing with short-term concerns and a long-term vision
- Reviewing curriculum and providing enhancements
- Developing strategic plans

- Meeting students' needs beyond the classroom by assisting students with personal and social needs—grief counseling, personal development, needs for work-appropriate clothing, and help with negotiating social systems
- Securing equipment and resources
- Helping with recognition, awards, and scholarships
- Offering team training—partners can help focus and deliver training and workshops for teachers and student leadership. (It is also critically important to take the time to train and orient the partners to the school setting.)
- Focusing on outcomes and evaluations—clearly, educational reform is demanding more accountability for positive student outcomes. Partners can identify research trends and conduct evaluations that are both anecdotal and statistical. Postsecondary partners may be a particular asset here.
- Securing paid and nonpaid job experiences for students.

BUSINESS BASICS

These valuable contributions to your improvement plans will rely heavily on partnerships. As we can see from one school's experience, schools in the twenty-first century will increasingly be driven by partnerships. As Dr. Mildred Musgrove, former principal of Anacostia Senior High School in Washington, DC, so adeptly points out,

> The millennium brings with it increasing demands on schools to do more than they are now to prepare students for the world of work and for educational experiences beyond high school. As educators we must accept that we can no longer work in isolation to help our students meet the challenges they face. We are already experiencing the increased demands on us to do more to raise the academic achievement of our students. The public has grown impatient with the state of public education in this country. It is clear, educators are being asked to raise the bar for themselves and their students, and to fill the gaps left by some families and some agencies.
>
> Those of us who are principals know, perhaps better than anyone else, that we are being asked to accomplish more with limited, and in some cases, no resources. If we do not turn to our communities to help we will fall short of our goals.

Indeed, educators across the country are turning to their communities to establish a broad range of partnerships that go far beyond even the wildest imaginations of educators of the past. The concept for educators and business and community leaders has evolved from a paternalistic "adopt us" attitude to one of full working agreements. In these, principals and the range of partners (families, business, community organizations, FBO, and postsecondary institutions) have had to learn new ways of working together, developing a vision and sharing responsibility for the growth and development of students.

In Raymond E. Callahan's (1964) *Education and the Cult of Efficiency*, listed as a "Book of the Century" by the Museum of Education at the University of South Carolina, he discusses the role of school administrators in the early part of the twentieth century and documents the influence of business management practices and philosophies on

American schools. This influence was the genesis for practices that have continued to impact the way we do business in education today—namely, classroom management practices, individualized curriculum, efficiency of education, and standardized qualifications.

A thoughtful approach, blending business and educational practice, allows administrators to be both more efficient and more educationally effective. Principal Musgrove adopted this approach and saw tangible payoffs in her school. Anacostia High School is among the most challenged in the nation. However, this school of five career academies can point to business partnerships and supports in each of them. The partners add depth to the school's ability to begin to turn around high dropout rates and low test scores. At her school, Dr. Musgrove relied on partners to provide job shadowing, mentoring, and internship experiences for her students *and* staff; to develop *and* deliver courses along with her regular faculty; to assist with the development of technology skill development; to raise scholarship money for students; and to provide guidance to her and individual academy teams by serving on advisory boards. While this is an extensive list of assets, Dr. Musgrove was quick to point out that

> We can provide solid evidence of our partnerships, but the greatest service these partners provide is intangible. Business and community partnerships provide students with the sense that there are caring adults throughout the community who want to see them succeed. There is no way that school alone could get that critically important message directly to students.

Marianne Becton, Director of Strategic Alliances for Verizon Washington, reinforces that commitment to student success. Ms. Becton highlights Verizon's role in making a major difference in Washington and as a vested partner in the educational reform movement in the District of Columbia. Becton cochaired the District's Local Partnership Council and believes that kind of commitment by businesses to the education process is the key to successfully preparing our youth for careers in the twenty-first century. "Education in general, and public education, specifically, is the cornerstone of our culture and an absolute necessity for economic prosperity," states Becton.

Today's partnerships supersede the traditional role of businesses, the occasional forays into schools for special programs and activities. Successful partnerships involve the training of educators and administrators, as well as students, and involve all levels of a company, not just its executives. These partnerships are more about shared responsibility than corporate donations.

As one of the largest employers in the District of Columbia, Verizon has considerable real estate, capital, and human investments in Washington, DC. Many of its employees work and live in the District. Their commitment to education is driven by their responsibility as good corporate citizens and, even more, by the understanding that today's students will be tomorrow's employees, consumers, regulators, and neighbors. On a more immediate basis, business partnerships make a difference by training current students and improving the quality of their lives and their communities today.

Ms. Becton works with diverse stakeholders who share a common vision of changing how and what students are taught in our public schools. In addition to curriculum content for technology courses, the stakeholders focus on using technology to improve teaching techniques and learning across all subjects. Their goal is to prepare our students as continuous learners who are workforce-ready.

Ms. Becton sees it clearly:

> Teachers face major challenges, a fact that impacts teacher training, recruitment and retention. Without support from the community at large, including business, all of our students will suffer. We seek to attract other businesses to make the same commitment that Verizon has made. As a leader in the business community, we sponsor mentoring, job shadowing and internships for our students and encourage our business partners to do the same. In a highly competitive and record high employment marketplace, some businesses may find it difficult to commit human resources to these kinds of programs. But we all realize that money alone will not cure today's education problems. Instead, a commitment to make a difference in someone's life is the impetus we seek to foster among our colleagues. We encourage our employees at all levels to volunteer as tutors and mentors, a commitment that money cannot buy.

The Verizon team understands that success can be elusive and is not immediate. They have made a long-term commitment to partner with the school system to ensure success. During their tenure with partnering with Washington, DC, schools, they have been able to identify some very practical guidelines for successfully engaging other business and community organization to support schools. The list is helpful to businesses which are involved with schools. For educators seeking to expand or refine their partnerships, knowing what business thinks works best is critical. Here are Verizon's Business Basics of Partnerships:

- Take a leadership role in governing bodies.
- Use your CEO as a cheerleader.
- Challenge competitors and other businesses to make similar commitments.
- Engage employees at all levels of the organization to volunteer.
- Partner capital resources with human resources.
- Find education stakeholders at all levels: principals, other administrators, teachers, aides, and mostly students.
- Find external stakeholders throughout the community: other businesses, organized labor, CBO, faith-community, postsecondary institutions, and others.

Increasingly, corporations, unions, professional associations, government agencies, postsecondary institutions, and nonprofit organizations are investing in the community through a commitment to education. In fact, some are redefining their mission statements specifically to join their corporate mission with a direct impact on the communities they serve. Several years ago, the Community Development Specialist at Integris Health, a not-for-profit health care system in Oklahoma, shared the Integris story: "The mission of Integris is to improve the health of the people *and of the community* it serves." This mission guides Integris's decisions and actions, guiding every partnership. They call this commitment *returnship*. Simply stated, *returnship* is giving back in a financial, emotional, physical, and spiritual way a portion of what we have received from the community.

Like Verizon, Integris is in it for the long haul with school partnerships and school supports. A particular partnership with Putnum City High School's Health

Academy put it on the map as one of U.S. Secretary of Health and Human Services' Health Career pilot site programs. This innovative partnership with the school has students and teachers in academy programs involved in a variety of ways at the hospital, including organ donation and retrieval with the Oklahoma Organ Donor Network. According to Putnam City Schools, "There is simply no way the value of Integris' commitment to education and the students can be assigned a dollar value. The rewards, the challenges and the opportunities for students and staff offered through real partnership are simply priceless."

While we can point to extraordinary examples of partnerships from coast to coast like those with Verizon and Integris, and we can hear the accolades from educators, the establishment of such exemplary programs still seems elusive for many educators. As we noted in Chapter 4, some studies point out that 90 percent of school business partnerships fail within the first year. Part of that failure is due to a lack of understanding of the nature of partnership, and part of it is due to a failure to understand the very different worlds of school and business.

Traditionally, we think of partnerships as only those involving business, but today's school climate calls for more. Whether it is partnerships between teachers of different disciplines, between teachers and business/community partners, between students and their community-based adult role models, or between families and school staff, each partnership adds individual depth to the life of the school and brings about successful outcomes for students. Establishing successful partnerships is just like establishing any relationship. It takes time, clear communication, flexibility, and constant attention. Partnership relationships are the essence of these learning communities, and specifically of career academies. Without the strong support of the community in a strategic, clear, measurable plan, school reverts to "school as usual."

People commit to getting involved in school partnerships for a variety of reasons that range from being "good corporate citizens" to enhancing the mission of their own organization. Corporate culture and practices will define the parameters under which an organization may become involved in your work. The more aware you are of a specific organization's practices, the more effective you will be in your ability to attract and manage your partnerships. For example, business partners are strongly driven by time and cost efficiency. Meeting times are measured in "time is money," and it is important for schools to realize that an hour-long meeting of multiple partners is viewed as an expenditure of literally hundreds or thousands of dollars. Government partners, on the other hand, must tailor their involvement to how the task furthers the mission of their agency, bureau, or department and live within the parameters set by federal ethics and performance mandates. Community-based organizations (CBO), such as many nonprofits, will be interested in enhancing the life of the community by generating or applying their current resources to the mission at hand. Postsecondary partners have a range of interests from "corporate" commitments to recruitment, to research designs, and placements for graduate student practicum experiences. Important to the partnership strategy should be the inclusion of parents and alumni. This most frequently overlooked resource should be surveyed as to their interests and careers, where they work, whether they can serve as speakers or as workplace hosts. In making a selection of who you should approach for support, you should become familiar with some of the individual characteristics and philosophies of the varied individuals and organizations available to help you meet your *continuous improvement* goals.

KEY INGREDIENTS IN CREATING AND SUSTAINING PARTNERSHIPS

Know That You Do Not Have to Forge Partnerships on Your Own

Become familiar with those who are responsible for creating and sustaining community partnerships for your school district. There will certainly be a central office staff person designated as having this responsibility. There is a growing national interest in creating or designating independent intermediary organizations that help broker effective relationships and resources between schools and business. It will therefore be important to quickly identify whether there is an intermediary organization, or public education network affiliate, identified in your district which facilitates school improvement, grants, education policy, or partnerships. Identifying those who are tasked with supporting the schools will make developing a partnership strategy smooth. These individuals will help you align your needs to existing and potential partnerships. They will also be able to assist you in determining whether there is competition for certain resources or a protocol to follow in approaching partners. In addition, they may serve as brokers, negotiating the varied worlds of corporate and organizational cultures and making the match between school and partner.

Other Organizations

There are other organizations which can help identify and broker resources at little or no cost to schools and districts. Local Chambers of Commerce frequently assume responsibilities for building a bridge between community groups and education. In addition, exemplary organizations such as the National 4-H Council and many of its local councils, and Junior Achievement (JA) hold at their very center the forging of effective educational partnerships between schools and their communities.

Building Your Partnership Team

Identify the knowledge, skills, and abilities you are working at inculcating in your students and staff, then set out to build your partnership team. If you did not conduct the partnership audit and the set of guiding questions discussed in Chapter 4, please refer to it now. In the Tool Kit, this is found in [4.1 Initiative and Partnership Identification and Alignment] on the second tab of the Excel file. Catalog all your partnerships, formal and informal. Begin to think of the multiple consultants you may hire as partners in the process as well. In listing your partners, be as specific as possible about how these partners help you meet your mission and goals. After you have done this, determine—again through the lens of the guiding question—what is missing. From that point, you can hone a strategy for continuing and expanding your work with partners.

Identify What You Need to Accomplish

Create a partnership strategy. Set a goal. Refer back to [6.1 SLC Pathways Course and Experience Planning] and [4.2 or 4.3 the SLC Punch List], review the list of partnership possibilities above, and talk with both the Continuous Improvement Team and each SLC to learn of their needs and plans. Use these tools to focus your work and plan. In developing business and community partners, it is critical that the mission be clear. If it is unclear why you are establishing the partnerships, it is going to be impossible to find common ground on which to build.

STRUCTURES AND STRATEGIES

Once you have proceeded this far in your work on partnerships, you will want to determine how you want your partnerships structured. As we mentioned in Chapter 3, there are informal and formal partnerships. Not every encounter with partners will have to be solidified into a formal agreement and the development of an advisory board. However, you will want to consider the establishment of a cadre of true partners that will make a long-term commitment to supporting your effort. Indeed, successful organizations like the NAF insist that the establishment of formal partnerships and a supportive board must be the first step in the establishment of academies.

Regardless of the formality of your partnerships, you will want to ensure that you have practices in place that keep students, staff, and families safe. Several states now require fingerprinting and background checks for anyone who has the opportunity to be directly in contact with students. Several even have regulations for how families can be contacted and can access information about their child. Identify regulations within your district, plan for how they will impact you partnership plan, and communicate how they will be addressed openly.

When partnerships fail, it is often because the "cultures" of work and schools are so different that they lead to missed communication and missed opportunities. Schools need to have a better understanding of the time sensitivity, value-added, and financial sensitivities of business and community organizations. In a like manner, nonschool entities need to have increased awareness of the demands of working in frequently underequipped buildings, with perhaps several thousand young people, with hundreds of adults, and very rigid schedules. So a first key to a successful partnership with schools and community organizations must be to take the time to get to know each other's organization, its needs, and its resources. Create time for potential partners and partners to visit classrooms and talk with students and teachers. Teachers, as you will see below, also gain important experience from time in workplaces other than their own.

Teachers also benefit from one-on-one partnerships. Teachers around the country are reporting the need for, and the benefit of, having work-based mentors to help bring relevance to their curriculum. Through no fault of their own, teachers were not prepared to build career awareness of all aspects of the industry for all students into the high school classrooms. As teachers continue to be asked to do just this in increasing numbers, they have reported that the partnering of their skills with those of other professionals engaged in a career area related to their academy/SLC's discipline has been invaluable. Teachers can best understand the value of the SCANS and industry standards discussed in Chapter 6 when they have experience with worlds of work beyond education. Today's teachers will want to incorporate partnerships in their efforts to incorporate real-world and project-based examples into their curriculum. This teaming with partners is a challenge for many at the high school level where traditionally teachers have been divided into subject area departments. Applying teacher-specific subject knowledge to an SLC theme can be a challenge; however, as we saw in Chapter 6, partners can help. Teachers can benefit immensely from job shadowing. They quickly gain information on careers and industries that are readily incorporated into their classrooms. To encourage the "two-way street" discussed earlier, partners should be encouraged, whenever possible, to shadow at the school site. Most partners will be astonished at the pace of a teacher's day, the early start, the afterschool meetings, the multiple demands, limited time to return phone calls or check on e-mail. The business communities' understanding of the culture of school is vastly different than the realities faced by those who work in schools every day. Strive to make shadowing a regular part of your planning for both educators and partners.

As you fine-tune your goals, you will ultimately seek to establish a formal relationship with some partners and create an advisory board. You will want to have agreements and understandings of any parameters set by your district under which boards can work in your school. You will also want to ensure from the start that participation on the board has real meaning and substance. Partners should not be asked to simply rubber stamp principals' decisions or be asked to work on efforts that will then be wasted because there is no follow-through at the school level.

In establishing a partnership, board roles should be clearly established, a regular meeting schedule should be set, officers elected, and operating practices put in place. In some instances, the board may wish to establish itself as an independent 501(c)(3) nonprofit organization that would allow it to attract grants and scholarships to the program independent of school system funding.

WORK-BASED LEARNING

Perhaps the most distinct contribution of the School-to-Work initiative was the critical element of linking students' school-based learning with real experiences in the workplace, thus providing students with opportunities to meet, and form relationships, with adult role models. This section links closely with the next chapter's focus on the student experience. In exit surveys conducted with students, many define their relationship with their business hosts as among the most important of their high school careers. Regardless of your determination to have a career-focused or CTE completer sequence as part of your SLC design, you will want to ensure a broad range of experiences beyond the classroom and in multiple worlds of work is included. These experiences should be increasingly comprehensive, build skills over time, and be focused on developing students' skills. In the case of career-themed and CTE programs, these work-based experiences are essential. The result should be students who are positioned to seek *and maintain* employment and postsecondary experiences.

In this section, we have outlined the basics for work-based programs. The comprehensive sequence of activities, implementation steps, skill standards, and evaluations is captured in *Insights, Shadows, and Mentors: A Comprehensive Series of Work-based Learning Experiences* (Sammon & Donegan, 2006), noted in the Resources section.

THE "WHY" OF EMPLOYABILITY SKILLS

Connecting students to the workplace has profound results. These experiences have the following impacts:

- They enhance the curriculum in ways "class" cannot—they bring *relevance* to coursework. Please refer to Chapter 6, on curriculum, and this chapter, on partnerships. Design programs to meet the specific goals you have for your students.
- They build self-esteem—as students gain skills both in preparing for and actually participating on the job, they become more self-reliant, composed, and confident.
- They provide substantive links to partners—your community base of partners should seek tangible links to the program and to youth.
- They are ranked consistently high by students. Exit surveys indicate that the workplace experiences, and links to adult role models, are among the top components of a student's high school experience, keeping them focused and in school.

THE "WHEN" OF EMPLOYABILITY SKILLS

Partner surveys indicate that the most successful student programs are designed so that they are increasingly complex in nature. Partners want to start working with students as early in their high school careers as possible. It is one reason that we created the Brief-cases program discussed in Chapter 6. When students are involved early on with employers and partners, the results are clear:

- The longer the exposure at worksites, the greater a student's personal and professional development.
- The longer the exposure, the greater the commitment and involvement of the partners is in the SLC.
- The earlier the experiences begin, the more developed a student's appreciation for work becomes.
- While the goals and practices of employability programs have been discussed, it is truly in the practice of the developmental steps and the strict attention to detail that the success or failure of the programs lies. For the program to succeed for all stakeholders, the work-based component must be introduced appropriately.

DEVELOPING WORK-BASED EXPERIENCES

Determine an appropriate introduction to work-based experiences through in- and out-visit programs with employers. This will entail some of the same steps that we have followed in other chapters: assessing what is already in place, capturing the best practices and what is making them work, and developing a training strategy so that the program is understood and accepted. This is best accomplished by the following tenets: use both a school-based and work-based approach for teachers and students and work toward ensuring that the work-based programs follow the following pattern:

- Address issues of liability, exposure, and student safety.
- Create designs that include increasingly demanding interactions and accountability measures based on specific SLC goals.
- Understand and respect the fact that the students are young people, not young professionals; rather, they are young professionals in the making. The programs need to be developed so that the students succeed. This means having experiences which meet their skill and development level.
- Tie the work-based experiences to school learning. It cannot be stated often enough that there needs to be a clearly defined link between the school learning and the workplace learning. If the two activities are performed in separate silos, they both lose relevance and importance.
- Work to ensure true teacher buy-in.
- While staff development is addressed in other chapters, it is important to have a specific staff development approach that addresses the importance of work-based learning. Involving teachers in advisory boards, mentorships, and their own work-based job shadowing and externships, as well as involving partners in the curricular life of the school, as described in the section on brief-cases in Chapter 6, will help tremendously.
- Develop clear lines of responsibility.
- Determine which staff can be responsible for the many detailed tasks that ensure work-based program success. Sample tasks follow:
  - Developing a calendar of coordinated activities
  - Defining the specifics of the school program
  - Preparing students with "soft skills"
  - Serving as a student advisor
  - Coordinating with partners/business hosts
  - Working on student résumés, cover letters, thank-you notes
  - Assisting with service learning and work-based academic links
  - Handling the preparation and follow-up activities.
- Constantly monitor for success and failure. Any program that involves students, schools, and businesses—and therefore a variety of "cultures"—will have many challenges that can stand in the way of success. The work-based programs are highly visible programs that stretch and stress an individual's patience. Because these programs take a great deal of time, and are subject to changes on all sides of the equation, it is imperative that a regular set of checks and balances be put in place to monitor the programs.
- Agree at the outset that there will be failures and that these will be addressed immediately. Have a strategy in place to address such issues as students not showing up for an assigned shadows experience. In this example, have in place a system to check students in and out of school, make phone calls to the host sites, and work with the host sites in order that they understand that these are first and foremost students. That type of close contact with the hosts, along with strategies that are in place or quickly developed in response to challenging situations, will keep the overall program from failing. Business hosts will be more responsive and understanding when they can see the specifics of the school situation.

- Be flexible and adaptable to change. Be prepared to alter and adjust your program in a manner that makes the most sense for success. In one work-based program, students had traditionally gone to school in the morning, then to their work assignments in the afternoon, and then returned to school for afterschool activities. Students did not like the schedule because of bus fare costs and travel time. Employers did not like it because the students sometimes arrived late and needed to leave early. Schools, however, did like it. They were used to having the students come to school in the morning, take attendance, and then leave for the day. It took a two-hour planning meeting before a student suggested, "Let's just change schedules and have the students' classes scheduled in the afternoon next semester. That way we save on bus fares, we're not going back and forth, and our bosses aren't always wondering if we have to leave early for something back at school." It made perfect sense once it was said out loud. The student, not the adults, had the answer, and the success and satisfaction rate of the program improved.

The CASN Web site, previously mentioned and included in the Resources section, has a variety of downloadable forms and materials related to the establishment of boards that are extremely worthwhile.

At a Glance: Summing It Up and Next Steps

Partnerships can make a powerful difference in the way *continuous improvement* and SLC goals are met. Assess the current partnerships for your school and build a database of your current resources. Track the number and types of partnership contacts and opportunities you generate in a year. Determine whether you will create or utilize districtwide, schoolwide, and/or SLC-specific advisory boards. Designate a point of contact for working with partners. Make sure the contact person has the requisite skills of knowing how to interact with the business community, and respond in a timely manner. Ensure that this person is provided with the time and supports for making phone calls, attending meetings, and communicating on paper and via e-mail. A single point of contact will make it easier for everyone to know who is coordinating activities, resources, and needs. In approaching a potential partner, see whether you have an "in"—a parent who may work at that site or perhaps an alumni link. If not, start with the organization's Community Relations Office. If the organization is not large enough to have a Community Relations Office, try the Personnel Office.

The primary rule is to establish a true partnership by taking the time to learn about each other's needs and interests and then developing a common vision and shared responsibility for the effective education of youth. Do not "over ask" for things, items, or support. Find the right match for potential partners' interests and your needs and you will get the "yes" you need to build the partnership.

Time needs to be taken to develop a team attitude and to build an understanding of the two very different cultures of school and nonschool work environments. Provide partners with data about school and student outcomes. Partnerships need to be constantly evaluated and assessed. Everyone needs to be flexible to adjustments that need to be made. Always have clear, honest communication about challenges, pitfalls, problems, and successes. Say "thank you" often and in a variety of ways. Make partnerships a two-way street. Invite partners to plays, concerts, and sporting events. Make your JROTC cadets available for partners' retirement ceremonies and special events. Offer your choir for holiday parties. Be creative—the possibilities are limitless.

At a time of increased demands on all educators and increased expectations for teacher accountability and student success, it is only through the establishment of truly successful, comprehensive partnerships that schools will be able to provide students a full range of high-expectation opportunities for learning. It will be through partnerships that teachers will receive the richest and most sustained training. And it is through partnerships that principals will be able to continue to lead their schools creatively. In the next chapter, we will focus on the most important aspect of our work—the student experience. After all, they are the central players on the team.

9

The Student Experience

Making It Personal

The secret in education lies in respecting the student.

—Ralph Waldo Emerson

Chapter 9 Road Map

Purpose	To expand on the possible structures and practices that contribute to personalization and attention to a student-rich experience.
Stage of Implementation	Establishing Structures, Engagement and Commitment—focus on personalization.
Process and Action Steps	Review all work to date through the lens of what students experience. Create successful work-based placements. Begin to hone a culture that encourages and listens to the student voice.
Tool Kit	9.1 Placement Checklist
Reflective Practice	What evidence do we have in policy and practice that we hold students at the center of our work in a high-standards, respectful way? What evidence do have that we do not? Are there real ways for students to have input in creating, enhancing, and altering school culture and community?
Outcome	Final decisions will be made on polices and practices related to SLC and personalization for all students. Strategies will be in place for successful work-based learning.

It has taken over one hundred pages of this text, and countless hours of your time, to come to the point where we focus specifically on the student experience. Many federal and state initiatives call for the needs of all students to be addressed, and while some would argue that that legislation is sometimes difficult to understand, the wording is clear. "All" means *all:* students with special needs, speakers of languages other than English, out-of-school youth, academically high-performing students, teen mothers, students in nonpublic schools, adjudicated youth, students in public charter schools, those advancing to postsecondary education, and those who will be going directly to work all need to be able to access and benefit from the our educational system. In many ways, this should have been the first of our chapters because, at their core, SLC nurture a student in a unique setting to reach personal and academic success. At the center of this work is a belief in and commitment to the tenet that all students deserve our best work, our unwavering respect, a rigorous curriculum, and tiers of support as they travel through our high schools. The inclusive language of *all students* is the focal point for SLC. *Continuous improvement* means focusing on *all* students. In this chapter, we will build on multiple tools and your work to date. While this may in some ways be a mechanical chapter about the student experience, focusing on school-based and work-based components of SLC, please keep in focus the reason we put so much emphasis on the details: to provide a rigorous, relevant, personalized education that reaps results for *each* student.

SCHOOL-BASED STRUCTURES

Facility Design and SLC Identity

There is a great deal of debate about facilities design and costs as they relate to creating SLC. Regardless of the decision you have made to separate your SLC from each other, or to create a separate ninth grade, every SLC will benefit from having its own area of the building in which to hold its classes and establish its own identity through such indicators as signs, ID tags, and—when desirable—uniforms or "SLC attire."

Many schools feel that the assigning of a class area, wing, or floor to an SLC is a difficult task because of the placement of such key resources as science labs, music rooms, or art suites. A schoolwide facility team can usually work out the issues of space after a careful walk-through of the building, studying floor plans, and setting class schedules. Naturally, there will be incidents when students and classroom space cross over between SLC, but the goal is to establish a learning area that promotes a sense of community and minimizes movement in the building.

Student name badges with photos can be developed specifically for each SLC. If your students are participating in job shadowing or internships, the ID tags will make it easier for students as they arrive at work-based experiences, many of which now require a photo ID (for government agencies, a valid government-issue ID may be required). The ID also makes hall monitoring more effective as staff can tell at a glance, usually by the color of the ID, whether a student is in the approved area.

Many SLC also choose to create a logo or "learning signature" that can be used on signs welcoming students and visitors to the SLC, on promotional brochures, letterhead stationery, business cards, certificates, and on "SLC attire."

Selecting the Students

All of the work to date has set the stage for selecting and welcoming students to your SLC. As you move forward, please keep in mind that the single best indicator of how a student will perform in an SLC is that the student has chosen to be there. As part of your planning process, have the SLC teaching team meet and discuss what type of student would best benefit from the type of learning environment it is creating and how it can ensure that all students succeed. Has the team considered students' career areas of interest and learning styles? Is it working with guidance and using the Holland Interest Inventory or a similar instrument as a guide? How do the mission and commitment statements the team has already created attract students? How will those mission statements be in evidence each day, in each classroom? Is the team paying attention to potential racial, ethnic, or gender biases when it considers potential students? Has it considered course prerequisites? Does it have an idea of the types of SCANS and "academic" skills that are important for the SLC? The team should be able to articulate these areas in discussion with families, partners, and students.

Once the team has a clear vision of its program elements and the students it seeks, a policy needs to be set for awareness and application. We highly recommend a student application process as part of the selection criteria. The application absolutely should not—and in the case of any federally funded SLC may not—drive a decision on student acceptance. Perceived academic ability and skill cannot be the indicators of acceptance. You will want to ensure equity and not create a "smart kid academy." Rather, the application process reinforces a thoughtful process about what the high school experience should comprise and lead to for *all* students and their families. The more the school can reinforce the lessons of the real world, such as college and job applications, the more students will gain skills and confidence in their abilities. A simple application form that reflects student name, ID number, contact numbers, grade point average, extracurricular activities, and interests sets the right tone and allows teams to acquire vital information about potential students. A note of recommendation from a teacher, counselor, or community person is also an important component of the process. Students should also be asked to submit a copy of their transcript. This helps in two ways. First, they get used to the process of organizing transcripts. Second, they get to see—perhaps for the first time—how their student record is catalogued. Of utmost importance is a short writing sample that invites the student to describe why he or she wants to attend the SLC.

Those SLC housed in schools with a ninth grade academy will undoubtedly have built in some bridging activities with the current freshman class by engaging these students in field trips, service learning, assemblies, and other awareness activities. Those schools with designated nine to twelve structures will want to build strong alliances with feeder pattern schools in order to create a series of activities and media that build awareness and generate interest in their programs.

Students should be encouraged to rank their SLC choices as not all students will get their first choice. The work you do with the middle schools and the ninth grade students in preparing them for making smart SLC selections will undoubtedly include work with guidance counselors and families. While we would like to believe that students always pick their SLC based on this hard work, it is likely that they will select their SLC based on a friendship or other relationship, or at the direction of a parent.

If you are moving from a traditional school to wall-to-wall communities immediately, you will need to determine how student interest will balance with numbers of students in SLC. In our experience, the numbers of students seeking entrance to specific SLC tends to balance out across all SLC. You will also want to determine which activities you will include at the start of your program and which ones you will want to include later on so that neither you, nor the rest of the school, is overwhelmed. This is where the Punch List will come in handy.

Once the application process is established, applications should be submitted and reviewed. Whenever possible, include families and partners in an interviewing process of the students. The idea is to continually reinforce life lessons and to build, from the very start, a sense that being in the SLC is a special, distinct experience—that selection comes with rights and responsibilities and is a privilege.

While there are few absolute deadlines in the SLC planning process, student selection is one that must occur in tandem with the school cycle of building the master schedule—usually in February and into the spring of each year. If you are using an interest inventory, you will need to ensure that this is purchased and scheduled. The drive for the midwinter process is to guarantee that the master and student class schedules can be set in a timely manner.

Once students are selected, they and their families should be notified and an orientation program that involves families, faculty, school staff, and upper-level students should be planned. It is a time for celebration, course selection, communicating the mission, and building a team of this new part of the SLC "family."

A Transfer Strategy

How do we address a student's request to move from one SLC to another? This is a frequently asked SLC design question. Students who change their career or SLC interests, and those who move from school to school, cause a special challenge in the establishment of stable, consistent SLC. Both situations need to be addressed and prepared for in a thoughtful way. Today our schools are highly transient places. One school in Muskegon, Michigan, noted that, at the end of the academic year, not one of the kindergarten students who had begun the year had concluded it with the class in June. Families move; students drop in and out; migrant labor is a norm in many communities; students move between family members; and some are in and out of the juvenile justice system. The result is that students move in and out of high school at amazing rates. Schools, struggling to design increasingly comprehensive programs that build on experiences and result in a specific skill set, certificate of mastery, or portfolio experience, find themselves with the added challenge of meeting the educational needs of a student who transfers into a program in the later years of high school. These situations point out the need to have three transfer strategies in place.

First, internal to the school, a policy on student transfers between SLC needs to be established. While there will be an exception to every rule, there does need to be some operating principle that indicates a decision point of "no return" after which students can no longer easily transfer between programs simply on the basis of a change of academic or career interest. Various programs may have varying levels of flexibility in allowing changes between programs. Counseling students about the broad theme of the SLC and "all aspects of the industry" can frequently re-engage a student's interest in a specific program. The guiding forces here should be the student's well-being and his or her ability to continue to be actively involved in a meaningful education. One consideration in a transfer strategy between SLC within a building is a student's ability to finish a prescribed "completer sequence," major, or pathway. Most programs opt for a policy that asks all students to stay in the SLC for the full academic year, allowing only one change across SLC during the high school years.

Second, in addressing transfers between schools, districts with multiple high schools would benefit by establishing a policy on schedules, credits, and educational experiences. For one school within a district, for example, to move to a block schedule without realizing the potential impact on a student's ability to accrue credits should they transfer to a different district school can be troublesome. Close coordination between the establishment of new or changed programs in your SLC and district policies and practices will obviate the need for complex transfer interventions. In a like manner, whenever possible you will want to send your students off to other schools with a complete record of the SLC experience that includes not only the academic credits earned but documentation of the work-based, service learning, portfolio, and other experiences that have been the total of their educational experience.

A third approach includes a documented effort for how to transition transfer students *into* SLC programs when they come to you from other schools. This strategy will need to include careful review of student records, sensitivity to student interests, and a specific practice for student orientation.

PERSONALIZING THE LEARNING EXPERIENCE

Students and faculty unfamiliar with the SLC "culture" will be unfamiliar with the myriad of practices that other practitioners and your own teams have worked so hard to establish. They may be unused to, and untrained in, basic expectations and traditions and will need an orientation to bring them "up to speed." Many of these traditions are captured beautiful in Peggy Silva and Bob Mackin's *Standards of Mind and Heart: Creating the Good High School* (2002). We have captured some of the key personalization elements for you below.

Welcome!

In a time when an increased number of students are "welcomed" to school by a metal detector and school security, an important practice being employed by the best of schools is a means to greet the students each morning. This usually entails a cycle of faculty members *and administrators* agreeing to stand in the SLC area each morning and welcome students *by name* as they enter the SLC area *and* as they enter each class. To be truly personal—the intent of the entire SLC—this practice should not be about focusing on the deficits of hats, belts, IDs, and the like. One of the principals with whom we work said he had read a research study that documented the number one question students are asked in school. Take a moment and think what the question might be. It is "where are you supposed to be?" This principal suggested that if he got each teacher to simply ask instead "What are you reading?" "Are you having a good day?" or "How is it going?" *before* asking "where are you supposed to be?" school climate would improve! This is a time to "catch students doing something good," notice successes, connect informally with students, and set high expectations. This is a great time to ask what students are learning, to prime them with an excitement for an upcoming project or activity, or to offer opportunities for extra help.

Putting the "Home" in Homeroom

In the chapter on professional practice, we discussed teachers serving as advisors and guides. As more and more schools opt out of homerooms—traditionally used for the business of running schools—and choose instead to implement advisory programs, we see a new opportunity to provide students with a home base and a place to stay connected to school and a caring adult. There is more information on advisories in the Resources section. There implementation, while widely called for in almost all program designs, is decidedly uneven. Not surprisingly, the results are as well. One reason is that few programs start their planning with the five key dimensions of advisory in mind: purpose, organization, content, assessment, and leadership.

The advisory period should be a time for taking stock, realizing who is attending and who is not, looking at grades, identifying strategies students need to succeed, welcoming students who have been missing, and sending out feelers for information on students who may need assistance. High standards and support—both personal and academic— are the primary goals of advisory. It is a time to match talents and abilities with needs and deficits. This is a great place for teachers to "ZAP" students. Again, with the dual focus of attention to data and consistent support of students, teachers monitor students' grades well before they are in danger of failing a course. Zeros Are Not Possible (ZAP) is a simple technique that directs students to the extra help they need to get back on track quickly. When advisory does not seem to matter to students, they will tell you it is because it does not seem to matter to the teachers. Advisory raises questions of "extra preps" and a change of requirements around the practice of teaching. The "culture" of the SLC should be clearly reflected in advisory. It should be a place to which students want, and need, to stay connected. A skillful teacher can create a sense of belonging and accountability among the students.

Student-Led Conferences

Preparing students to assume a role in making decisions about their futures, having them process how and what they learn, and providing a platform for engaging families and partners in a student's academic life are all goals of student-led conferences. During the student-led conferences, students present samples of work to their invited guests. It is part exhibition and part assessment. These conferences take preparation. Students engaged in them will need your support in looking at and assessing their own work and setting goals for improvement. A typical "script" for a conference would include the following points:

- These are samples of work from the following class or classes . . .
- To complete this class I had to . . .
- I am proud of this piece of work because . . .
- The strength of my work in this class includes . . .
- The weakness of my work in this class is . . .
- If I were to take this class again, I would do the following . . .
- Please give your feedback on what I have presented to you.

Student Organizations and Afterschool Activities

Not all activities during students' high school experience should be narrowly focused on either their intended career focus or academic interest. High school is a time to explore interests, build skills, and build relationships. For many, the public high school experience will be their last opportunity to explore and indulge their talents and interests. That said, there are some natural matches between career themes, student interests, and the wide array of school activities, clubs, and community/afterschool activities. In planning to build students' skills, or in planning on providing them with a comprehensive opportunity to explore their chosen career field, practitioners will want to make every attempt to suggest and match student interest to the offerings in the school and the community. As we noted in the chapter on pathways development, this is the time to discern the natural extracurricular links to the sequences you created.

SERVICE LEARNING/COMMUNITY SERVICE

"Giving back" to the community through dedicated volunteer service has become a national trend. School systems, determined and mandated to address issues of "character education," have begun to require service hours for graduation. These volunteer experiences are perfect occasions to expand student understanding of "habits of the mind and habits of the heart."

The SLC experience provides the opportunity to maximize the benefit of community service for students, teachers, and the community by doing four things:

1. Matching the type of student volunteer experiences students seek to their area of interests or chosen career area

2. Expanding the SLC's ability to place students in work-based experiences

3. Building students' skills and knowledge through a range and depth of volunteer experiences

4. Using a graduation requirement for completion of service hours to further develop a student's knowledge, skills, ability, and self-esteem.

While the terms "community service" and "service learning" are sometimes used interchangeably, there is a distinct difference between the two experiences. Community service is a matter of donating your time and skills to a certain effort. Certainly, there is new learning taking place, but it is frequently unrecognized and uncataloged. Service learning, by design, brings the all-important *relevance* to the volunteer experience. By taking service experiences and tying them directly to the curriculum and the skills that we want students to "know and be able to do," the entire educational community becomes involved in expanding students' volunteer experience and matching it to their career and educational goals. The difference in the experiences can be seen easily in the following example.

A Public Service Academy student chooses to assist in a "Christmas in April" house refurbishing project. In a community service activity, the student attends the event and has his or her hours documented. In a service learning scenario, the student does the same service but also makes correlations to the curriculum and to the careers that are in evidence. The possibilities are limitless. How many gallons does it take to paint a room that is 11 × 16 feet? What is the cost to paint the room (did they include brushes, drop cloths, pans, etc., in the budget)? What were the environmental conditions and laws that affected the house (lead paint, zoning issues, etc.)? What jobs were in evidence in the house refurbishment (e.g., military personnel, carpenters, plumbers, public relations)? What technology was in evidence? How is the experience documented and evaluated (e.g., written report, video, speaker/presentation)? What new skills were acquired (e.g., teamwork, time management, resource management, carpentry)? How does the community commitment to refurbish the house happen, through what nonprofit agencies, with what government support? How does this event tie to my public service academy program?

The difference between the two experiences, as you can see, is profound and clearly linked to both academic and industry skill standards.

THE SENIOR EXPERIENCE

The twelfth grade year is gaining new attention from educators across the nation. This pivotal year in a young person's life is the bridge between childhood and young adulthood. It is a time of retesting limits, gaining new independence, creating a life plan, and moving into a world with new rights and responsibilities. Increasingly, as educators are becoming more responsive to this adolescent stage of development, and as block schedules are allowing for students to finish required coursework in a condensed period of time, schools will want to revisit their expectations for twelfth grade students. Rather than being a year of coasting to graduation, as it is for many students, the senior year can be one of high expectations.

There are already excellent models for senior projects in place at schools across the country. The best programs capture a combination of work-based experiences, service learning, research, presentation, and technology applications that result in an exhibition which builds on the combined experience of the student, and demands a synthesized outcome that reflects a balance of "academic" and "real world" experiences. Frequently, the result is a senior project and portfolio that reflect all aspects of the student's study. The project is then presented to a review board.

Portfolio completion, college and job search, stress and time management, work-based learning, and a time for reflection are all being incorporated into senior experiences.

STUDENT VOICE

For over a decade, schools have been working to create more personalized learning environments that focus on students. However, remarkably absent from almost all of this work have been the active participation and the boisterous voices of our students. How odd it is that, in a design that has worked so hard to put in multiple levels of varied challenges and supports to students, we have all too often left them to be the silent and passive recipients of plans made by adults! In every instance where I have had the opportunity to involve students in my work, it has been enhanced by their insights. We have touched on some of the critical ways students' voices can be heard here and in Chapter 5. NWREL, noted in the Resources section, serves as an excellent site for helping schools find, nurture, and bring to the fore the benefits of listening to student voice. While the video tools and the tool kit are not available at this time, the Web resource is still valuable. Moreover, ask students what they believe to be true about their opportunity to share in creating personalized structures that meet their needs.

In the last chapter on partnerships, we discussed work-based learning and the importance it plays in partnerships that lead to creating relevant and rigorous learning environments. Here, we want to look at these experiences from the student's perspective.

MORE ABOUT WORK-BASED LEARNING: BRIEF, PERFORM, AND DEBRIEF *EVERYTHING*

As you plan to include successful work-based activities for students, it may be helpful to remember that this single triad of activity is essential to effective work-based learning programs. Students succeed if they know what to expect and if they are guided in how to connect the experience into new knowledge.

Brief

Students benefit from specific preparation. They need to have information and skills at their fingertips in order to transition into this new experience. In preparing students for a business site visit, for example, it is not enough to say "wear work-appropriate attire." Appropriate workplace attire is vastly different when visiting the work yards at the public utility than when you are visiting their corporate offices.

Here is a list of skills to develop and needs to address that will support student success:

- Time management skills
- An up-to-date résumé with current phone contact information
- Good eye contact, posture, and a firm handshake (the so-called "soft" skills)
- An understanding of why they are in work-based programs
- An appreciation of the time and commitment it takes on the part of the hosts to participate in these programs
- Place and dates of assignment(s)
- The time they start and finish
- The person to whom they will report
- The job, tasks, and activities they will be engaged in
- What they need to bring (photo ID for clearance, transportation and lunch money, résumé, writing materials)
- The person they call if they run into a problem
- How they get to the workplace
- How they should confirm and prepare for the experience
- What will be expected of them after the experience.

Perform

The on-site component is clearly where the essential learning will take place for students. These work-based experiences need to be closely developed and tailored to meet real outcomes. Employer hosts will need guidance and support to make the student experiences a balance of hands-on learning, professional development, time on task, and basic/routine assignments. The range of possible activities is truly endless. We have placed students in police cars, in hospital operating rooms, behind the scenes at the zoo, in senate office buildings, in federal and state agencies, and in the White House. At times, the work-based assignments are exciting. At times, they are mundane. It is all part of the learning about work that helps students make positive postsecondary choices and gain skills while they do it.

Debrief

After each activity, students need to be helped to make the continued connections from their work world to their school world. Each activity provides a different opportunity for a different type of reporting and debriefing structure: new skill acquisition suggests revisions of résumés; oral presentations on work-site experiences give students a forum to develop their public speaking skills; a newly acquired technology- or industry-related skill provides the opportunity for the student to teach others at school what they have learned; and regular thank-you letters develop positive habits and good writing skills.

Shared failures and successes allow students the opportunity to brainstorm better response strategies and to celebrate their accomplishments. In general, effective debriefing also gives the program organizers important information on how to fine-tune and tailor the program for increased learning and student success. The nature of reflective practice, which we have reinforced throughout this book, suggests that you look at all aspects of the work-based experiences: did we have clear goals, are we seeing results, were the student sufficiently prepared to succeed at the placement, were there program elements in place to support the host, are teachers using these experiences to deepen student learning, and are the administrative structures in place to support everyone's success?

A WORD ABOUT PLACEMENTS

In placing students at worksites, you will want to review aspects of your plan for diversity and cultural sensitivity. If you are placing students with physical challenges, you need to ensure that the worksite is equipped to meet each student's particular needs for accessibility. Special education students, even with profound challenges, can be paired with other students and succeed well in the workplace. In placing students who are speakers of English as a second language, you will want to be aware not only of their perhaps limited English proficiency, but also of cultural practices that may impact their participation (e.g., women traveling unsupervised on public transportation).

We would be remiss if we did not at least acknowledge the specific challenges faced by schools in suburban and rural communities when it comes to placing students in the workplace. Placing students in work-based experiences in nonurban areas poses transportation and partner challenges. The absence of public transportation, long commute times, and the lack of available partnership sites sometimes make it impossible to provide substantive work-based experiences. Some communities have attacked this problem by working on summer and holiday placements for their students. Others have embraced the establishment of school-based enterprises and electronic mentoring programs as vehicles for student exposure to work-based experiences. Regardless of the approach taken, developing an effective strategy for student experiences will demand thoughtfulness, commitment to partnership development, and inclusion of creative uses of technology.

JOB SHADOWING

Job shadowing is the act of pairing an individual (the learner) with a professional (the host) in a specific career area for the purpose of the learner gaining understanding, insight, and skills related to the host's industry and profession. Job shadowing can be for any length of time, but is usually a one- to three-day experience.

Job shadowing is usually the first intensive, hands-on workplace experience for students. It is within the context of job shadowing that students learn not only the important lessons of specific industries and individual careers, but also begin to make the critical distinction between what they like and what they dislike about these same areas. The defining of likes and dislikes is as important as any other lesson learned in career awareness and skill building and, perhaps most importantly, impacts a student's ability to make positive postsecondary choices.

Of all the work-based experiences, job shadowing is the one that is most time intensive and has the greatest exposure for school programs. Taking the time to ensure that you have the basics in place and have reviewed the "Placement Checklist" (Tool Kit Snapshot 9.1) before sending students into a shadows assignment will be worthwhile.

Tool Kit Snapshot 9.1	Placement Checklist

Placement Checklist

☐ Determine with the school team at what grade level and on how many occasions your students will be performing shadows.

☐ Review the school calendar and set dates for these activities so that they do not conflict with other school events (Advanced Placement tests, standardized tests, holidays, homecoming, other SLC program events, etc.).

☐ Determine who will be responsible for handling the pre- and follow-up activities (briefing/debriefing).

☐ Calendar all shadows dates. Make sure to place the critically important briefing and debriefing activities on the master calendar.

☐ Create permission slips for students specifically related to job shadowing. Students may travel on their own, using public transportation. They participate in activities that are not directly supervised by school personnel. Check on school and district policies for clearances and insurance that protect the student, the school, and the host. Since shadowing should be a prescribed part of your district's approach to education, the district's liability coverage *should* extend to the student. However, it is important to determine whether this is the case. You must ensure that all involved parties have an understanding of how the shadows program works and that the students are engaged in a nontraditional field experience.

☐ Beginning with the partnership audit you have already conducted, create a database of your school's supporters who can serve as shadows hosts. Include families, partners, alumni, and others. Work with the available district staff, chambers, and any designated partnership intermediaries to enhance your list.

☐ Begin to develop your business partners and contacts. Ascertain that they have an interest in working directly with students. Tell them of your willingness to work within the parameters they set (taking only the number of students they set, on only some of the dates, during specific times, with specific supports from you). Share with them that you are available to conduct an orientation for their staff on the shadowing program and will supply them with tips on how to work with students. Let them know that you will be having the students contact them before the program begins and that they will be asked to do a very short evaluation of the students' performance at the conclusion of their visit. Work with the hosts to create a day for the students that is part

hands-on, part observation, part discussion, and part interview. Your goal for shadows is to create an experience where the student gains real insight into and understanding of the various worlds of work. It is also important that you stress that the host's involvement is critical to developing the workforce of tomorrow and that the host's willingness to work with students who have an array of interests and skills will help transform them from professionals in the making to young professionals.

☐ Survey your students. Ask them what particular careers interest them within their industry theme. Once surveyed, you have a base from which to work for all your future placements. Do not be surprised if a student in a business SLC indicates that he or she wants to be an artist or if a student in a transportation SLC states an interest in cosmetology— these young people will have many interests. In a like manner, do not be surprised when, for example, a student in a law SLC indicates that his or her *only* interest is in being a lawyer and when you hand out the first shadows assignment with a lawyer, the student indicates that his or her interest has changed to a forensic scientist or ballistics expert.

☐ Create a database of all of your students, their dates of birth, student ID numbers, family contact information, and areas of interest. Having this on hand will make the entire shadows management process move more smoothly, and it will prepare you for the next steps of mentorships and internships.

☐ Prepare students with the "soft skills" they will need to succeed at shadows: teach them about using the transportation system and discuss and practice handshakes, phone skills, workplace diction, eye contact, and being on time.

☐ Develop individual résumés.

☐ Lay out the plan for their shadows experience and build the critical links between their school and workplace experiences.

☐ Develop a contract with the student that is signed by the student, a representative of the teaching team, and a family member. The contract should lay out the expectations and the ramifications of involvement in shadows.

☐ Match the students and their hosts at least two weeks before the students are to arrive and shadow. Send the hosts brief student bios or résumés so that the hosts can tailor the day to the students' interests.

☐ Prior to the placement visit(s), have students review their assignment, plan for how they will arrive at the work site (this may entail arranging transportation or transportation costs), determine what is appropriate workplace attire, and plan what to wear. They should also have a specific plan and requirement to call the host prior to the visit to confirm all the information with which you have provided them. These prework/briefing steps are critically important to ensure the success of the day and to building the students' skills. In many instances, students will not have appropriate workplace attire and you may need to creatively work with faith-based organizations (FBO), professional associations, friends, and others to secure a supply of clothing for the students.

☐ Have an established policy on emergency, weather, and other cancellation possibilities.

☐ On the day of the visit, you may want students to arrive at school prior to their setting out for the workplace. This gives you an opportunity to do last-minute checks on attire, transportation money, and possible truancies. Regardless of whether you have students arrive at school first, you will still want to call the hosts the morning of the visit to confirm student attendance, thank them for their participation, and contact any parents/guardians of students who chose not to participate.

☐ While on site, students should conduct *informational interviews* with their hosts, as well as participating in the activities the host has planned. The opportunity to discuss a prepared set of questions will give the students a focus for their visit and build their self-confidence.

☐ Following the visit, ask the host to complete a brief assessment of the visit and the program and fax the results to you. Students should also complete an assessment, make a presentation to the class, or otherwise chronicle their experience. They must write a letter of thanks to the host. Each of these activities, while obviously good business practice, builds the relevance between school and work that is so central to the theme of the SLC.

☐ You will want to follow up with students who did not successfully complete shadows. Possible scenarios are assisting with strategies to address the students' deterrents to participation (e.g., issues with clothing, funds, child care, or fear). You can consider linking the work-based experiences with a series of positive reinforcements.

MENTORSHIPS

Internships and mentorships both have at their base a specific, nurturing relationship between a professional and a developing professional. The mentor takes on the role of a "seasoned guide" who agrees to support the learners in their development. Mentors need not be directly associated with a student's work setting. However, in placing students at work sites, you will want to encourage all workplace supervisors to also agree to serve as mentors. The goal for creating mentor relationships is to provide students with:

- An extended community of support
- Specific and continued work-based and career exploration activities
- A focus on future employment and postsecondary education.

Some of the considerations for planning strong mentorships for your students are catalogued below.

- *Mentors can be of any age.* Consider using college and graduate students in your mentors pool. Mentor activities will need to be laid out clearly, tied to the overall goals you have set for student achievement, and include clearly drawn lines of responsibility.
- *Training for mentors helps.* You will want to conduct specific mentorship training for all those who agree to serve students in this manner. As the relationship between the student and his or her mentor grows, you will want to ensure that the relationship is appropriately supportive and conducted within appropriate boundaries.
- *Virtual mentoring is becoming more popular.* A growing phenomenon in mentor relationships is that of electronic mentoring, where the bulk of the relationship, questions, suggestions, edits on papers, and the like can be conducted online through e-mail correspondence or blogs. In each case, you will want to institute a policy and a practice that all electronic correspondence is automatically copied to someone at the school for the protection of all parties.

You will want to ensure that the structure you develop for your mentorships follows the same practices outlined above for shadowing. These experiences should be briefed, performed, and debriefed. They must be regularly evaluated, and they must have specific ties to school-based learning.

At a Glance: Summing It Up and Next Steps

Many of us are drawn to working in high schools because of the energy that surrounds adolescents as they move into young adulthood. By including students directly in the work of continually improving schools, we are gaining not only the very real opportunity to improve our own practice, but continually reinforcing a belief that students can succeed at high levels and that their voice has value in our work. In many ways, they are the experts among us. Creating structures through practice, policies, and experience ensures that the SLC experience is indeed personalized. At this juncture, you will have addressed the key elements of an effective high school and an effective SLC—because the two are synonymous. You have also committed to a process in establishing these structures that has built capacity in staff at each journey point. You have made a commitment to focus on data, curriculum and instruction, partnerships, a climate for success, and, critically, personalization. Now, it is time to assess, celebrate, plan anew, and continue to build everyone's capacity to succeed—including that of the students.

10

Sustaining

The Experts Are Among Us

The most splendid achievement of all is the constant striving to surpass yourself and to be worthy of your own approval.

—Denis Waitley

Chapter 10 Road Map

Purpose	To create a focus on reflection that leads toward ongoing assessment, fine-tuning, study, planning, and *continuous improvement* that all lead to a sustainable program, school gains, and successful, *effective* SLC.
Stage of Implementation	Evaluation—focus on data, building capacity and a climate for success.
Process and Action Steps	Create a study process, activate Peer Review Team, assess progress, gather data, reflect on the data, utilize the past and newly introduced tools, use the opportunity to listen to student voices.
Tool Kit	Reference all previous Tool Kit tools 10.1 Listen, Learn, Lead 10.2 Prides, Pitfalls, and Priorities 10.3 Informational Interview Questions 10.4 Measuring Up Evaluation
Reflective Practice	What gains have we made and why? How has each of our roles shifted and created or detracted from our plan? How are the subsets of the organization (be they SLC or schools within a district) improved? Do we know why? Do we believe the changes we have made are sustainable—*how is this evidenced*?
Outcome	Data gains and losses will be documented. Roles and responsibilities will be assessed. A study process will be concluded that results in a plan for ongoing, *continuous improvement*.

Vision, leadership, planning, flexibility, innovation, collaboration, personal accountability, and adherence to data and instruction—these are the elements that have brought you through this work and to this chapter. It will take all of these, and a thoughtful process of reflection, to bring you to the stage of your work where you can begin to expect that the efforts already accomplished are taking hold. After the work you have put in so far, the list should not surprise you. Simply establishing the SLC is only the beginning. Each program will need time to grow and mature. Practices will need to be tried, failed at, re-tuned, and refined. The individual efforts of a single SLC will need to be woven into the fabric of success for a whole school. In a like manner, successes at one school need to be documented and shared with its district and the nation. This chapter will outline and detail the steps necessary to ensure that you and your program meet the mission of not only creating SLC but documenting their successes and challenges as you work to see that the redesigned school thrives and flourishes. It is likely that your successes will be uneven as each SLC and school has its individual strengths and weaknesses. It will be very useful to have a healthy sense of competition and a commitment to lessons learned so that all schools meet their goals for every student and teacher.

We have moved from *formation,* to *study and assessment,* to *establishing structures,* to *engagement and commitment,* and have arrived at *evaluation.* This is the place when a great deal of hard work has already been accomplished. By this time, you have evidence of structural and cultural shifts within the organization. Now is the time to ask what the gains are. It is time to return to your mantra of Chapter 2 and ask, *"As evidenced how? What would it look like? What data do we have that what we are saying is real?"*

Successful organizations pay attention to their core mission and the elements of the organization that support it. In the case of SLC, the characteristics that create a true sense of community, and those you have worked hard to create up to this point, must be present. The regular cycle of schools—changing initiatives, the ebb and flow of funding streams, and the rotation of administrators and faculty—makes it very easy to get off task and to return to school as usual. As you move to the stage of evaluation and assessment, you must watch for "slippage." Without this ongoing commitment to taking stock of where you are and how far you have developed or deviated from your original plan, you will find that program elements and student successes quickly fall by the wayside.

In one of our early site implementations, we were able to measure marked increases in graduation rates over a three-year period. After that, however, graduation rates began to plummet, down 10 percent one year, an additional 4 percent the year after, and an amazing 15 percent the following year. The incredible gains of an almost 60 percent increase in graduation rates were being quickly eroded. The school hit bottom when the rate leveled out at just 25 percent over the initial baseline graduation figure. The causes were clear. The school had stopped paying attention to the practices that it had established to ensure success. Multiple changes of principals, failure to place students in programs based on their interests, and the lack of orientation and training of new staff caused several calamities including erosion of partner interest and support. The entire well-designed program began to unravel.

This is the time to revisit [2.2 Data Tracking Tool]. The feature that allows you to watch for average and net changes is critical in informing programmatic and personnel supports. Please remember that the whole-school sheet is designed for year-to-year analysis; however, the ninth grade sheet encourages a progress period-to-progress period review. If you have not already taught or empowered individual groups on how to garner, interpret, and apply the lessons evident from data, you must do this now. Keep in mind, as you work through this chapter, that SLC are designed for everyone's success—students, staff, and practitioners. Hopefully, you have already set both a measured pace and a tone that will breed success. While this is a chapter on sustaining, you also know—because you are committed to *continuous improvement*—that the real work of "reforming" schools is never done. Keeping things moving and setting the bar for the next focus of improvement and achievement will take continued attention to detail. However, like much else, it is not rocket science.

REVISITING THE PRACTITIONER'S ROLE

Throughout this book, you have learned about SLC implementation through the five bins of work and through the stages of formation, establishing structures, and engagement and commitment. You have been given tips and directions on how to accomplish specific objectives. In an earlier chapter, we suggested that you find your way to this page as a primer for what would come. As you arrive here, now in sequence, you will want to reflect on how well you have performed, and you will want to take stock of how your role is changing as you move into another stage of school improvement. As a practitioner—whether you are the principal, district leader, school improvement facilitator, program coordinator, consultant, board member, or member of a school improvement team, your overall success rests on being adaptive to the needs of your school and in your ability to do the following.

Continually Refine Your Own Role

Your job description alone will not define you. You will need to craft a specific role at your site to align with the school's specific "culture" and management style. The more clear you are about what you want your role to be and what you will accomplish, the more you will be able to be both a support and a leader in the SLC process. Moreover, you must model for others that roles and responsibilities are not stagnant. As you move more deeply into the redesign work of becoming a model school, and as new and sometimes competing initiatives pull at the fabric of what you are trying to accomplish, your own role will change. You will need to smoothly move from a role as resource provider and facilitator to a hands-on champion working on projects and tasks.

Take Charge

It is sometimes frustrating to wait for others to help you accomplish your tasks and realize your vision. You will often need to "lead the cause" for effective implementation. While you will always want to strive for collaboration, you cannot let the nonresponsiveness of others deter you from meeting your mission. This entails your active involvement in school, districtwide, and national efforts. You will need to be the best advocate for your school's needs and seek out the resources, skills, and individuals to help. Organization of time and resources will be essential to your success.

Ignite Others' Passion

To truly engage others in a cause, you must first be able to engage their minds and hearts and then follow up with a plan. Years ago, I read a piece on leadership. In it the author noted that Rev. Martin Luther King, Jr., did not ignite a nation's imagination by stating, "I have a *strategic plan*." It was the idea of a reachable dream that captured our imaginations. As a practitioner, you will need to tap each person's desire to meet with success for students. You will succeed if each person sees their individual importance in the accomplishment of the plan.

Determine People Assets and Build Capacity

Look at the strengths and deficits of your team and those on whom you rely to accomplish your goals. Conduct assessments and a self-assessment such as those referenced in Chapter 5. Share feedback on the assessments across stakeholder groups and seek to redefine your role to developing needs. It is a basic management principle—though we sometimes lose it in schools—to match the talents of your team to the tasks that need to be accomplished. Committee and planning work gives people a chance to use a variety of their talents and increase their skills and abilities. Reach out and make some—perhaps obvious—matches for getting the work accomplished—for example, statistical reporting by the math faculty, leadership development handled by your JROTC program, differentiated instruction introduced by your special education faculty, report writing by the English Department, meeting the needs of ESL students by the Language Department. To succeed at what you are working so hard to achieve—*effective SLC that invoke a commitment to continuous improvement and student success*—you will need to have varied and deep skill sets evident across the faculty. Once you have established your goals and the tasks associated with them, you will want to match your and others' strengths to the tasks at hand.

Recruit

The best programs meet success by recruiting the necessary resources and individuals to succeed. Once you have done your people assessment, rigorously recruit the special talents and resources you need to meet specific outcomes. For practitioners, this recruiting role will take the shape of reaching out to school and the community, postsecondary partners, school board members, funders, families, and potential partners.

Create a Sense of Urgency and a Disciplined Approach to the Work

The growing body of data on our teachers leaving the profession, drop outs, and graduation and college remediation rates alone should instill an urgency to achieve measurable results quickly. Schools are facing the greatest challenge to their futures with increased demands for state performance tests. Approximately half of all current teachers will retire by 2010. As a practitioner, you will need to instill a sense of urgency and dedication to mission in all those that are responsible for carrying out the SLC implementation. We know from the research cited throughout this book that effective implementation of SLC is the single best chance we have as a nation to meet with success in our comprehensive high schools.

Assess Results and Hold Hard Conversations

Later in this chapter, we will discuss several means of gathering results. Be open to looking at all aspects of the school and to pinpointing the areas that are most in need of improvement.

Communicate

Effective organizations and teams succeed when there is clear, regular, and useful communication in place for all those involved and affected by the process, event, or activity. As a practitioner, you must ensure that communications about events, training, initiatives, and services get posted and announced for staff, families, students, and community partners and that each of these is clearly linked to your school redesign and the commitment to *continuous improvement.*

Plan as far out as possible; cross check all dates with school, public, and religious holidays as well as those for sports events, homecoming, prom, and standardized test schedules. Use multiple approaches to get your message out, including the school and district calendars, your school and district Web pages, newsletters, weekly bulletins, assemblies, e-mails, and Listservs. Make information accessible for those who benefit from translation services.

Celebrate!

In a climate focused on change, improvement, and meeting school benchmarks for AYP, it is sometimes too easy to focus on the negative. Moreover, the magnitude of the tasks required for improving schools through the creation of effective SLC can make it appear as if we have not already accomplished great things, instituted successful practices, and seen students and teachers soar with success. Throughout your tenure with the implementation process, make sure that you catalogue what you have. Celebrate your successful benchmarks, goals, and accomplishments, and recognize the personal commitments of the many individuals who achieve and contribute to this important reform effort!

WHAT WILL IT TAKE TO SUCCEED?

Regardless of your place on the continuum of SLC evolution based on the tool we introduced in Chapter 2, you must constantly address the fundamental tenets and principles of your redesign. Remember that [2.3 (or 2.4) Data SLC Implementation Assessment (With CTE)] provides both a base line of data for initial planning and a means for documenting challenges and growth. It is designed as a tool that provides practitioners with a means to review specific elements of their program. Its usefulness will be as broad as the intensity of the scrutiny for each question raised. It is the linchpin for knowing if you are achieving and sustaining the goals you set.

WHAT DO SUCCESS AND SUSTAINABILITY LOOK LIKE?

Critical to the success of your implementation will be the ability to demonstrate the gains made by the administration, teachers, partners, and students in meeting the mission you have set for your SLC (see Box 10.1).

Box 10.1   Your SLC Mission

- Increases in student achievement as measured by state tests, GPA, numbers of students in honors and advanced placement (AP), numbers of students completing dual enrollment courses, and graduation and college-going rates
- Increases in student and teacher externships in the business and labor community
- Evidence of integrated, career-focused curricula being used in the classrooms
- Evidence of substantive partnerships between schools
- Increases in enrollment and completion of postsecondary education
- Increases in successful employment and retention
- Reports from the employer community that there is a definite improvement in the quality of their young employees.

Since data collection is extremely time consuming and the data themselves are often considered sensitive or proprietary, you do not want to spend time duplicating efforts. The first line of attack for data collection should be the multitude of reporting materials that are required by the school district. Unless you are already in school administration, you may be unaware of all reporting requirements or results of testing and assessments that are returned to the school. Develop with the principal to get a schedule of what reports are required, when they are due, where they are housed, and the results for the past few years. You should also ascertain what the policy is on use and distribution of the data.

A key area for data collection will be your site's involvement in one of several efforts focused on both self-study and third-party evaluation. Your willingness to receive feedback will set the tone for others who will also be reviewed, and it will provide you with information to improve your own performance. The added benefit of seeking feedback, of course, is that you reinforce for everyone that their input is wanted and is needed in order for things to improve.

TAKING STOCK: STUDY PROCESS AND THE PEER REVIEW

In our work with schools, we engage in a process of focused reflection when we near the end of our contracted time or when the end of a funding cycle is approaching. *Taking Stock,* a study process, began as a way to codify which schools had met the benchmarks set in grants and grew into a powerful tool to validate participants' work, share promising practices, focus on areas of need, and celebrate years of working toward a common goal. The process is relatively simple. Each school creates a study team, and it reviews the goals set at the time the redesign work was begun. The team examines its data then and now and it begins to chart out successes and challenges. As the story of implementation emerges, so do key questions—for example, why did we see gains in year three? Did the initiation of our literacy program have an impact on instruction? The study process is aimed at getting the questions answered and for positioning schools for the next body of work.

We believe that the study process should first and foremost be nonevaluative, nonjudgmental, and nonpunitive in nature. There are formal assessments and reviews for that purpose. The study process that we encourage is decidedly one of reflection and an opportunity to share with colleagues and other schools engaged in a similar change process. It should be made as easy as possible by establishing a not-too-rigid structure of inquiry which includes the previously mentioned data and goals review, but also informational interviews of staff and students. The *Taking Stock* sessions that we facilitate have been as varied as the schools themselves. One school focused its entire study process on the issue of equity. The study team's focus was on which SLC were making gains, which were not, how students and staff were selected, how it was that they had inadvertently allowed a "smart kid" or a "special needs" academy to develop, how they were going to fix that. It was the process of disaggregating whole-school data into individual SLC data that unearthed the student disparities and made for an interesting study process. A second school took over a classroom and began posting an initiative and data timeline around the walls. Changes in staffing, additions or deletions of initiatives, and data gains and losses were each posted year by year as a pattern of successes and challenges emerged. Still other schools have looked at their goals in a very specific manner, documented structures and gains, and positioned themselves for next steps. Regardless of the approach or focus of the study process, the end result should be threefold. First, there should be presentations to groups that can ask hard questions, provide constructive criticism of past practices, and make recommendations for next steps. Second, there needs to be a presentation to the faculty that establishes the gains, challenges, and lessons learned as you move to continually improve. And, finally, there must be the creation of an action plan for *continuous improvement.*

STUDY TOOLS TO GET YOU STARTED

Listen, Learn, and Lead

The Tool Kit contains a MS Word file [10.1 Listen, Learn, Lead]. It is a *Taking Stock* graphic organizer aimed at facilitating the reflection and study process (see Tool Kit Snapshot 10.1). We suggest that you include selected readings as part of your study process. Select articles which are targeted at the specific goals and objectives you sought to accomplish. Take the time to use this organizer in a thoughtful manner. It will serve as a primary record of your work.

Tool Kit Snapshot 10.1 Listen, Learn, Lead

Listen, Learn, Lead!

Purpose: to help ensure that the myriad of activities, plans, and learning experiences undertaken during the SLC implementation process are woven into the whole of our plans for continuous improvement in each of our buildings and in each of our spheres of influence.

Process: In preparation for the *Taking Stock Study Process*, we are using this Listen, Learn, and Lead tool for reflection. The goal is that the organizer serves as a running journal of our work. We will work through the organizer to celebrate what we are already doing in regard to creating aspects of SLC, note areas where we need to improve, identify perceived barriers to success in this area, and set in place some planning items that will be reflected in upcoming staff development and school improvement plans.

Expected Outcome: Through a process of preparation, participation, and planning, we will be able to ensure that the multiyear investment of time and resources—and the rich information we will share—will have a direct application to our work and not serve as a stand-alone event, disconnected from the important work underway to continuously improve our high schools.

As we begin . . .

THE WHAT: Prior knowledge and wonderings		
The following represents my understanding of where we are in our SLC implementation and how far we have come:	These are the things we already have in place AND ARE WORKING in our school/district that support that understanding:	Here is what I would hope for and expect as a result of the SLC study process and follow-up planning:
•	•	•
•	•	•
•	•	•

From the readings		
Key elements that are evidenced in our work:	Key elements we want to learn more about:	Key elements that we want to include in future planning:
•	•	•
•	•	•
•	•	•

As we continue the process . . .

THE WHAT:		
Key points	New learning	Wonderings
•	•	•
•	•	•
•	•	•

SO WHAT:		
What do I need to celebrate?	What do I need to change/improve?	Who do I need to involve?
•	•	•
•	•	•
•	•	•

In order to sustain the work . . .

NOW WHAT:		
How will we ensure that this event is not an isolated professional learning experience?		
What are the real values of this learning—what should or should not be included in our plans for teaching and learning?	What are the perceived barriers to implementing/changing/improving?	To what am I personally willing to commit?
•	•	•
•	•	•
•	•	•

Action steps—involving everyone		
What	Who	When
•	•	•
•	•	•
•	•	•

Best and Worst of Times

The Tool Kit contains a very simple prompt to use in group discussions. [5.4 It Was the Best of Times] asks groups to simply chart what have been the best and worst aspects of the implementation process. This tool was originally introduced in Chapter 5. Garnering these data will offer you a valuable lens to look backward and forward for both process and programmatic changes. We have used it not only at the "end" of a process but also at the beginning to take the pulse of a group.

Prides, Pitfalls, and Priorities

The tool [10.2 Prides, Pitfalls, and Priorities], contained in the Tool Kit, is designed to "jump start" your review process (see Tool Kit Snapshot 10.2). It can be used at any point in a process of assessing where you are and where you need to go next to stay or get back on track and to sustain your work. Set up in three areas, "prides," "pitfalls," and "priorities," groups can quickly identify success and challenges. Hold deep conversations. Ask the group, "As evidenced how?" You can gage consensus around these elements and begin to position yourself for next-step strategies.

Interviews

There is no more valuable tool in the engagement and reflection process than encouraging those involved in the process to have their voices heard. I am constantly struck, when I conduct what should be routine question and answer sessions in schools, by how often administrators, faculty, and students comment that no one has ever asked their opinions before. Formal climate surveys and pretests/posttests that garner statistical data can and should be woven into the process; however, it is *active* listening to individual ideas and concerns that ultimately results in a win for continued efforts aimed at improvement. Conducting information interviews with targeted questions helps tremendously in a process of self-reflection. We have included [10.3 Informational Interview Questions] in the Tool Kit as a sample of what you might cover with administrators, teachers, SLC groups, and students (see Tool Kit Snapshot 10.3).

Data in a Day

The process of *continuous improvement* begins, ends, and begins again with data. The data elements that are most significant are those which can be measured in improvements in student outcomes as related to classroom instruction and successful postsecondary transitions. In Chapter 6, we focused on the *curriculum and instruction bin*. This book is not designed to provide the in-depth work required to improve classroom and instructional practices; however, assessing instructional practice and coaching teachers to success are at its core. Since in so many cases the SLC structural elements come into play before the instructional ones, and since changes in academic success take longer to take hold and reap results than climate changes, it is very likely that at this point in the book you have not done a whole-school assessment of teaching and learning. If you are using an instructional reform model such as *Co-nect* or *First Things First*, you will have access to their instructional assessment tools—the *Instructional Practices Survey* or *Measuring What Matters*, respectively. There are also excellent commercially available PDA-driven electronic

Tool Kit Snapshot 10.2 | Prides, Pitfalls, and Priorities

Prides, Pitfalls, and Priorities School/Program/SLC:	
Over the course of our redesign and reform effort, there have been great strides made through struggle and strategy and through trial and error. This document helps capture "lessons learned" from your work.	
PRIDES: areas where real success was seen with students, in data elements, in changes in the culture of teaching and learning, in terms of engagement of community . . .	**PITFALLS:** places where we really wish we had known better, not gone there, and still really need to improve
1.	1.
2.	2.
3.	3.
4.	4.
5.	5.
PRIORITIES: things strongly suggested in order to meet with the greatest success around data, instruction, use of time, faculty and community engagement, student support, roles and responsibilities	

programs such as TeachScape that help collect data in a myriad of formats by school, departments, subject area, and individual teacher. These instruments go well beyond a checklist of items and go much deeper than the "D and F" report assessments we conducted in Chapter 7. They go to the core of effective instructional practice, and you must do the same. Make sure you build in an instructional review process as part of your work. Begin with the essential issue of what good teaching looks like and how it is demonstrated. Do this in departments and in SLC. As referenced earlier, you will have multiple ways of assessing this through walk-throughs, looking at student work and teacher assignments, and through a data review. Undoubtedly, you will want to incorporate the work of Downey, Marzano, Bloom, and Wiggins and McTighe in your thinking. We suggest that, for the purpose of "data in a day," you build a rubric that allows you to quickly assess classroom environments for teaching and learning as well as classroom practices. These will include, minimally, that the teaching objective is posted, the teaching is on or above grade level standards, the materials are relevant, higher-order thinking (and teaching) are *evident*, and students are actively engaged in their learning. Other elements include the classroom environment and evidence of specific instructional strategies—such as cooperative learning and differentiated instruction. Make sure that part of your discussion about what good teaching looks

The reasons systems don't work is that those who are asked to implement and sustain them didn't create them.

—Julie Rosenberg

Principals

1. What problem, challenge, or enhancement did you/do you want fixed by SLC?
2. What was/is the driving force for redesign, reform, or *continuous improvement*?
3. How are you creating a climate for success?
4. What supports from district, staff, families, or community do you need most?
5. What are current staff needs for training?
6. What roles and responsibilities have been defined for implementation?

School Staff

Questions that relate to students

1. What do you want a student of this school to look like at graduation?
2. Are you currently enrolling students in classes that produce that?
3. If not, what do you want to offer and how can we ensure that students get it?
4. Can you do that under your current graduation requirements and schedule?
5. If not, what do you have to change to make it so?
6. What has the SLC structure done best in supporting you?
7. What has it hindered you from doing?

Questions that relate to faculty

1. What are your school's major strengths?
2. What areas of your school need improvement?
3. Of those needs for improvement, what are the highest priorities?
4. On a scale of one to ten, with one being low and ten being high, how would you characterize the school climate? Why?
5. What problem, challenge, or enhancement did you want/do you want fixed by SLC?
6. What is the driving force for redesign, reform, or *continuous improvement*?
7. What are current staff needs for training?
8. What roles and responsibilities have been defined for implementation?
9. What recommendations do you have for increased success?

Questions that relate to SLC teams

1. How do you define the SLC in regards to personalization, curriculum, partnerships, climate for success, and data?
2. Are the structures in place effective (common planning, student assignment, etc.)?
3. What type of student do you feel benefits most from the SLC? Why?
4. What has been a positive outcome of this SLC?
5. What is the biggest challenge you have dealt with in the creation of SLC?
6. What was the process for students choosing an SLC? Has it been effective? If not, what change would you recommend?
7. What problem, challenge, or opportunity for enhancements did you/do you expect the creation of SLC to solve for you?
8. What barriers (both internal and external) do you expect to face as you move forward with SLC?

Questions that relate to Curriculum and Instruction

1. How would you describe your involvement in reflective practice, professional learning communities, looking at student work, utilization of data to guide instruction, and the like?
2. What assessment strategies do you use to determine student achievement?
3. What instructional strategies do you employ to meet the needs of specific student populations (i.e., at-risk, special needs, limited English proficient [LEP] students)?
4. How effective has the use of instructional time been each day?
5. In your SLC, to what extent is the school's curriculum aligned across grades and subjects (how well do the subjects complement and reinforce each other)?
6. Where does work-based learning fit in the mission and expected outcomes of the curriculum?

Questions that relate to Families and Partnerships

1. How involved are families in your school community?
2. How supportive are families of your school's education program?
3. How are community partners involved in your school?
4. What is the balance of partners: postsecondary, business, faith-based organizations, families, community-based organizations?

Students

1. Of what one thing are you most proud as a student at this school?
2. What are your school's major strengths?
3. What areas of your school need improvement?
4. Why do you think the school is changing how it operates (school reform, SLC, schedules)? Does it seem to work?
5. Do you know to which SLC you belong?
6. What was the process for choosing your SLC? Did you like the process? Why or why not? If not, what change would you recommend?
7. What is one thing you like about being in an SLC?
8. What is one thing you dislike about being in an SLC?
9. What is your perception of students in (other) SLC?
10. Is what you take in school challenging to you or easy?
11. In your classes, what types of assignments interest you (OR get you excited about learning) and motivate you to complete them?
12. On a scale of one to ten, with one meaning "none at all" and ten meaning "very good," what effect has your SLC had on your school's attendance?
13. On a scale of one to ten, with one meaning "none at all" and ten meaning "very good," what effect has SLC had on your school's climate?
14. How well are you being prepared for life after high school? Give an example from your high school experience to support your answer.
15. Do you think students have a true voice in the school process?

like includes an examination of what an administrator or Peer Review Team member could expect to see and document in a classroom visit.

Build on your Peer Review Teams and your Instructional Team mentioned in Chapter 4; include your district curriculum and instruction personnel. Create a protocol that allows for quick classroom visits and documentation. In a commitment to creating a sense of inquiry, rather than one of "got you" evaluation, we suggest the following process. Communicate to the faculty that the teams are going to be visiting classrooms for the purpose of benchmarking where departments and the school as a whole sit on a continuum of successful instruction. The "what does good teaching look like" discussion has, hopefully, already transpired and taken hold. Discuss with the team what process will work best for gathering information. Prior to the classroom visits, departments should be invited to submit evidence of student work and teacher assignments that can be measured against the developed rubric. Then, team members operate alone visiting classrooms. No individual teacher name or course title should be documented. Rather, information should be gathered by department or content area. Communicate to the teaching staff that the "data in a day" process fully recognizes that they may have had their most brilliant moments of teaching just before the review team members came in to observe, and that is why everyone's head is down on the desk and the teacher is reading the newspaper. The purpose of the review is to take the pulse of the school on a given day where teaching may indeed be uneven across the school.

Team members visit classrooms, observe, take notes using the rubric you have created, talk informally to students, and then leave—all within ten minutes. With a review team of six, you can get to nearly ninety classes in a day. Information from the review of student work, teacher assignments, and classroom visits is tallied, by department, for each rubric item and across the school. The data are then presented to the whole school and individual departments for the purpose of discussion and setting goals. Including a "data in a day" review is a powerful tool for sustaining a focus on instructional practice.

Assessing the Players and Practices

In Chapter 5, you began to look at position descriptions for DIFs, ninth grade teachers, and Instructional Improvement Team members. These will have been fine-tuned from the drafts we provided for you in the Tool Kit. In addition, hopefully you have created one for yourself as the prime practitioner or driving force in the SLC implementation. This is the step for evaluation and assessment, and you should not be exempt from the process. Use the assessments for discussion and redefining of roles and responsibilities.

In addition to the previous section on determining people, assets, and building capacity, this is also a time to assess others who can help move the *continuous improvement* agenda forward. Remember the partnership audit document here. Ask what is working, what is not, what needs to be added, and what can be dropped. Lastly, have hard conversations about the consultants and technical assistance providers you hire to support your work. I have said in other forums that it is rare that consultant performance gets evaluated. Hold our feet to the fire and ask hard questions about missed benchmarks, ask us to partner on the planning for what happens next in terms of the support you seek, and assess the professional development activities we deliver. Perhaps the most important thing to ask of consulting relationships is whether they built your internal capacity to succeed on your own as resident experts.

The tool [10.4 Measuring Up Evaluation], located in the Tool Kit, is an evaluation instrument for assessing workshops and professional development activities. Because of the vast array of printer definitions, it is presented to you in Adobe PDF format. As a graphic organizer, it is wonderful for visual learners, students, and those of us who doodle at meetings. It is also remarkably simple for those of us who hate to read through long evaluation forms or wrestle with the Likert scale. Even in its simplicity, however, it should call you to look at what is still needed and at what should be followed up. The way we have used this form most effectively is to ask participants to take it out at the beginning of a session and to jot notes throughout the session in response to the prompts. At the end of the session, I ask my copresenters and our clients to circle up and read through all the evaluations, make observations on the evaluations, and then react to the sum of the comments.

Third-Party Evaluation Information

While performing your own internal assessment is critical, the most highly respected and useful data will be those compiled by an outside, nonpartisan, third-party evaluator. Many grants require or encourage outside evaluation and set specific parameters for assessment. Engaging an independent third party to conduct research, however, does not mean you are not involved in the process.

Through our site work, we have been directly involved in third-party evaluations conducted by organizations such as RAND, MDRC, and The George Washington University. In each case, it has taken practitioners' time to participate in interviews, distribute and collect surveys, and locate and catalog data from student records and school reports. In some cases, it has also demanded the acquisition of releases from students and parents/guardians/families for access to and use of records. Some evaluations have been started and completed in an academic year, while others have spanned half a decade. In each instance, the results have been invaluable. In addition to student achievement factors, the evaluation will undoubtedly help you measure the following:

- Adherence to the principles of your redesign
- Adherence to the commonly held beliefs and nationally agreed-upon definitions
- Family involvement in the academic and career development process
- Community involvement in the academic and career development process
- Student attendance, office referrals, truancy, promotion and graduation rates
- Increases in employment rate in growth industries
- Clear, focused, and sustained leadership and mission
- Professional development and common planning time
- Teachers placed in career theme work-based experiences (for academy programs)
- A demonstrated commitment to work-based experiences as equal to "academics"
- Community of supportive partners
- True, shared leadership by the partners and the school
- Communications tools to engage students and parents/guardians
- Schedules and structures that support integration, common planning, and significant time for career-focused field and work-based experiences

- Curriculum that is integrated, has high standards, and, for academy programs, has a career pathways sequence
- Student work-based experiences that match or exceed the school's, district's, or reform effort's requirements
- Accountability: clear lines of responsibility for programs, services, and activities, and a commitment to them
- Flexible funding: identification of the resources that can support both the mission of the SLC and working with partners to secure additional resources.

In structuring all your evaluations, including the high prescribed ones often included in grants, be selfish about including items about which you want to learn. In a recent Federal Smaller Learning Community award where schools must be measured on Annual Performance Review (APR) benchmarks, we worked with one district to also include the items that were relevant to its own learning—effectiveness of instructional improvement teams, implementation of career-focused programs, redesigning SLC, and changed administrative support practices. After all, it is district monies that fund the research. It is the district that contracts with the third-party evaluator. It is the district that should benefit from the lessons learned.

"We're Outta Here!" Survey

Of increasing interest to researchers is what actually happens to students once they leave high schools and the SLC. Of increasing interest to students is a high school experience that is truly rigorous, engages their imaginations, and provides them with real skills and opportunities. Build on your commitment to listening to student voices from Chapter 9. By securing the direct input of your graduating seniors, you can capture critical information on both of these areas. The additional benefit of surveying seniors is that you will have a means to continue to follow their progress, involve them with your current students, and activate them as alumni.

For schools with a highly transient student body, recognize the need to ask students to supply the names and phone numbers of several individuals who they believe will always be in touch with them. This simple feature alone has made a critical difference in tracking student outcome data. Once the data are gathered, with the appropriate security checks, you can use students and advisory board members to conduct an annual phone or e-mail survey of graduates, invite them to functions, and mark their progress. Over the four-year postgraduation period in which we conducted surveys at our first trial school, the results were nothing short of remarkable. Eighty-four percent of the students in the follow-up survey were either in school, at work, or dually engaged.

The types of data you will want to garner from students fall into four categories:

1. *Personal information:* name, address, social security number (if allowable), e-mail address, primary and multiple alternate phone numbers of individuals who know how to reach you

2. *Program information:* was the SLC experience important to your success, would you enroll again if you were starting high school today, what was

the most important part of the experience, what was the least, and was the coursework challenging?

3. *Educational outcomes:* GPA, SAT/ACT scores, certifications, scholarships, and awards

4. *Future plans:* after graduation, are you going to work, continue with school, or enter the military? Are you unsure? Are you pursuing a career/course of study in the same career area as the theme of your SLC?

At a Glance: Summing It Up and Next Steps

The one thing we know about schools and districts is that change is constant. Practitioners and other key partners must collaborate on a system of establishing practices that will ensure continuity. Practitioners will play a key role—and, indeed, be responsible for keeping the momentum and focus on the development of the SLC, as changes in school and school personnel shift. In addition to assessing your implementation process, you will want to "do the little things" that fine-tune and add depth to the success of a culture shift. Box 10.2 presents a list of strategies and elements that will build success.

Box 10.2   Strategies and Elements to Build Success

- Include students, teachers, parents/guardians/families, and community partners in all reporting and research. It will reinforce the value you place on their support.
- At least once a year, hold a staff/partner/stakeholder retreat to reinforce the "team" approach and to ensure adherence to the *continuous improvement* mission.
- Involve recent graduates in dialogue with current students. Inviting graduates back to share their stories about finding their way after high school as they take on new adult roles in jobs and college experiences will speak volumes to current students in your program. The SLC format, and good records of student exit outcomes, will help immensely in this process.
- Develop a policy and procedures or operations manual that catalogs all the events, contacts, and "how to's" of your implementation. Better yet, take advantage of shared drives, moodles, and blogs as online resources. Without a place to capture historical memory or institutional knowledge, much of the process of struggle and success will be lost. With the changes in personnel that are inevitable, and in the spirit of truly shared leadership, there must be a depository of knowledge and materials that is readily available and user friendly.
- Gather research on your program. Your "wins" will help you attract new resources; your deficits will allow you reevaluate and to plan effectively.
- Get the word out! Success breeds success. Failures bring new learning opportunities. As you move through the process of implementing and developing your SLC or academies, make sure that you share the information with your community and with educators across the nation. Have students involved in making public service announcements and videos. Send press releases. Submit applications to present your story at regional and national conferences.

THE JOURNEY CONTINUES

While we are concluding our work together, know that the journey for creating and sustaining your SLC is just beginning. It takes years to "get it right." It takes continued focus and attention to make sure that the gains, so passionately won, are sustained and serve as the seeds for future school improvements. As you endeavor to work to improve your school and increase options and expectations for students, you will meet with endless frustrations, great challenges, bureaucratic roadblocks, and "set in their ways" professionals. Couple this with the needs and demands of working with adolescents and changing educational initiatives, and your own school-based challenges increase a hundredfold. You will continually be tempted to return to "school as usual," to step back and hope that the next principal or superintendent or change initiative will somehow make your current challenge of redesigning and reforming and committing to *continuous improvement* unnecessary.

However, every day the numbers and the students tell the story. We are not now creating learning environments that result in students' abilities to learn, apply learning, and succeed. We are not now creating learning environments that capture students' imaginations and challenge them to do more. We cannot wait for this wave to pass over us. We can leave no child behind.

Hedrick Smith's PBS documentary *Across the River* highlighted positive contributions to the quality of life in Washington, DC's, most trouble community, Anacostia. The premise for the program was that in every city and community there is a world "across the river" or across the tracks. He focused on the work of the Public Service Academy at Anacostia High School. In this beleaguered community, he stated, there was hope in a sea of despair because students in the Public Service Academy were reaching nearly a 95 percent graduation rate compared with the 40 percent rate for the general student population. He cited the academy's small size, personalized atmosphere, high expectations, and close ties to adult role models and business partners as the keys to the academy's success. He dubbed those of us who worked in Anacostia "urban heroes." He focused on one young man, T. J. Reeves Thompson, who was tempted with dropout and school failure. The academy program's small learning environment and work-based learning model kept T. J. motivated and in school. He completed a successful internship with the U.S. Secret Service and graduated sixth in his high school class. According to T. J., the Public Service Academy taught him how to sit up straight, look people in the eye, be on time, and work hard. "They teach us about business, and run our school as if it was a business of their own," Reeves commented.

Smith concludes his documentary with an accolade and a challenge. He points out that the individuals we meet in the documentary want what we all want: safe neighborhoods, good schools, and better opportunities for their children. He states that the individual educators and support teams highlighted in the program are heroes. Smith points out that the gains come hard, but the question and the challenge is "will these urban heroes succeed and gain the support of the wider community, or be lost to the world *across the river?*"

Whether you are trying to implement your SLC in an urban setting, or perhaps in a less challenged community, the gains will still come hard. In each of our neighborhoods, we face very personal and real barriers to student success and truly effective schools. Yet in each of our neighborhoods we have the skills, abilities, and resources to not only succeed but to persevere. You will have to "find the gifts" in your community: the gift of an individual's talents and skills, the gift of new opportunities, the gift of challenge and growth, and the gift of knowing that it is possible to improve schools, communities, and individual students' lives. Perhaps most important will be to find and celebrate your own T. J. Reeves Thompson stories. Keeping focused on the students will keep all else in perspective when the adult issues become overwhelmingly ridiculous.

Done right, your SLC will be extraordinary places. They will be places that strive for excellence. Your partners, families, students, and faculty will find it contagious and exhilarating to be there.

Hopefully, *Small Learning Communities* and its Tool Kit have helped you effectively begin or enhance your SLC and, more specifically, commit to a culture focused on improvement. The tools and strategies used herein are based on current research, and specifically on what has worked for educators in schools across the nation. The work has been a true partnership with the schools and businesses we have served. We have learned that the process is never quite finished. Our journey with the American high school for nearly two decades now has been filled with remarkable stories of teachers and students, of families and partners, of administrators and central office staff—all who have taken great risks, worked tirelessly, failed, and succeeded.

In one of the very first years of our work in Washington, DC, there was a student named Damon. He was a senior who was working at an internship at *The Washington Times.* One day he called his supervisor, and said he would be detained. Because close communication and partnership are at the very heart of SLC, the supervisor, Nick, picked up the phone. He let us know that Damon was doing well and was modeling good business practices by calling and saying he was running late. Six days later, we again heard from Nick. He reported that he had not heard from or seen Damon since he had received the call last week. He reported that Damon's mother had called and could not locate him. Calls to school and to friends resulted in no clue as to his whereabouts. Finally, two days later, Damon had placed a second call to his workplace and said he had indeed been *detained.* He had been incarcerated for car theft. Nick's first reaction was that trust had been broken—that, regardless of the outcome, Damon could not return to work at *The Times.* After some discussion, however, we looked at the whole picture. Damon had not called his mother, he had not called his school, and he had not called program supervisors. He had called Nick, however. Could there be any question of the importance of the role he was playing in that young man's life? Once we saw the power of the impact on Damon's life, we saw the whole picture. And remember, SLC are about the *whole* picture. With this understanding, we were faced with only one alternative: to realize that each of us has the opportunity to positively impact the lives of students. Because Damon was in a career academy, and there were supports in place, he was able to successfully find his way back to school, work, and graduation. The charges against him were dropped. He was able to go on to college. He—and we—were able to find the gifts.

Creating and sustaining *effective* SLC take time, patience, courage, and great attention to detail. This book and its accompanying tools are geared to arm you with what you need to succeed. Let them serve as a vehicle that promotes your work, but do not get so mired in the details that you loose sight of the fact that SLC are, in their simplest form, a vehicle for creating success for students and for empowering teachers and administrators to create the schools of which they dream!

As you continue on your journey, remember to find the gifts, celebrate the successes, and share your story. When we have done this work well, we realize that the experts are truly among us, and the journey continues!

Resources

Advisories That Work!

http://www.gmspartnersinc.org/downloads/#donegan

Based on research that highlights five key areas for successful advisories— "purpose," "organization," "content," "assessment," and "leadership"—this comprehensive guide contains nearly 90 lessons, a special section on freshman orientation, implementation strategies, resources, handouts, and rubrics for assessment.

American Youth Policy Forum

http://www.aypf.org

A national organization providing professional development activities for federal policy aides and staff of national organizations in areas of youth development, including education, school-to-careers, employment and training, and learning through service.

Association for Supervision and Curriculum Development

http://www.ascd.org

Through "smartbrief," provides a free daily summary of the top stories in education.

Bill & Melinda Gates Foundation

http://www.gatesfoundation.org/Education/

Through its partnerships in communities across the nation, the Bill & Melinda Gates Foundation is committed to raising the high school graduation rate and helping all students—regardless of race or family income—graduate as strong citizens ready for college and work.

Bloom's Taxonomy

http://www.officeport.com/edu/blooms.htm

Bloom identified six levels within the cognitive domain, from the simple recall or recognition of facts as the lowest level, through increasingly more complex and abstract mental levels, to the highest order which is classified as evaluation.

Breaking Ranks I and II

National Association of Secondary School Principals
http://www.nassp.org

These reports outline a vision for educational reform grounded in the experiences of those most involved in American high school. They set out a series of recommendations as a template for action. NASSP represents more than 41,000 middle-level and high school principals.

Career Academy Standards of Practice

http://www.hsalliance.org/_downloads/home/Career_Academy_National_Standards_of_Practice.pdf

Developed by an informal consortium of career academy organizations, the Career Academy Standards of Practice are framed around ten key elements of successful implementation, drawn from many years of research and experiences from all parts of the country.

Career Academy Support Network

http://casn.berkeley.edu

Housed within the Graduate School of Education at the University of California, Berkeley, the network's purpose is to support the growing number of career academies developing around the country, fostering their growth and improvement.

Career Clusters Institute

http://www.careerclusters.org

Career clusters provide a way for schools to organize instruction and student experiences around sixteen broad categories that encompass virtually all occupations from entry through professional levels. Resources such as knowledge, skills, and brochures are available for each of the sixteen clusters. Click on the cluster icon for access to resources. The sixteen clusters are:

1. Agriculture, Food and Natural Resources: http://www.careerclusters.org/clusters/anr.cfm

2. Architecture and Construction: http://www.careerclusters.org/clusters/ac.cfm

3. Arts, A/V Technology and Communications: http://www.careerclusters.org/clusters/av.cfm

4. Business, Management, and Administration: http://www.careerclusters.org/clusters/ba.cfm

5. Education and Training: http://www.careerclusters.org/clusters/et.cfm

6. Finance: http://www.careerclusters.org/clusters/f.cfm

7. Government and Public Administration: http://www.careerclusters.org/clusters/gpa.cfm

8. Health Science: http://www.careerclusters.org/clusters/h.cfm

9. Hospitality and Tourism: http://www.careerclusters.org/clusters/ht.cfm

10. Human Services: http://www.careerclusters.org/clusters/hs.cfm

11. Information Technology: http://www.careerclusters.org/clusters/it.cfm

12. Law, Public Safety, Corrections and Security: http://www.careerclusters.org/clusters/lps.cfm

13. Manufacturing: http://www.careerclusters.org/clusters/m.cfm

14. Marketing, Sales and Service: http://www.careerclusters.org/clusters/mkg.cfm

15. Science, Technology, Engineering and Mathematics: http://www.careerclusters.org/clusters/sre.cfm

16. Transportation, Distribution and Logistics: http://www.careerclusters.org/clusters/t.cfm

Career and Technical Student Organizations

http://www.ed.gov/about/offices/list/ovae/pi/cte/vso.html

CTSO develop citizenship, technical, leadership, and teamwork skills essential for students who are preparing for the workforce and further education. They provide a unique instructional method for attaining the competency goals and objectives identified in each course.

Coalition of Essential Schools

http://www.essentialschools.org

For over twenty years, CES has been a national leader in public education transformation. Guided by the Common Principles, CES strives to create and sustain a *network* of personalized, equitable, and intellectually challenging schools. The Small Schools Project, part of CES Northwest, provides coaching, professional development, and a Web site at http://www.smallschoolsproject.org.

CORD, Leading Change in Education

http://www.CORD.org
P.O. Box 21689, Waco, TX 76702-1689, 254-772-8756 (voice), 254-772-8972 (fax), E-mail: webmaster@cord.org

CORD is a national nonprofit organization dedicated to leading change in education through projects and programs that prepare students for the technological workplace of the future. Whether developing curricula, delivering professional development workshops, creating new applications of technology, conducting applied educational research, or facilitating education and employer partnerships, CORD strives to empower educators to make meaningful connections between school and work for the benefit of students. To accomplish this mission, CORD assists educators in schools and colleges in three areas: curriculum development, professional development, and Tech Prep leadership.

Cross City Campaign for Urban School Reform

http://www.crosscity.org
407 S. Dearborn Street, Suite 1725, Chicago, IL 60605, 312-322-4880

The Cross City Campaign for Urban School Reform is a national network of urban school reform leaders from seven cities: Baltimore, Chicago, Denver, Los Angeles, New York, Philadelphia, and Seattle. They comprise parents, community members, teachers, principals, central office administrators, researchers, union officials, and fundraisers working together to improve public schools and education for urban young people. We support efforts to create high-quality schools that ensure educational success for all urban young people.

Current Literature on Small Schools

http://www.ael.org/eric/digests/edorc988.htm

Mary Anne Raywid. ERIC Clearinghouse on Rural Education and Small Schools Office of Educational Research and Improvement, U.S. Department of Education, January 1999.

This digest presents a brief overview of research literature on the effectiveness of small schools. It then describes current topics researchers have begun to explore, including discussion of associated policy issues, individual successes and failures, and essential elements and other implementation considerations.

Education Week

http://www.edweek.org

Education Week is American education's newspaper of record—see *Teacher Magazine*, edweek.org, and *Agent K–12*. It publishes periodic special reports on issues ranging from technology to textbooks, as well as books of special interest to educators. The primary mission is to help raise the level of awareness and understanding among professionals and the public of important issues in American education. Covers local, state, and national news and issues from preschool through the twelfth grade.

First Things First—Institute for Research and Reform in Education

http://www.irre.org/ftf

First Things First, a framework for school reform, has one goal: to help students at all academic levels gain the skills to succeed in postsecondary education and find good jobs. In the process, FTF helps districts and schools meet the requirements of NCLB.

GMS Partners, Inc.

http://www.gmspartnersinc.org

GMS Partners, Inc. was established in 1987 with the single purpose of having a positive and powerful impact on education in America. By partnering with schools, businesses, and community organizations that understand the critical relationships between schools, community development, and issues surrounding youth, GMS has been able to make a positive difference in school systems in over thirty states for nearly twenty years. GMS Partners works at the national, state, district, and school levels with a focus on secondary school improvement. Through a process of analysis, diagnosis, strategic planning, facilitated work sessions, professional learning opportunities, coaching, and tool development, we help schools and communities build capacity, enrich their climate, focus on teaching and learning, and reach their continuous improvement targets.

Great Schools

http://www.greatschools.net/
   Great Schools is an independent nonprofit organization committed to providing parents with information and tools to choose schools, support their children's education, and improve schools in their communities.

High School Alliance

http://www.hsalliance.org
   The National High School Alliance (HS Alliance) is a partnership of nearly fifty organizations representing a diverse cross-section of perspectives and approaches, but sharing a common commitment to promoting the excellence, equity, and development of high school–age youth.

High Schools of the Millennium: Report of the Workgroup

http://www.aypf.org/pubs.htm
   The report, produced by the American Youth Policy Forum (see above), argues for a new vision of high school, one that uses all the resources of the community to create smaller learning environments, to engage youth in their striving for high academic achievement, to support them with adult mentors and role models, and to provide them with opportunities to develop their civic, social, and career skills.

Improving Low-Performing High Schools

http://www.mdrc.org/press_releases/17/press_release_17.html
   Recent research on three high school reform models from MDRC (formerly the Manpower Development Research Corporation) offers hope that programs can improve low-performing high schools. Together, these three interventions are being implemented in more than 2,500 high schools across the country, and various components of these models are being used in thousands more schools. Each model has been the subject of rigorous evaluation by MDRC, and each has been shown to improve some measures of student success. The new report offers lessons from across these three studies on:

- Creating personalized and orderly learning environments
- Assisting students who enter high school with poor academic skills
- Improving instructional content and practice
- Preparing students for the world beyond high school, and
- Stimulating change in overstressed high schools.

The report asserts that structural changes and instructional improvement are the twin pillars of high school reform.

MDRC's research suggests that transforming schools into SLC and assigning students to faculty advisors can increase students' feelings of connectedness to their teachers. Extended class periods, special catch-up courses, high-quality curricula, and training on these curricula for teachers can improve student achievement. Furthermore, school–employer partnerships that involve career awareness activities and work internships can help students attain higher earnings after high school.

Indiana Workforce Development Career Majors

http://www.in.gov/dwd/partners/tech_ed_career_majors.html

Career Majors increase high school students' motivation and achievement by helping them make the connection between what they are learning in school and their future opportunities.

Insights, Shadows, and Mentors: A Comprehensive Series of Work-based Learning Experiences

G. Sammon, and B. Donegan, Fort Worth, TX: Upstream Press, 2006.
http://www.gmspartnersinc.org/downloads/#sammon4

Built from the highly successful work-based learning program that help transform one of the nation's toughest high schools, this detailed guide, with downloadable and adjustable files, leads teachers, partners, students, and families through a multistage work-based learning experience solidly grounded in industry skill standards, SCANS, and WorkKeys.

International Center for Leadership in Education: *Creating Small Learning Communities*

http://www.icle.net/slc.html

This resource kit offers a wealth of practical advice, suggestions, and tools to establish a successful SLC or enhance an existing one. The text and accompanying CD-ROM contain many handouts, tools, and worksheets, such as questions and answers to prepare for those many meetings, forms to modify and use in planning processes, and checklists to keep track of progress and measure your success.

Jobs for the Future

http://www.jff.org

Jobs for the Future (JFF) believes that all young people should have a quality high school and postsecondary education, and that all adults should have the skills needed to hold jobs that pay enough to support a family. As a nonprofit research, consulting, and advocacy organization, JFF works to strengthen our society by creating educational and economic opportunity for those who need it most.

Junior Achievement, Inc.

http://www.ja.org

Brad Kaufmann, Director, Public Relations, Junior Achievement Inc., One Education Way, Colorado Springs, CO 80906

JA currently reaches more than 3.5 million students across America through programs in grades K–12. JA's ultimate mission is to ensure that every child in America has a fundamental understanding of the free enterprise system so that they are prepared to meet the challenges of the global economy.

Manpower Development Research Corporation (MDRC)

http://www.mdrc.org

MDRC has brought its unique approach to an ever-growing range of policy areas and target populations. Once known primarily for evaluations of state welfare-to-work programs, today MDRC is also studying public school reforms, employment programs for ex-prisoners and people with disabilities, and programs to help low-income people succeed in college.

National Academy Foundation

http://www.naf.org

NAF's public-private partnerships have been transforming inner-city high school education for more than twenty years. Through an innovative educational model, NAF's small public school–based "learning communities" empower high school students to become active citizens who successfully go on to higher education and professions of their choosing. The NAF model works by bringing business people into the public schools and introducing disenfranchised youth to the world of business. Through the academies, educators and business people work as partners by investing in and developing America's youth.

National Career Academy Coalition

http://www.ncacinc.org

The mission of the NCAC is to create and support a national network of existing and emerging high school career academies.

National Center for Education and the Economy

http://www.ncee.org

P.O. Box 10391, Rochester, NY 14610

A not-for-profit organization based in Washington, DC, the National Center is organized to provide resources to schools, districts, and states interested in standards-based reform. Currently, it provides products and services in the areas of New Standards, America's Choice, and Workforce Development

National Governors Association

http://www.nga.org

NGA is the collective voice of the nation's governors and one of the most respected public policy organizations in Washington, DC. NGA provides governors and their senior staff members with services that range from representing states on Capitol Hill and before the Administration on *key federal issues* to developing policy reports on innovative state programs and hosting networking seminars for state government executive branch officials. The NGA Center for Best Practices focuses on state innovations and best practices on issues that range from education and health to technology, welfare reform, and the environment. NGA also provides management and technical assistance to both new and incumbent governors.

National School Reform Faculty

http://www.nsrfharmony.org/default.html

At the heart of the National School Reform Faculty (NSRF) program are the concepts of facilitative leadership and critical friends. Critical friends, an essential ingredient for learning communities, is best achieved through providing deliberate time and structures to promote adult growth that is directly linked to student learning. Facilitative leadership skills are needed to engage school communities in this practice and are valuable for all leaders—school leaders, classroom teachers, and district administrators. One common example of this work is a CFG. This site is designed to provide information about critical friends and facilitative leadership, provide updates on news from the National Center and upcoming events, offer a national connection to NSRF Centers of Activity, and make resources available.

Northwest Regional Education Lab

http://www.nwrel.org

NWREL has been tasked by the U.S. Department of Education to monitor, support, coach, and study the federal SLC initiative. This site has extensive information, materials, and tools that support SLC implementation as well as lessons learned from promising sites, extensive information on comprehensive school reform, and student voice.

Promising Practices: Successful Texas Schoolwide Programs

http://www.utdanacenter.org/products/products.html#star
Dr. Joseph F. Johnson, STAR Center at the Charles A. Dana Center, The University of Texas at Austin

Schools where almost all students live in low-income situations can be schools in which almost all students achieve high levels of academic success. This is known not in theory, but in the practice and the results generated by real schools in Texas.

Small Learning Communities Meet School-to-Work: Whole-School Restructuring for Urban Comprehensive High Schools

http://www.csos.jhu.edu/crespar/techReports/Report31.pdf
Center for Social Organization of Schools, 3003 North Charles Street, Suite 200, Baltimore, MD, 21218, 410-516-8800/410-516-8890.
Report No. 31 by Nettie E. Legters, January 1999, CRESPAR, Johns Hopkins University
   Research on school size has spawned a widespread movement toward smaller schools and the creation of self-contained "houses," "charters," or SLC within large high schools.

Small Learning Communities: Self-Assessment in Five Domains of Research-Based SLC Practice

http://www.nwrel.org/scpd/sslc/SelfAssessment.pdf
   This self-assessment tool allows you to take stock of SLC organization and functioning in five domains of practice. The domains are: Interdisciplinary Teaching and Learning Teams; Rigorous, Relevant Curriculum and Instruction: Inclusive Program and Practices; Continuous Program Improvement; and Building/District Support.

Small Schools Workshop

http://www.smallschoolsworkshop.org/
   This is a group of educators, organizers, and researchers based in the College of Education at the University of Illinois at Chicago. The Small Schools Workshop collaborates with teachers, principals, parents, and district leaders to create new, small, innovative learning communities in public schools.

Stanford University School Redesign Network and Toolkit

http://schoolredesign.net/srn/study_kit.php
   Responding to the need for new school models that are designed to teach all children to high levels, the School Redesign Network serves as a resource for communities working to improve their schools. The Network is a learning collaborative which helps leaders of districts, small schools, and large schools that are redesigning to develop a deeper understanding of the features that effectively support excellence and equity in schools.

Index